Zionism at the UN

Eliahu Elath

Zionism at the UN

A Diary of the First Days

translated from Hebrew by Michael Ben-Yitzhak

foreword by Howard M. Sachar

The Jewish Publication Society of America

Philadelphia   5736 / 1976

English translation copyright © 1976
by The Jewish Publication Society of America
First English edition
All rights reserved
Originally published in Hebrew by Dvir, Tel Aviv, 1971
ISBN 0-8276-0083-6
Library of Congress catalog card number 76-708
Manufactured in the United States of America

Designed by Adrianne Onderdonk Dudden

Grateful acknowledgment for permission to reprint the photographs
following page 82 is made to the Zionist Archives and Library, and for
the photographs following page 204 to the United Nations.

Acknowledgments

My first expression of thanks goes to Professor Moshe Davis of the Hebrew University of Jerusalem. His encouragement led to the translation into English of this book, which I originally wrote in Hebrew (*Yoman San Francisco,* Dvir, Tel Aviv, 1971).

I am grateful to the Memorial Foundation for Jewish Culture for their assistance. I am especially indebted to Mrs. Shulamit Nardi and Professor Nathan Feinberg, who read and commented on my manuscript, and to the Institute of Contemporary Jewry for their help.

It is with great grief that I acknowledge my deep gratitude to the translator of the book, Michael Ben-Yitzhak, who met an untimely and tragic death in July 1975 during the terrorist assault in Zion Square in Jerusalem.

Contents

Illustrations follow pages 82 and 204

Foreword HOWARD M. SACHAR

On November 10, 1975, the United Nations General Assembly issued a resolution branding Zionism as "racism." The condemnation in fact was but one of a long, if recent, series of United Nations proclamations and pronunciamentos intended to isolate Israel in the international community. In this instance, however, the resolution reflected more than the transformation of the United Nations into a sounding board for its aggressive Third World majority of Afro-Asian-Communist members. By the appalling militancy of its own anti-white and anti-Jewish racism, the resolution all but wrote finis to a dream once cherished by men of goodwill everywhere. Was it barely thirty years ago, in May and June of 1945, that the statesmen of the victorious Allied and associated powers gathered in San Francisco to lay the foundations of a new world order? From the vantage point of the 1970s—and most particularly in the aftermath of the statement of November 10, 1975— it is all but impossible to grasp the near-mystic hopes that were enshrined in the deliberations that produced the United Nations Charter. More than an instrument of collective security was to be formulated. A mighty edifice of peace and freedom, of justice and dignity, was to be erected for Great Powers and weaker nations, for sovereign states and colonially mandated races alike.

The Zionists were among the welter of delegations that converged on San Francisco to plead their special causes and to press their—often fragile—claims to national recognition. No people had a more anguished vested interest in winning international support than the Jews. The balance sheet of the Final Solution was even then being compiled, and the numbing magnitude of this genocide was only belatedly coming to light. Of the more than five million Jews who had been immolated in the Nazi inferno, perhaps half that number could have been saved had the gates of Palestine remained open during the war. Those gates had been slammed shut, of course, by the British white paper of May 1939, a policy document that in effect froze the Holy Land's existing population ratio, with its two to one Arab majority, and foreclosed any additional growth of the Jewish national home.

Accordingly, the Arab diplomats who convened in San Francisco were intent upon ensuring that the demise of the Jewish national home be given international sanction. Their strategy could not perhaps take the form of a head-on assault upon the Palestine Mandate. Winston Churchill in any case had stated emphatically that all questions regarding mandated territories would remain for the time being within the purview of Britain and France. What the Arabs demanded, rather, was recognition of the preeminent rights of majority peoples in mandated lands. Had this simplistic, although superficially logical, doctrine been incorporated into the trusteeship chapters of the Charter, the guaranteed status of Palestine's Jewish minority under the Balfour Declaration would have been repealed. It was on forestalling that possibility, on warning friendly delegates against Arab objectives and tactics, that the Zionist representatives at San Francisco now concentrated their efforts. In defending their rights under the Balfour Declaration, moreover, the Zionists hoped not simply to preserve and enlarge their foothold in Palestine, but eventually to achieve nothing less than a Jewish state in the Holy Land. This was the essence of the Biltmore Program, adopted in May 1942 by an Emergency Zionist Conference and thereafter accepted as the official Zionist platform.

As it happened, the Arabs did not win acceptance of their views in the trusteeship chapters of the Charter. This failure reflected less the other delegations' pro-Zionist sympathies than their plain and simple unwillingness to offend the British or to involve themselves prematurely in the complex Palestine issue. The significance of the Zionist diplomatic effort at San Francisco, therefore, is to be found not in what the Jews actively accomplished but rather in what they learned from their first encounter with the Arabs before an international assembly—and in the prefigurations of far more dramatic confrontations to come in the United Nations of subsequent decades.

Eliahu Elath's description of these events of May–June 1945 is uniquely perceptive. Although nothing is added in hindsight—this is a diary, not an autobiography—the book is fascinating in its account of the vicissitudes of small-power diplomacy. Ironically, the Arabs themselves fell into that category. Sovereign they were, and their combined delegations totaled fully 10 percent of the representatives officially accredited to the San Francisco conference. Nor were the Big Four insensible to the importance of Arab friendship and Arab oil. Nevertheless, when it suited Britain, the United States, France, and the Soviet Union to write the trusteeship chapters according to their own strategic purposes, not a single non-Arab delegation ventured to cast a negative vote. The distance between the incipient United Nations of 1945 and the Third World forum the UN has become today is more than one of three decades. It is one of light-years of perception and influence.

The Zionists were in no position to draw consolation from this initial Great Power predominance, however, or even from the decisive voting strength of the Anglo-Americans and their protégés in Western Europe, Asia, and Latin America. If the British insisted in 1945 that the Palestine Mandate be left to their own discretion, their policy hardly represented an orientation in favor of the Jewish national home. The newly emergent Arab League was altogether a creature of Anthony Eden, after all, and it represented Britain's hope of developing a network of well-disposed client nations throughout the Middle East, answerable to London's strategic and economic needs. In large measure those needs coalesced around the fathomless oil resources of the Persian Gulf.

Neither were the Americans oblivious to the importance of Arab friendship. Elath understood well that however much politicians like Harold Stassen, member of the United States delegation, expressed a tolerant understanding of Zionist aspirations, the long-range contours of American Middle East policy were more likely to be shaped by men like Foy Kohler, Philip Ireland, and other State Department professionals. "When the conversation turned to the Palestine question," Elath observed, "I recognized at once the British influence on them both. Each emphasized that the United States can follow no course in the Middle East without full coordination with its British ally. . . . Although neither Kohler nor Ireland mentioned the word 'oil,' it was perfectly clear what was meant by the 'legitimate interests' of the United States in the Middle East."

Indeed, the concern for Arab goodwill was not expressed by career diplomats alone. It is worth noting that the advocates of a pro-Arab policy included, besides the Arab and Muslim delegations themselves, a wide complex of American vested interests, the most substantial of which were oil companies with extensive wells and pipelines in the Middle East. These corporations were not unimaginative or ungenerous in financing Arab propaganda. Often, too, their senior officials were made available to Arab delegations for public-relations assistance. Similarly, working in intimate collaboration with the Arabs were front organizations such as the Near East College Association (its publicity orchestrated by Lowell

Thomas), the Near East Foundation, the Council for Near Eastern Affairs, the Arab-American Mining Company Institute, the Institute of Arab-American Affairs, as well as the Washington-sponsored Foreign Service Education Foundation.

Against this formidable array of interlocking governmental and oil personnel, what did the Jews have at their disposal in San Francisco? Those in quest of a smoothly functioning propaganda machine capable of moving and shaping events would have been astonished at the Zionist lobby's pitiable lack of structure and discipline. To be sure, the sheer number of Jewish special-interest groups exceeded that of any other delegation at the conference. But in fact this was a principal source of Zionist weakness. For one thing, many of the Jewish factions clamoring for attention were not overtly Zionist at all. They ranged from socialist-Yiddishist elements to the non-Zionist American Jewish Committee to the bitterly anti-Zionist American Council for Judaism. Worse yet, the Zionists themselves were dispersed among parallel, and often competing, bodies. Thus B'nai B'rith and Hadassah, the American Jewish Congress and the World Jewish Congress, the American Jewish Trade Union Committee for Palestine and individual Zionist parties (Mizrachi, Poalei Zion, General Zionists) were all present and active. While loosely organized in the American Jewish Conference, each nevertheless insisted on maintaining a separate delegation at San Francisco. Singly or in tandem, all conducted propaganda efforts of their own.

Even the "official" Jewish Agency was divided into Palestinian and American sections, the former represented at the conference by Reuven Shiloah, Gershon Agron, and Elath, the latter by Nahum Goldmann. While many of the American Zionist groups also functioned under the umbrella structure of the American Zionist Emergency Council, their confederative relationship soon was undermined by rivalry between the council's cochairmen, Stephen S. Wise and Abba Hillel Silver. Witnessing this chaos of duplication and competition, Elath could only reflect sadly:

Our Jewish pluralism stems evidently not so much from schisms in ideology or organization as from the basic lack of an internationally recognized Jewish body enjoying official authority and prestige among the family of nations. Only a Jewish state will serve this need and possess the moral, if not always officially recognized, right to speak on behalf of the Jewish people as a whole.

It was wishful thinking. Elath's illusion of future Zionist discipline was belied by his own shrewd and sharply drawn vignettes of the leading American Zionist spokesmen at San Francisco. The brilliant, multilingual statesman Nahum Goldmann, for example, emerges in these pages as the most astute and knowledgeable of the "maximalists," those committed to the Biltmore Program of a sovereign Jewish commonwealth in Palestine. On the other hand, newly declassified State Department material reveals that Goldmann, losing his nerve in 1948 at the prospect of war in Palestine, actively cooperated with Secretary of State George Marshall in attempting to persuade David Ben-Gurion to delay independence for Israel. For that matter, Goldmann in later years became a frequent public critic of Israel's sovereign policies. At San Francisco, too, the mighty tribune Stephen Wise, long a champion of democratic, mass action within the American Jewish community, appears in 1945 as a classic shtadlan, favoring the discreet, behind-the-scenes approach to key government officials. By contrast, the fiery Cleveland rabbi Abba Hillel Silver, whose political maximalism and oratorical skills were transcended by an amour propre uncommonly engorged even for the rabbinate of that generation, broke with Wise, ostensibly on the issue of mass action (but more probably out of personal rivalry), and fractured the American Zionist Emergency Council during the period of its most critical activity. If Elath noted glumly that one must take care to avoid becoming involved in American Jewish politics, he failed to anticipate the post-Israel terrain still to be claimed by the American Jewish leadership. With or without Israel, that collection of monumental dais-sitters and resolution-pronouncers would not shrink to life-size for years or even decades to come. Long after the birth of the gallant and widely admired Israeli republic, an agglomeration of American Jewish organizations and their rotating presidents would continue to arrogate to themselves the privilege of defending Israel's cause in clamorous public rallies and near-hysterical full-page newspaper advertisements— thereby reviving precisely the image of a hyphenated and aggressive Jewish conspiracy that a sovereign Jewish nation had been established to dissipate.

Yet Elath was dead accurate when he observed that the most crippling weakness of this diffused Zionist lobby at San Francisco was its exclusive obsession with Jewish moral and legal claims to a homeland, a fixation uninfluenced by even the most superficial awareness of the complexities of Middle Eastern politics. "To reach an effective and working relationship with people like . . . Kohler one has to possess firsthand knowledge and personal experience in the fields they deal with," Elath commented. "As a matter of fact, in all the American Zionist bodies represented here I have not yet met a single person with the requisite level of either background knowledge or practical experience in Arab or Middle Eastern affairs," he went on. Elath's indictment is echoed in State Department correspondence relating to Palestine in the decisive years 1945–48. Time and again exasperated references appear—less to the intransigence of American Zionist demands than to the parochialism of American Zionist information. The Jewish Agency's knowledgeable Palestinian emissaries were hardly less adamant than the American

Zionists in their desiderata; yet it was the former, not the latter, who won the respect and the occasional concessions from hard-bitten government professionals in Washington and London.

Surely none of these emissaries were more highly regarded than Eliahu Elath himself. Born in Russia, where he was an early member of the Zionist pioneers' organization, Hehalutz, "Ilyusha" Epstein (his name was Hebraized only decades later) settled in Palestine in 1925. After working as a farmhand in Rehovot and B'er Ya'akov, as a construction laborer in Transjordan, he eventually attended the Hebrew University, then studied at the American University of Beirut in 1930. Elath's background in the Middle East subsequently included numerous journalistic and Jewish Agency missions to Arab capitals. From 1934 to 1945 he served as director of the Middle East division of the Jewish Agency's Political Department. Arriving in San Francisco with these credentials, then, and with a formidable linguistic virtuosity in Russian, Hebrew, Arabic, English, and French, he was a man who understood with relentless accuracy how little moralistic or legalistic issues dictated the policies of foreign governments. Moreover, Elath's discernment was broadened by the personal access he, more than any of the American Zionist representatives, could win to the members of other delegations.

Elath's accounts of these meetings sustain their relevance even in the late 1970s. If they reveal the single-minded pro-Arabism of the British, for example, they also cast a penetrating light upon French outrage at British machinations in the Levant, the circumspect Arabophile "neutralism" of Iran and India, the perturbed sense of Christian beleaguerment of Ethiopia and Lebanon. The comment Elath attributes to a journalist attached to the Turkish delegation, a veteran of

Middle Eastern diplomacy since 1914, is worth reading and rereading in the context of Kissinger shuttle diplomacy. "Every time the Arabs were mentioned in today's conversation," Elath noted "he warned us not to depend on any agreement made with them—even one 'signed by all the kings, the emirs, and the pashas in the Arab world.' According to him, since the dawn of history Arab tribes have fought among themselves and then broken every treaty they ever put their signature to, because every peace settlement in their eyes is no more than a truce. This attitude of mind, he said, is as true now as it ever was, and time has changed nothing of substance in the mentality of their leaders."

Elath's contacts were based upon more than his far-reaching experience in Middle Eastern diplomacy, however. Those who have known the man over the years would agree that his personal qualities of temperateness, open-mindedness, and gentle charm must have contrasted vividly with the often overpowering intensity of the American Zionist delegates. These attributes, no less than Elath's insights into the Arab mentality, won him important friendships. Thus his initial discussions with Harold Beeley (of the Colonial Office) and Foy Kohler (of the State Department) began on the purely professional level and ended with long and mutually appreciative dinner conversations in San Francisco's Chinese restaurants. Other acquaintanceships blossomed into guest visits at the homes of such pro-Arabists as Archibald Roosevelt. Most impressively of all, they led to teas, lunches, and dinners with many prominent Arab officials and journalists. The latter included personalities Elath had met during his earlier years of study and diplomatic apprenticeship in the Middle East, among them Hashim Jawad and Dr. Fadhil al-Jamali, secretary and secretary-general, respectively, of the Iraqi foreign ministry; Ali Jawdat Pasha al-Ayubi, Iraqi minister to the United States; Dr. Farid Zeineddine, adviser to the Syrian delegation and later his country's deputy foreign minister; Mahmoud Abul Fath, an eminent Egyptian senator; Mahmoud Fawzi, counselor of the Egyptian delegation in Washington, and ultimately his nation's prime minister; Faris al-Khouri, the Syrian prime minister. While few attitudes were changed during Elath's courteous and lengthy parleys with these and other distinguished Arabs, the simple fact of the meetings offered telling evidence of the civilities that once could be observed between political adversaries—and of the tragic gulf that since has made an Arab and Israeli appearance in a room together virtually unthinkable.

Of all these exchanges, none were more poignant or prophetic than those between Elath and his Lebanese counterparts, most particularly the noble Maronite scholar and statesman Dr. Charles Malik. "In our talks Malik always impresses me with his tolerant opinions on religion and society," Elath recalled, unwittingly describing a mirror image of himself. "He is a gallant opponent, and his attitude to those with whom he has ideological differences is one of moderation and respect." So it was with other Maronite Lebanese whom Elath came to know well, among them Saloum el-Mokarzel, president of the National Lebanese Society of America. Indeed, no people understood better than these talented Levantine Christians—not the Ethiopians, not the Armenians, not even the Jews—that the Middle East was a heterogeneity of cultures and religions. No greater tragedy could befall the region's plenitude of minority civilizations than to succumb to Muslim domination or to its preliminary stage, the facile Western stereotype of the Middle East as essentially an Islamic preserve. "El-Mokarzel spoke about anxiety in the Maronite community . . . over the recent events in Lebanon," recalled Elath, "which point to the intention of Lebanese and Syrian Muslims to undermine the Christian character of the country and ultimately incorporate it into a 'Greater Syria.' " The date was 1945. It could as easily have been 1976, as the danger approaches the threshold of realization. If the Western Christian world appears unlikely to exert itself in behalf of its imperiled coreligionists, how much more remote the chance—then as now—that it would bestir itself to protect the Jews.

Some Zionists grasped the fact that ultimately it was less the decisions taken by gentile statesmen at international conclaves than those taken by the Jews themselves in Palestine that would make or break the Zionist claim to sovereignty. Elath's diary concludes early in July 1945 soon after the arrival in New York of David Ben-Gurion. The flinty chairman of the Jewish Agency executive did not underestimate the importance of a well-planned and efficiently executed campaign for support in the United Nations, in the United States, and elsewhere. But typically "B.-G." had made the trip from Jerusalem with the central purpose of mobilizing American Jewry for a vast fund-raising and arms-gathering effort in behalf of the Yishuv. In the end, it was there, on the soil of Eretz Yisrael itself, that the issue would be forced—by the courage and dynamism of the Jewish people on the spot. As the interview between himself and Ben-Gurion ended, Elath was moved to comment: "Ben-Gurion's remarks reminded me of John Stuart Mill's comment that 'when the object is to raise the permanent condition of a people, small means do not merely produce small effects; they produce no effects at all.' " In the context of modern Jewish history, it was this perception that became the most meaningful accomplishment of the Zionists, and most especially of the Palestinians among them. They thought, and acted, in terms of heroic solutions.

Zionism at the UN

Introduction

I

This book records in diary form the events I was involved in, the activities in which I participated, and the impressions I gathered as an emissary of the Political Department of the Jewish Agency for Palestine* to the United Nations Conference on International Organization (UNCIO), meeting in San Francisco in the late spring and early summer of 1945. The conference was convened to draft the charter of the new international organization that was to replace the League of Nations, an organization that had ceased functioning with the outbreak of World War II. I arrived in the United States on April 28, 1945, and proceeded almost immediately to San Francisco. The present memoir ends with my becoming, in July 1945, director of the Jewish Agency's Political Office in Washington, a position I held until the declaration of Israel's independence on May 15, 1948.

There were three of us representing the Political Department of the Jewish Agency at San Francisco: the late Gershon Agron (then Agronsky), editor of the *Palestine Post*, the late Reuven Shiloah (then Zaslani), a senior member of the staff

---

*Article 4 of the Mandate for Palestine granted the Jewish Agency the right of "advising and cooperating with the Administration of Palestine in such . . . matters as may affect the . . . Jewish national home and the interests of the Jewish population in Palestine. . . ." The agency headquarters were in Jerusalem.

in the department, and myself, the person responsible for relations with our neighboring countries. Our task was to consult with and assist the Jewish Agency representatives in the United States who were working at the United Nations conference to defend the rights of the Jewish people and those of the Jewish national home, as recognized by the Balfour Declaration and embodied in the Palestine Mandate held by Great Britain. Since the Jewish Agency had no official standing at the conference, our work had to be done outside the conference itself by unofficial means.

There was a special reason for an active Jewish presence at the San Francisco meeting: the threats to our vital interests posed by the participation in the conference of delegations from five Arab states. These five states constituted the Arab League, which had been set up a short time before and had taken a hostile attitude toward Zionism and the Jewish national home. It was expected that the Arab delegations at the conference would miss no opportunity to jeopardize the rights that had been ensured by the Palestine Mandate, to subvert the position of the national home, and to undermine its future.

The political aspirations of the Zionist movement in Palestine had by then been crystallized and made public. In May 1942 an Extraordinary Zionist Conference had been convened at the Biltmore Hotel in New York, one of the most fateful gatherings in Zionist history. At the inspiration of David Ben-Gurion, then chairman of the executive of the Jewish Agency, who was present, the Biltmore conference called for the establishment of a Jewish commonwealth in Palestine. It also demanded that the gates of Palestine be opened to Jewish immigration and that the Jewish Agency be given authority to handle matters of immigration and the development of the country, including the reclamation of unworked and unsettled lands for the settlement of new immigrants. The Biltmore Program, although not yet endorsed officially by the World Zionist Congress, became the guideline for planning Zionist policy to achieve its ultimate objectives.*

However, at San Francisco the issue as far as the Zionist movement was concerned was not the Biltmore Program but the fate of the Palestine Mandate, the last remaining "A" Mandate of the League of Nations. The conference had, to examine, among other matters, the status of dependent territories and make arrangements for the international trusteeship system to become part of the United Nations Charter. The proposals of the Dumbarton Oaks conference of October 1944, for the structure of a general international organization, contained no provisions concerning the disposal of the former mandated territories, and the fate of none of these territories was to be specifically dealt with by the conference.

*The Biltmore Program was a direct response to the white paper issued by the British government on May 17, 1939, which formed the foundation of a policy intended to appease the Arabs by betraying Britain's moral and legal obligations toward the Jewish people, as defined by the Balfour Declaration and contained in the League of Nations Mandate for Palestine. At its cabinet meeting on March 15, 1939, the British government had decided on the following basic elements for its policy in Palestine. (1) An independent state, with a large Arab majority, was to be established in Palestine within ten years. Meanwhile, gradual progression toward self-government was to take place, by means of the appointment of Palestinians to various ministerial offices. (2) In order to retain the prevailing ratio of two to one in favor of the Arab population, Jewish immigration to Palestine was not to exceed a total of seventy-five thousand persons, spread over a period of five years. After that time no more Jewish immigrants were to be allowed in without Arab consent. (3) In order to protect Arab villagers against the allegedly large-scale eviction caused by Jewish land purchase, the Palestine high commissioner was to have special powers to restrict land transfer to Jews (Great Britain, Public Record Office, Cab. 23/98 11[39]-5). At its meeting in June 1939 the Permanent Mandates Commission of the League of Nations denounced the white paper as inconsistent with the terms of the Mandate.

There was also no provision requiring the Mandatory Powers to transfer to the new trusteeship system the territories for which they were responsible. The relevant decision in the matter was left in their hands. Transition from mandate to trusteeship was not intended to be automatic. To dispel any doubts and prevent speculation on the subject of Palestine, Prime Minister Churchill announced in Parliament, on February 27, 1945, that the San Francisco conference would not concern itself with the Palestine problem and that its solution would be postponed until after the war.

The danger that the Jewish Agency faced at the conference was not, therefore, an overt attack by the Arabs on the Palestine Mandate or, more directly, on its clauses dealing with the rights of the Jewish people and the Jewish national home. Even if it had been open to them, for tactical reasons it is doubtful if the Arabs would have chosen such an approach. But they could confine themselves to the overall principles that the trusteeship system should adopt and induce the conference to draft general clauses that in practice would undermine the sui-generis provisions of the Palestine Mandate. This was a real threat, particularly since many delegates at San Francisco were representing their governments for the first time at an international gathering and presumably knew nothing about the vicissitudes of the Palestine Mandate or the course of events regarding the Mandate of the League of Nations throughout the years 1920–39. At best, their knowledge was scanty and superficial. This ignorance would make it easier for the Arabs to succeed in their machinations.

In these circumstances we had to warn friendly delegations about the real objective and possible tactics of the Arabs. We had to muster all our forces to guarantee that any change in the form and substance of the League of Nations mandates, as far as the Palestine Mandate was concerned, would fully respect the rights proclaimed in the Balfour Declaration and embodied in the Palestine Mandate, if it was eventually transferred to the trusteeship system. In protecting these rights we would not merely be preserving the status quo, but increasing our chances of progress in future stages of the struggle for a Jewish state in Palestine.

Needless to say, in concentrating our efforts on the defense of our rights under the Mandate our task first and foremost was to explain the Zionist case to the conference delegations. We had to clarify for them all aspects of the Palestinian question and the objectives of the Zionist endeavor to set up a Jewish state in Palestine. The demand for a Jewish state was made clear in the Jewish Agency's memorandums to the conference, in conversations with the members of delegations, and at press conferences. This information campaign also proved to be a valuable long-term investment: its effect could be detected during our struggle at the United Nations in the fateful years of 1947–48.

II

The situation of the Jewish representatives attending the San Francisco gathering was markedly different from that of the Arabs. The five Arab delegations had at their disposal all conference facilities, including the large staff of technically qualified personnel attached to the office of the secretary-general of the conference. As full members of the conference, the Arab delegates could conduct their business with other delegations through normal diplomatic channels. It was otherwise for the representatives of the various Jewish bodies. We had to search out every suitable opportunity to advance our objectives and to seize on every contact or sign of understanding and sympathy in influential circles or by individuals, whether in national delegations, in public bodies, or among the host of journalists covering the proceedings. What the Arabs could do by right of their official status in the conference itself we had to try to do by partisan means, our chief weapon being the ability to persuade anyone who would listen of our needs and of the justice of our cause.

Our suspicions about probable Arab tactics were quickly realized in the opening stages of the discussions at the UNCIO Trusteeship Committee on the principles of the trusteeship system. As we had foreseen, the Arab plan was to propose to the committee general principles and guidelines on trusteeship whose effect would be to annul the rights granted the Jewish people under the Palestine Mandate. The Arabs demanded the introduction of a clause authorizing the United Nations Charter to recognize the rights of only one people in a mandated territory. If the Arab proposals were adopted, the legal foundations of the Palestine Mandate and of the national home would be shaken, and the recognition of the historic aspirations and rights of the Jewish people as a people in Palestine would be undermined. The intention of the Arab delegations was to confer on the Arab majority in Palestine the sole right to decide the political future of the country and its national character.

A most important factor working in our favor, in fact a decisive one for the outcome, was that the British, French, and American delegations at the conference all strongly opposed the Arab designs. It emerged that the Arab proposals to the committee would adversely affect important interests of these powers in areas they either ruled directly or possessed considerable influence in. The proposals also contained, in their opinion, a threat to the peace and stability of countries in Asia and Africa made up of diverse racial, tribal, or national populations. Incidentally, the fact that the Arabs argued their case on grounds of principle and that on no occasion during the deliberations in the Trusteeship Committee did they refer to Palestine only increased British, American, and French opposition and, consequently, our chances of success.

I need hardly add that the British delegation's concern,

which flowed partly from the broad, continuous colonial administration of territories in the British Empire, also stemmed from their fear that any material change in the terms of the Palestine Mandate might open a Pandora's box of further changes—including some that could adversely affect the position and privileges of Great Britain as a Mandatory Power. The Great Britain of Churchill, then at the height of its standing and prestige in the world, would have found no difficulty in rallying support for its views on subjects on the conference agenda, quite apart from that supplied by the British Commonwealth delegations. Because both Great Britain and the United States (the latter exerting a powerful influence at San Francisco) opposed the Arab intentions, the number of states that were prepared to vote them down multiplied, especially among the Latin American countries, members of the Pan American Union, which constituted a big voting bloc at the conference.

At the very start of the deliberations of the Trusteeship Committee the Arabs suffered total defeat on matters of substance affecting the future of Palestine, presented to the committee in the "Working Paper for a Chapter of the Charter on Dependent Territories and Arrangements for International Trusteeship." Only the Arab delegates voted in favor of their own proposals. Those voting against included the delegates of all the five Great Powers. It certainly appeared that the Arab maneuver had no chance of success and that the committee's decisions would be passed on without further difficulty to the next stages of formal procedure: Commission II of the General Assembly and then the plenary session of the conference. However, to the surprise of the committee, and indeed the entire conference, the delegation of the Soviet Union suddenly changed its tune, and at a subsequent session of the Trusteeship Committee joined the Arab bloc by questioning the decision it had previously supported and voted for; it called for further discussion of the clause, which, as passed, would ensure the rights of the Jewish people and the Jewish national home in Palestine if put under a trusteeship.

It had been thought that Soviet opposition to the Arab stand at one stage of the Trusteeship Committee's discussions, on a point directly linked to the Palestine question, did not mean its fundamental support for Zionism. Equally, when the USSR later supported an Arab amendment that it had rejected only a few days previously, it was doubtful if any pro-Arab motives were involved. The Soviet tactics could be better explained as exploitation of the committee's discussions affecting Palestine to highlight the differences of opinion between the Arab League —making its debut at an international gathering—and Great Britain, the Arab League's patron, on a matter of great importance to both parties; it also gave the Soviet delegation a chance to use their flexible position on the issue at the right moment to bargain with the British on matters concerning the Soviet Union.

III

As it happened, the Arab stratagem failed despite Soviet support, and the Arabs achieved none of their aims at San Francisco on matters affecting Palestine. In the United Nations Charter the conference confirmed the rights of the Jewish people in Palestine, even if the Palestine Mandate was eventually replaced by a trusteeship. It was not so much what the Arabs did that surprised the Jewish and Zionist representatives in San Francisco however, for an Arab move on Palestine had been expected; it was Soviet opposition on a matter vital to the future of the Zionist cause and the Jewish national home in Palestine that caused concern. The Soviet Union had become a leading world power in the aftermath of Hitler's defeat. The USSR had contributed much to the Allied victory, and the Soviet Union had gained standing and prestige that increased its influence in international affairs. True, the inconsistency the Russians showed at the Trusteeship Committee deliberations could be interpreted as tactics rather than as evidence of any considered and settled policy on the Palestine question. This became still more probable when the Russians made no further attempt to give the Arabs any special help in later committee discussions on clauses that affected the Palestine Mandate.

Nevertheless, there were grounds for concern that Soviet behavior might here prove a guide to what would happen at future stages of our political struggle, particularly as there were no means to verify the Russians' position: there was no contact with Moscow, and the Soviet delegation avoided any real communication with the Jewish representatives at San Francisco. As a matter of fact, uncertainty about the Soviet stand on the Palestine question lasted until Andrei Gromyko's famous speech on May 14, 1947, at a special session of the United Nations General Assembly, a speech that, in the words of Moshe Sharett, "came as a great surprise, as a bombshell."* This was the first time that the Soviet Union's attitude to the national aspirations of the Jewish people in Palestine had been stated at an international forum, and moreover, at a UN session, dedicated to the Palestine question itself. However, the course of events after the San Francisco conference showed that what had occurred there was not a precedent on the Palestine question; the positions taken then were not sustained by either Britain or the Soviet Union.

At San Francisco concerns about the Jewish people and the national home dovetailed with Britain's interest in safe-

*Moshe Sharett, *Bi'Sha-ar Ha'umot 1946–1949* (At the Threshold of Statehood, 1946–1949), Tel Aviv: Am Oved, 1958), p. 73.

guarding the integrity of the Palestine Mandate. The Soviet Union, adhering to its long-established, uncompromising ideological and political anti-Zionism, took the opportunity to undermine British prestige in the eyes of the newborn Arab League, which had emerged on the international scene with Britain's blessing. Yet little more than two years later it was the USSR that supported the creation of a Jewish state at the Lake Success session of the United Nations General Assembly, and this time it was Britain that opposed the move and placed obstacles in the way of implementing the decision. At San Francisco the British position on matters of vital importance to the Zionist cause and to the future of the Jewish national home in Palestine was crucial to us, while the Soviet opposition at that juncture was without impact on its outcome. However, when the Palestine question was placed by the Mandatory Power on the agenda of a special UN General Assembly in 1947, "for consideration of the above question," and more particularly in the stages subsequent to the decisions of that assembly, the Soviet Union's role became crucial on a number of occasions, as important as the British position had been at San Francisco. On both occasions, however, Soviet tactics were motivated primarily by considerations of short-term policies in the Middle East and in its relations with Great Britain.

IV

The United States emerged from World War II as the strongest power in the world, militarily and economically. U. S. armed forces were based on all five continents, and the country had become involved in problems beyond its traditional concern for the security of the American continent and the oceans that touch its shores. Its participation in the United Nations conference at San Francisco represented the opening of a new chapter in American foreign policy and signified the end of the interwar period of isolationism. The United States had made a great contribution to the establishment of the new world organization and to the determination of its responsibilities and guiding principles. New York was chosen as the permanent site of the organization headquarters and as the center of most of its sections and agencies. By joining the organization the United States had pledged itself to join with other countries in the preservation of peace and security and the development of understanding and cooperation within the family of nations. The chief architect of America's new internationalism, President Franklin Delano Roosevelt, had died. Roosevelt's successor was Harry S. Truman. In the eyes of the general public in America and abroad he seemed at that time to possess neither Woodrow Wilson's intellectual gifts nor Roosevelt's diplomatic skill. Yet he bore, at a fateful moment for mankind, the historic responsibility to achieve what these two men had labored for but had not managed to realize.

Many delegates at the conference in San Francisco, not least the Americans, were still in doubt as to the new president's aims: would he remain loyal to Roosevelt's vision, broaden his predecessor's aspirations, and continue an active American international role? Or would he opt for a return to an isolationist position? At San Francisco, the United States position in the Trusteeship Committee discussions affecting the future of the Palestine Mandate was certainly friendly and helpful to the Zionist cause. But this did not necessarily mean it would remain so if the rift between the Zionist movement and the Mandatory government widened, or if embittered Jewish-Arab relations intensified the opposition of Arab states to Zionist aspirations.

The San Francisco conference still gave no clear answer to these questions, or to many others about the principles and intentions on which United States foreign policy would be based. It was also unclear what policy the United States would follow with regard to the Middle East, either inside or outside the United Nations. On the other hand, there were already several disturbing facts regarding American activities in the region and their possible effect on the Palestine question. The most significant of these activities was the economic and military involvement of the United States in Saudi Arabia.

After meeting with King ibn-Saud in February 1945, President Roosevelt said in his message to Congress: "Of the problems of Arabia, I learned more about that whole problem, the Muslim problem, the Jewish problem, by talking with ibn-Saud for five minutes than I could have learned in exchange of two or three dozen letters." The president's remark shocked Zionist leaders, who suspected that the fanatical and militantly anti-Jewish monarch had extracted an understanding from the president at the expense of vital interests of the Jewish people in Palestine. The reassurance President Roosevelt gave to Zionist leaders of his firm support for Zionist aspirations in Palestine did not dispel the concern of the Jewish public regarding what had taken place at the meeting between Roosevelt and ibn-Saud. The escalating activity of American oil companies in the area and the increase in political and military initiatives by the State Department and the army underscored the fact that the United States had entered the Middle East and the Arab world, where it now had important economic and strategic interests. It was a foregone conclusion that these interests would be taken into account in the determination of American policy in the entire area, including Palestine.

V

Present at the San Francisco conference were representatives of many Jewish communal and Zionist bodies, both in and outside the United States. Among them were the Jewish

Agency for Palestine, the American Zionist Emergency Council, the American Jewish Conference, the World Jewish Congress, the American Jewish Congress, the American Jewish Committee, the Board of Deputies of British Jews, the World Council of Jewish Women, the American Jewish Trade Union Committee for Palestine, the Canadian Jewish Congress, and others. Latin American Jewish organizations also sent representatives. In all, more than twenty Jewish public bodies were represented. They were busy distributing to the conference delegates various appeals and proposals on matters, Jewish or general, that they regarded as important. While no Jewish organization had any official standing at the conference, among the advisers to the United States delegation were representatives of the American Jewish Conference and the American Jewish Committee, whose advice was sought on subjects of interest to the Jewish people. The leaders of these two organizations could utilize their status with the American delegation in approaching delegations from other countries at the conference.

A lack of concerted action highlighted the divisions in Jewish ranks, divisions that not even the grim events in Europe had managed to bridge. Yet at this first international gathering after the end of the Nazi and Fascist nightmare, the Jewish presence at San Francisco was demonstrating the central place that Palestine occupied in its claims. What was especially impressive was that this was true not only of the Zionist bodies but of the most prominent Jewish organizations, which had previously shown no interest in or had even opposed a Zionist solution as the source of hope and inspiration for a homeless people in its centuries-long search for national dignity, peace, and security. This represented more than simply a moral victory for the Zionist idea. In thus augmenting its strength the Zionist movement furthered its claim to embody the national struggle of the Jewish people for its historic rights in its ancestral land. This achievement had a considerable influence on public opinion and greatly strengthened the Jewish Agency's standing among the United Nations conference delegates, thereby easing its task at San Francisco.

This gain, however, could not wholly offset the damage done to the coordinated effort of the Jewish Agency and other Jewish organizations by the representatives of a number of Jewish bodies who worked independently in San Francisco. Their activities usually embarrassed conference delegates who, although ready to assist the Zionist cause, often found it difficult to do so when they had to thread their way through the many conflicting proposals for the solution of the Jewish problems with which they were bombarded, including the Palestine question. The confused situation was frequently exploited by those hostile to the Zionist cause, who pointed to the lack of unity in Jewish ranks on the Palestine question and to divisions among Zionists themselves.

VI

Five Arab states—Egypt, Iraq, Saudi Arabia, Syria, and Lebanon—had full rights at the conference, although only Egypt and Iraq had been members of the League of Nations. They held added prestige as the second largest geographical bloc among the forty-nine delegations attending the conference, the first being the Pan American Union. Since 1941 the British government had actively supported the establishment of the Arab League. The United States attitude to the Arab intention to set up a bloc for social, economic, and cultural cooperation was sympathetic and positive, as expressed in Washington's dispatches to the Arab states in October 1943 and July 1944. The Arab delegations, therefore, expected encouragement and assistance from both the British and the

United States conference delegations. The conflicting, and on occasion strongly conflicting, points of view in the Trusteeship Committee did not, however, affect the basic aspects of the Arab-British understanding, which was supported by military and political arrangements in the area. The American attitude was expressed through special attention paid to the Saudi Arabian delegation.

The main opposition to the Arab League at San Francisco came from the Soviet Union and from France. Both powers regarded the league as a British tool. In the eyes of the French it violated their historic position and traditional cultural and political influence in Syria and Lebanon. The Soviet Union saw in the league a result of the British intention to secure total domination of the Middle East and a threat to Soviet security interests in the area.

The French delegates at San Francisco were among the most sympathetic to Zionist aspirations. They supported the Jewish Agency's demands to the conference, and the French representative on the Trusteeship Committee was among the first to oppose anything in the amendments offered by the Arab delegates that might damage Jewish interests.

The China of Chiang Kai-shek, which was one of the five Great Powers, had no direct political or military interest in Palestine, the Arab League, or the Arab states' objectives at the conference. Nevertheless, anything tending to strengthen the position and influence of Asian states in world affairs was welcomed by the Chinese. In the course of the conference proceedings the Arab states usually enjoyed the willing support of the Chinese delegation.

As for the smaller states attending the conference, the Zionist demands for the preservation of the rights of the Jewish people as embodied in the Palestine Mandate, as well as in the Biltmore Program, were received by most delegations with sympathetic understanding and support. This attitude was particularly strong among the delegations from liberated Europe and most delegations from Latin American countries.

The Arabs' neighbors, Turkey and Iran, had reason for concern at the appearance of an Arab bloc at the world forum, prompted by considerations of prestige and anxiety over Arab intentions. This was particularly evident as the large Arab presence impressed other delegations; they were seen as representing the majority of the states of the Middle East, not simply as the members of the Arab League. Throughout the conference the Turks and Iranians treated the Arabs with respect, but behind the scenes they worked ceaselessly to undermine the Arab League's attempt to gain recognition as a regional organization enjoying special status in the United Nations.

Although some of the delegates from Turkey and Iran expressed private sympathy for the Zionist cause, there was no reason to expect their delegations to support Zionist aims. Both Turkey and Iran at that time faced the threat of Soviet designs on their territorial integrity, and neither could do without the help of Great Britain, then the leading military power in the region. A further consideration was that despite their hostility to the Arab League and to Arab designs in world affairs, they did not want their relations with their Arab neighbors to suffer because of a pro-Jewish stand on the Palestine question.

Like Turkey and Iran, Greece adopted a reserved position on the Palestine question. There was concern for the welfare of the large and wealthy Greek community in Egypt and fear that a careless move might adversely affect the position of Greeks living in Arab countries.

Arab unity at the conference was far from complete. On matters of seniority and prestige, the mutual jealousies and rivalries among Arab delegations and within delegations were as evident as was their unity on other occasions, best demonstrated during the Trusteeship Committee discussions affecting Palestine. On most occasions the Egyptian delegate acted as the spokesman for the entire Arab bloc, both at the conference itself and in the Arab League's contacts with the press; its representatives always found time to stress Egypt's central role in the league and its emerging leadership of the Arab bloc of states. When I asked a good friend, an Egyptian senator, how it felt to be an Egyptian in the Arab League, he defined Egypt's role: "We will play the part in the Arab League that Britain does in the British Commonwealth."

What in fact happened in San Francisco was that the Arab delegations failed to achieve their aims on the two important points on which they agreed: they could not (1) advance United Nations recognition of the league as a regional organization, a point that the United Nations conference itself was not empowered to decide; or (2) insert clauses in the Trusteeship Chapter of the United Nations Charter that would annul the historic rights of the Jewish people in Palestine and undermine the future of the Jewish national home.

VII

This book comprises material drawn from a diary I kept at the time, as well as my reports to the Jerusalem and London offices of the Jewish Agency. In assembling the volume I have been greatly aided by rereading the letters I wrote during the period to my wife in Jerusalem. I have also found it useful to insert into the text part of a letter to Ze'ev Sharef, then secretary of the Political Department of the Jewish Agency, in which I summarized my impressions of the United Nations conference after my mission in San Francisco had been completed.

It should be noted that there already exists a small library of books on various aspects and stages of the Zionist political struggle in the United Nations leading to the establishment of the state of Israel, including personal accounts by participants in the events.* However, to the best of my knowledge, no other Jewish representative at the San Francisco United Nations Conference on International Organization has set down his impressions and recollections of the proceedings. The purpose of this memoir therefore is to fill, however incompletely, a gap in the general story of the Zionist struggle in the fateful years 1945–48. The San Francisco conference can be regarded as the prelude to the momentous events that followed. At a time when relations between Zionism and the UN have fallen to their lowest ebb, it is to be hoped that these recollections will serve to remind present-day readers of the Jewish achievements at San Francisco and show how these contributed to the ultimate outcome of the Zionist struggle in the United Nations.

*See, for instance, Jacob Robinson, *Palestine and the United Nations: Prelude to Solution* (Washington, D. C.: Public Affairs Press, 1947). Chapter 1 of this comprehensive and well-documented volume deals with the discussions in the Trusteeship Committee of the United Nations conference affecting the Palestine Mandate.

San Francisco, April 30–May 25, 1945

1 In the Corridors

On February 23, 1919, a Jewish delegation, led by Chaim Weizmann, appeared before the Council of Ten of the Peace Conference in Paris. Recounting the immemorial attachment and historic claim of the Jewish people to the land of Israel, it presented the case for the establishment of a Jewish national home in Palestine. As Nahum Sokolow reminded the council, declarations favorable to the Jewish national aspirations had been expressed by various governments following the issuance of the Balfour Declaration by the British government on November 2, 1917. Thus the Jewish question, and its national and international aspects relative to Palestine, were formally submitted to an international forum convoked to settle the problems of a world shaken by the cataclysm of World War I.

Twenty-six years later, in the wake of another even more terrible world conflict, delegations from forty-nine states gathered in San Francisco on April 25, 1945, to "reaffirm faith in fundamental human rights, in the dignity and worth of the human person, in the equal rights of men and women and of nations large and small"—principles to be incorporated in the Charter of the new world organization that was coming into being. But in San Francisco, unlike the Paris of 1919, there was no place at the conference table for one small nation, the Jews, a long-suffering people who had just endured their greatest travail.

For the Jewish delegations unofficially assembled in San Francisco to plead the cause of their people as best they could, the occasion was marked by a growing sense of despair, fed by the news pouring in daily from abroad —revelations about the horrors of the death camps, the plight of the survivors, the increasing tensions in Palestine. Nevertheless, it was also felt to be a time of unparalleled opportunity and a prelude to historic achievement, as for the first time on the international scene Jews and Arabs confronted each other about the future of Palestine.

23

Monday, April 30, 1945

I arrived at the Padre Hotel late this evening from New York, where I had stayed before coming to the United Nations[1] Conference on International Organization (UNCIO) here in San Francisco. I will serve as adviser to the delegation of the Jewish Agency for Palestine. Along with other Jewish organizations, the agency holds a watching brief at the conference over the rights and needs of the Jewish people in a world emerging from the destruction caused by the war—a war in which the Jews suffered more than any other people. In particular, the Jewish Agency has the task of protecting the interests of the Jewish national home in Palestine, of ensuring that they will not be undermined by any international arrangements worked out by the United Nations Organization when it falls heir to the League of Nations and its institutions, including Permanent Mandates Commission.

Moshe Shertok[2] sent me to San Francisco at the suggestion

[1]The term "United Nations" was applied in the 1939–45 war to those countries that fought against Germany and its allies. The name was later taken over by the international organization set up in San Francisco.

[2]Afterward Moshe Sharett (1894–1965); member of the Jewish Agency executive and head of its Political Department in Jerusalem (1933–48); Israel's first foreign minister (1948–56); second prime minister (1953–55); chairman of the Jewish Agency executive (1960–65).

of Dr. Chaim Weizmann,[3] who attributes much importance to the conference. My coming here was also supported by Eliahu Golomb,[4] with whom, a few weeks ago, I traveled from Jerusalem to Tel Aviv. We talked about events in the Arab world and the fact that there would be five Arab states, with the same rights and privileges as other participants, at the San Francisco conference: Egypt, Iraq, Saudi Arabia, Syria, and Lebanon. The Arabs will doubtless use the high international standing and importance of the conference to further their political influence, which suffered because of the wartime collaboration of many Arab leaders with Fascist Italy and Nazi Germany. One of the Arab aims that clearly emerged from the Annex Regarding Palestine, in the Pact of the League of Arab States at their congress in Cairo last month [March 1945], will be to change the international status of Palestine to their advantage. Nor can there be any doubt that Britain will stand alongside the Arab League. Led by the foreign secretary, Anthony Eden,[5] the shapers of the pro-Arab policy and its supporters in the British government have encouraged and actively assisted in founding the league. In the face of expected threats from the Arab states, we have been forced to launch an effective response in the United States. This country's public opinion has always been sympathetic to Zionism, and American influence in world affairs, which was higher than ever during the war, is now

[3]Chaim Weizmann (1897–1952); born in Russia; active in Zionist movement from its inception; migrated to Britain (1904); president of the World Zionist Organization (1920–31 and 1935–48); first president of the state of Israel.

[4]Eliahu Golomb (1893–1945); prominent leader of the Jewish labor movement in Palestine and one of the creators of the Haganah.

[5]Earl of Avon, Anthony Eden (1897–   ); British foreign secretary (1940–45, 1951–55); Conservative prime minister (1955–57).

reaching its peak with the approaching victories in Europe
and the Far East.

The San Francisco conference was discussed early in April in
the Political Department of the Jewish Agency in Jerusalem,
and one of the practical conclusions we reached was the
decision to mount a wide-ranging and thorough information
campaign directed at the member states of the conference,
exposing Arab collaboration with the Fascists and Nazis, as
opposed to the many valuable contributions that the Yishuv
(as the Jewish community of Palestine is called) has made to
the war effort of the democracies. It was thought that only
our people in Jerusalem are sufficiently acquainted with the
subject and possess the required knowledge and information
on Arab affairs to carry out this task properly and effectively.

Information reached Jerusalem from the United States that
Nahum Goldmann[6] and Louis Lipsky[7] will be in San Fran-
cisco during the conference, as the representatives of the
Jewish Agency, and that Jewish and Zionist leaders from the

[6]Nahum Goldmann (1894–   ); representative of the Jewish
Agency for Palestine to the League of Nations in Geneva (1934–40);
member of the executive of the World Zionist Organization and the
Jewish Agency (since 1934); played a major role in the Reparations
Agreement with West Germany; chairman (since 1936) and president (since 1953) of the World Jewish Congress; president of the
World Zionist Organization (1956–69).
[7]Louis Lipsky (1876–1963); became editor (1901) of the *Mac-
cabean,* the official monthly of the Federation of American Zionists,
and also of its successor, the weekly *New Palestine* (until 1928); early
Zionist theoretician in the U.S.; president of the Zionist Organization of America (ZOA) (1925–30); national U.S. chairman of Keren
Hayesod; founding member of the Emergency Council for Zionist
Affairs; founder of the American Jewish Conference and cochairman (1944–49) of its Interim Committee; chairman of the American
Zionist Council (1949–54); chairman of the American Zionist Committee for Public Affairs.

United States, Canada, Great Britain, and a number of South American countries will also be coming to the conference, representing their respective organizations. We were also informed that the Jewish Agency will have no official standing at the conference and that only two Jewish organizations in the United States itself—the American Jewish Conference and the American Jewish Committee—have been invited by the State Department to act in an advisory capacity to the American delegation at the conference. Under the circumstances, all other Jewish bodies, including the Jewish Agency, will apparently have to rely on these two American Jewish organizations to use their official standing and personal influence on the United States delegation in favor of the Zionist cause. Among the leaders of the American Jewish Conference and its spokesmen there are prominent Zionists, and doubtless we can obtain help from its representatives as advisers to the American delegation. However, we cannot take for granted the assistance of the representatives of the American Jewish Committee.

In view of the vital importance of a strong Zionist representation at San Francisco, it was decided to reinforce our presence here with people from Jerusalem. Gershon Agronsky,[8] Reuven Zaslani,[9] and I were chosen to go to the conference, which opened on April 25. Reuven was the first of us to leave for America.

[8]Afterward Gershon Agron (1894–1959); founder and editor of the *Palestine Post* and, later, the *Jerusalem Post;* mayor of Jerusalem (from 1955 until his death).
[9]Afterward Reuven Shiloah (1909–59); senior official of the Jewish Agency for Palestine and later an official in the Ministry for Foreign Affairs of Israel.

Tuesday, May 1

Today is my first day at the conference. For the last five days representatives of forty-nine states have gathered here in San Francisco and have been discussing matters of the highest importance to the world now free from the Nazi danger. Judging by the list of members of the delegations, it is a most impressive gathering of distinguished personalities. Some were famous in prewar political life in their own countries and at the League of Nations, but the majority of them are new faces in public life who have acquired influence during the war years or have risen to power as a result of revolutionary changes in the regimes at home.

On April 24 I flew from Lydda to Cairo, and after two days Gershon and I managed, with the help of the American embassy, to obtain seats on a military plane to Miami. Our numerous stops en route made the distance and the time in flight between Cairo and Miami seem even longer than they actually were; war conditions still prevail in all the airports where we had to change planes.

Early on April 28 I landed on American soil, the beginning of my first visit to the United States. I have a formal tie with the United States, since the diploma I earned at the American University of Beirut accords me the privileges of a graduate of an institution of higher learning in New York State. But it has contributed little to my knowledge of America and its people.

We flew from Miami to New York and went straight from

the airport to the home of Meyer Weisgal,[10] secretary-general of the Jewish Agency's American office, who is a friend of Agronsky's. He informed us about the latest developments in Jewish affairs in the United States and at the San Francisco conference. We had known before we left Jerusalem that the Jewish Agency failed to secure any status at the conference. Britain opposed us on this point, and no other country would support the agency's claims in the matter against the wishes of the Mandatory Power. There is no Jewish delegation in San Francisco that is recognized by the United Nations. The Jewish voice can be heard only by the United States delegation—and then only when it is invited occasionally, along with other public, religious, and professional groups, to advise on matters affecting special interests.

One of the two Jewish organizations with the status of adviser to the United States delegation is the American Jewish Conference. Much of its membership is Zionist or at least friendly to Zionism. Henry Monsky,[11] the president of B'nai B'rith and chairman of the American Jewish Conference, works closely with the Zionist groups and organizations present at San Francisco, and coordinates his activities on matters related to Palestine with theirs.

The other Jewish organization with similar status vis-à-vis

[10]Meyer Weisgal (1894–   ); came to the U.S. (1905); emigrated to Israel (1949); editor of the *Maccabean* (1918–21) and the *New Palestine* (1921–30); national secretary of the ZOA (1921–30); secretary-general of the American Section of the Jewish Agency (1943–46); personal political representative of Chaim Weizmann in the U.S. and author of books about him; chancellor (since 1970) of the Weizmann Institute.

[11]Henry Monsky (1890–1947); president of B'nai B'rith (from 1938 until his death) and chairman of the American Jewish Conference from its inception (1943) until his death. The AJConference disbanded in 1949, following differences over the organization's functions and activities among the organizations that had set it up.

the American delegation is the American Jewish Committee. This body originally participated in the work of the American Jewish Conference, but broke away after refusing to cooperate with the majority of the AJConference in the proposal to strive for the establishment of a Jewish commonwealth in Palestine in the spirit of the Biltmore Program.[12] The American Jewish Committee has a much smaller membership than that of the combined organizations represented by the American Jewish Conference, but it wields considerable influence on the general American public and press, and some of its leaders have good personal connections in the higher quarters of the government, including the State Department. Heading the American Jewish Committee's delegation at San Francisco is its president, Judge Joseph Proskauer,[13] who led those opposed to the resolution on the Jewish commonwealth in Palestine at the American Jewish Conference sessions in New York.

The Jewish Agency's representatives in San Francisco are Dr. Nahum Goldmann and Louis Lipsky. They are assisted by Dr. Jacob Robinson,[14] head of the Institute of Jewish

[12]The Biltmore Program, adopted by an Extraordinary Zionist Conference in New York on May 11, 1942, read in part: "The Conference calls for fulfillment of the original purpose of the Balfour Declaration and the Mandate, which, 'recognizing the historical connection of the Jewish people with Palestine,' was to afford them the opportunity, as stated by President Wilson, to found there a Jewish Commonwealth."

[13]Joseph Meyer Proskauer (1877–1971); attorney and member of the N.Y. State Supreme Court (1927–30); president of the American Jewish Committee (1943–49).

[14]Jacob Robinson (1889–   ); specialist in international law; founded the Institute of Jewish Affairs (1941) and was its director (until 1947); special consultant on Jewish affairs to the chief of counsel for the U.S. in the Nuremberg war criminal trials; helped organize the Human Rights Commission of the UN (1946); legal adviser to the Israeli delegation to the UN (1948–

Affairs of the World Jewish Congress, and Arthur Lourie,[15] director of the American Zionist Emergency Council (AZEC). Robinson is an expert international lawyer, who served as counsel to the Lithuanian delegation at the League of Nations and also, when required, at the World Court. His broad knowledge and rich practical experience are invaluable to our delegation, all of whom are public figures and all, on the whole, amateurs in international legal matters and diplomatic procedures. The arrival of Reuven Zaslani, who preceded us to San Francisco, was of considerable help to the delegation. I find it hard to understand why Eliezer Kaplan,[16] who is in Saint Louis, is not here in San Francisco. Is the political front less important than the financial matters to which Kaplan is devoting all his time and energies? As a Palestine member of the Agency's executive he could contribute both knowledge and prestige to our delegation and would be able to glean the personal impressions so valuable for the future of our relations with the new world organization.[17]

---

57); after 1957, adviser to the Conference on Jewish Material Claims against Germany; drafted the Israeli-German Reparations Agreement and advised Israelis on questions of documentation and law regarding the Eichmann case; currently coordinator of research activities and publications on the Holocaust for YIVO and Yad Vashem.

[15]Arthur Lourie (1903–   ); born in South Africa; political secretary of the Jewish Agency's London executive; director of the AZEC; later Israel's ambassador in Canada and the United Kingdom; deputy director of the Ministry for Foreign Affairs.

[16]Eliezer Kaplan (1891–1952); labor leader and first finance minister of Israel; born into a prominent Zionist family in Russia, he was active in Zionist affairs from his youth; served as a delegate to all Zionist Congresses, beginning with the eleventh (Vienna, 1913); emigrated to Palestine (1923); member of Jewish Agency executive (from 1933), heading its Finance and Administrative Departments; became deputy prime minister of Israel shortly before his death.

[17]The Jewish Agency executive did not then include a

In the short time we had in New York, Agronsky and I managed to meet with several people who provided us with useful background knowledge on the San Francisco conference. Agronsky, who was born in Russia and came to America as a child, conferred with a number of his colleagues in the newspaper world. He has seen to it that more detailed material on Palestine will be published than has previously been possible because of the strict wartime press censorship on news from Palestine. That sort of information includes vital Jewish contributions to the war effort of the Allied troops stationed in our area, knowledge of which has never reached the public outside Palestine—economic, scientific, and technical assistance that could not be obtained otherwise in the entire Middle East.

---

fully powered representative of the American Zionist movement. From 1935 on Lipsky was the American representative of the Jewish Agency and had only advisory status on the executive on matters affecting his work. Dr. Goldmann, too, was still not a full member of the executive. Beginning in 1935 he served as the Jewish Agency's representative at the League of Nations at Geneva; after his appointment to this position the Zionist Congress allotted him a seat on the Jewish Agency executive in London with the right to advise on questions connected with his post. Only at the August 1945 London meeting of the Zionist Council did Goldmann and Lipsky become full members of the Jewish Agency executive, with voting rights on political subjects. The meeting also conferred similar rights on Dr. Stephen Wise and Dr. Abba Hillel Silver, then joint chairmen of the American Zionist Emergency Council. With Dr. Israel Goldstein representing the Zionist Organization of America, Rose Halprin of Hadassah, Hayim Greenberg of Poalei Zion, and Leon Gellman of Mizrachi, they constituted the Zionist body that conducted the political work of the Jewish Agency in the U.S. until the 1946 Zionist Congress.

We left New York for San Francisco, where the United Nations Conference on International Organization has opened a new chapter in the history of a world striving for peace and stability and facing challenges of decisive importance for the future of humanity. One of the most urgent problems awaiting solution is that of the survivors of the Holocaust. Will the conference rise to this challenge? Will it understand the problem and draw the necessary practical conclusions affecting the future of Palestine, the only country where their national life and dignity can be fully restored?

Wednesday, May 2

This morning I went to the Butler Building, the meeting place assigned to the delegations of the Jewish Agency and the other Jewish organizations. I have been informed that their members get together daily to discuss the previous day's happenings and the agenda for the coming day, and I have been invited to join them.

The first person I saw was Nahum Goldmann. I got to know him in 1937, when the Political Department of the Jewish Agency in Jerusalem sent me to Geneva for the League of Nations Permanent Mandates Commission discussion of the Peel report on partition of Palestine. My duty there was to assist Dr. Goldmann, at that time the Jewish Agency's representative on Geneva, in explaining to members of the commission our views on the subject.

This morning Goldmann introduced me to Dr. Stephen

Wise,[18] Louis Lipsky, Rose Halprin,[19] Henry Monsky, Judge
Morris Rothenberg,[20] Dr. Israel Goldstein,[21] Herman Shulman[22] and his wife Rebecca,[23] and many others, among them
American members of the staff of the Jewish Agency and the
American Jewish Conference, who came to the meeting. I
had never taken part in a World Zionist Congress or convention, and this was my first opportunity to meet the spokesmen and leaders of American Zionism, including Wise and
Lipsky, who were among the founders of the Zionist organization in the United States.

At the meeting Agronsky reported on the situation in
Palestine and I answered questions on developments in

[18]Stephen S. Wise (1874–1949); prominent Reform rabbi; a
founder and the first secretary of the Federation of American Zionists; founder of the Jewish Institute of Religion; founder of the
American Jewish Congress and its president (1925–29 and 1935–49);
cochairman of the American Zionist Emergency Council; a founder
of the World Jewish Congress (and its president until his death).

[19]Rose Halprin (1897–   ); national president of Hadassah
(1933–34, 1947–52); member of the Zionist General Council (1939–
46); treasurer of the AZEC (from 1942) and vice-chairman (1945–
47); chairman of the Palestine Committee of the American Jewish
Conference (1943–46); member of the Jewish Agency executive,
American Section (from 1946), and its chairman (1956–60).

[20]Morris Rothenberg (1885–1950); labor lawyer, appointed
judge of New York City Magistrates' Court; president of the Zionist
Organization of America (1932–36); president of the Jewish National Fund (1943–49); active in rescue and resettlement of Holocaust refugees; chairman of Executive Committee of the American
Jewish Congress.

[21]Israel Goldstein (1896–   ); Conservative rabbi and Zionist leader; president of the American Jewish Congress (1951–58);
president of the ZOA (1943–45); honorary president of the Jewish
National Fund; member of the Jewish Agency executive (1948–49).

[22]Herman Shulman was a member of the Executive Committee of the AZEC and of the interim and administrative committees
of the American Jewish Conference. He died soon after the San
Francisco conference.

[23]Rebecca Bildner Shulman (1896–   ); national president
of Hadassah (1953–56); attended nearly every Zionist Congress,
beginning with the sixteenth (Zurich, 1929).

the Arab camp. From the numerous reports at the meeting I realized how much activity has been generated at UNCIO by numerous Jewish groups and delegations, including those who are, I gather, working independently of the rest. In addition to the delegations representing world and American Jewish organizations, who have been coordinating their activities on general Jewish and Palestine issues, there are no less than twenty various Jewish groups, most with no public standing or real significance in Jewish life; they are active in the lobbies of the conference and among its participants, advocating all kinds of solutions for Jewish problems, including that of Palestine. The haphazard activities of these groups have already caused much confusion and embarrassment to the delegations attending the conference, even to those prepared to help the Jewish cause, while making the activities of the Jewish Agency and its associated bodies more difficult and on occasion less effective.

Among the groups that work on their own are Agudath Israel, the American Jewish Committee, the New Zionist Organization, the Hebrew Committee of National Liberation, the Committee for International Peace, the Jewish Labor Committee and—working against our goal—the American Council for Judaism.

On the other hand, the World Jewish Congress, the American Jewish Congress, the Canadian Jewish Congress, the Board of Deputies of British Jews, the American Jewish Trade Union Committee for Palestine, and the World Council of Jewish Women all work in conjunction with the Jewish Agency and the American Jewish Conference. (The Trade Union Committee was formed in the spring of 1944 by Zionist members of the Jewish Labor Committee, under the chairmanship of Max Zaritsky, president of the United Hatters, with Philip Murray, president of the Congress of Industrial

Organizations [CIO], and William Green, president of the American Federation of Labor [AFL], as honorary chairmen.) The Zionist parties in the United States (Mizrachi, Poalei Zion, and the General Zionists) and Hadassah have their own delegates in San Francisco in addition to their membership in the American Jewish Conference. So do B'nai B'rith and others who are members of the American Jewish Conference. I doubt whether any other nation on earth has as many delegates in San Francisco as does the Jewish people. Yet the Jewish representatives are confined to the corridors. Our Jewish pluralism stems evidently not so much from schisms in ideology or organization as from the basic lack of an internationally recognized Jewish body enjoying official authority and prestige among the family of nations. Only a Jewish state will serve this need and possess the moral, if not always officially recognized, right to speak on behalf of the Jewish people as a whole.

At the morning session I also met Samuel Bronfman, Samuel Zacks, and Saul Hayes, of the Canadian Jewish Congress, and Abraham Moss, Maurice Perlzweig, and Alec Easterman, of the World Jewish Congress in England. I was glad to see Dr. Jacob Robinson who, in addition to his post in the World Jewish Congress, is also serving here as legal adviser to the Jewish Agency on all matters connected with the United Nations conference.

I lunched with Herman and Rebecca Shulman and Isaiah (Si) Kenen,[24] who is the official in charge of public relations

[24]Isaiah Kenen (1905–   ); director of information for the American Emergency Council for Zionist Affairs (1943); secretary of the American Jewish Conference (1943–47); director of information for Jewish Agency delegates to the UN (1951–54); executive vice-chairman of the America Israel Public Affairs committee (1954–75); editor and publisher of *Near East Report* (1957–75).

of the American Jewish Conference. In the course of our discussions the Shulmans filled me in on some of the problems currently facing American Zionism.

Thursday, May 3

At our morning meeting Monsky, Goldstein, and Perlzweig reported on their talk with Peter Fraser,[25] New Zealand's prime minister and minister of external affairs, who serves as chairman of the Trusteeship Committee (Committee II/4) here at the conference. This is the most important committee from our point of view because it deals with matters connected with the League of Nations mandates and their future. The talk with Fraser was friendly. After expressing warm appreciation for the way Jews greeted New Zealand soldiers visiting Palestine, he emphasized that when the committee discusses mandate issues he will be on guard to see that the rights of the Jewish people assured by the Palestine Mandate will not be undermined. He expressed his readiness to be guided by our representatives on all matters affecting us and on our requests to the committee. Our representatives explained to Fraser the character of the Palestine Mandate, emphasizing that the concept of the Jewish national home embraces the entire Jewish people, and is not

[25]Peter Fraser (1884–1950); born in Scotland, emigrated to New Zealand (1910); joined the Labour party and became a member of several governments; prime minister (1940–49); friend of the Jewish people and a supporter of Zionism throughout his public and political life.

related simply to the Yishuv. This point was apparently new to Fraser. He mentioned that in the statement he made to the Trusteeship Committee a few days ago on the future of the League of Nations' legacy, he had emphasized the need to consult the wishes of the indigenous inhabitants and to let them share in deciding the fate of the territory in which they live, now subject to the Mandatory regime. His meeting with the Jewish representatives, he went on, has shown him that his definition would give the Arabs of Palestine a decisive vote in the future of the country, contrary to the Balfour Declaration and the rights of the Jewish people according to the Mandate. As the meeting ended Fraser asked for details of the circumstances of Lord Moyne's murder and sharply criticized terrorist acts in Palestine.

Perlzweig then told us of his meeting with a member of the South African delegation. He was impressed with the delegate's friendly attitude to Zionism.

I visited the Opera House, where UNCIO is convening, this afternoon. The corridors, which are long and wide, were crowded with men and women of every race, many dressed in national costume, including the delegates from Saudi Arabia, who wear traditional Arab robes and kaffiyehs. The din reminded me of New York's Times Square, which I experienced on my first day in America as, feeling desolate, I searched hopelessly for the subway platform I needed to get where I wanted to go. I had no entry pass to the public gallery of the conference hall and had to content myself with what I saw in the corridors.

Goldmann talked to me this evening about my proposed activities in San Francisco. He told me that as early as when the preparatory work was being done for the conference it had become clear that the Palestine question would not be on the agenda and that no decision would be taken on the matter. It has been agreed by the Great Powers that no territorial questions will be dealt with, and they seem ready to prevent any such questions from being raised in the course of the debates. The matter affecting us directly is the new trusteeship authority within the United Nations Organization for the territories formerly under League of Nations mandates. It is vital for us that under any new arrangement for these territories the special character of the Palestine Mandate be recognized, and that neither the rights of the Yishuv nor the legal status of the Jewish national home, as laid down in the Palestine Mandate, should be altered or injured in any respect. Our best efforts at present are being devoted to this purpose. Although we do not want a trusteeship regime to replace the existing Mandate and aspire for the establishment in Palestine of a Jewish commonwealth, our main and urgent objective at this conference must be to protect the present international status of Palestine. Any undermining of that status could have disastrous effects on the position of the Jewish national home and might adversely affect our chances in future political struggles for our rights in Palestine in a final settlement of the problem.

Goldmann said how pleased he is that I have come and emphasized the importance of having conference delegates receive firsthand information on the Arab demands and their significance for our future in Palestine. Most delegates have scant knowledge of the Middle East and of our problems. He attached special value also to my explanation of the prevailing situation in the Arab states and matters affecting relations with our neighbors.

Friday, May 4

My first job was to telephone Judge Proskauer, president of the American Jewish Committee, to request a meeting. I carried a letter of introduction to him from Dr. Nelson Glueck,[26] director of the American School of Oriental Research in Jerusalem. The judge invited me to join him for breakfast at his hotel.

When we met he at once asked whether "the Zionists have already managed to incite you against me," and if the name of his organization had been known to me before I arrived in America. He explained that his overriding concern now is the fate of the survivors of the Holocaust and his wish to find shelter for them. His concern gives him a yardstick by which to measure the programs that any Jewish organization, Zionist or not, puts forward to the same end. He criticized the Zionist leadership for proposing "hairsplitting" programs instead of uniting world Jewry behind efforts to revoke the restrictions of the notorious white paper of May 1939, on Jewish immigration to Palestine and transfers of land to Jews there. He underlined his and the AJCommittee's opposition to the white paper "as a

[26]Nelson Glueck (1900–71); Reform rabbi; director of the American School of Oriental Research in Jerusalem (1932–33, 1936–40, 1942–47); president of Hebrew Union College (from 1947) and of the combined rabbinical school, Hebrew Union College–Jewish Institute of Religion (from 1949); established the Jerusalem campus of the Reform rabbinical school; wrote extensively on his finds relating to biblical archaeology.

product in the true tradition of Munich" and his willingness to work for its cancellation.

I asked him why the AJCommittee did not join the united Jewish front set up by B'nai B'rith and other Jewish organizations in the United States, including the Zionists, in the establishment of the American Jewish Conference. He replied by explaining in detail what took place at the Pittsburgh conference of that body in January 1943 and at the New York conference seven months later, and dwelt on his opposition in principle to a body with a political program claiming to represent American Jewry. In American Jewry, he went on to say, organizations differ in their political outlook, and sometimes their members hold conflicting views on various subjects. Therefore there is no group in America, nor indeed could there be one, that can speak for every Jewish organization and claim to represent American Jewry in its entirety. The right of every public Jewish group and organization to its own opinions must therefore be respected, and each group must also take into account the views of its own minority and allow members to hold whatever opinions they choose, in addition to the objectives of their own organization. The American Jewish Committee has in its ranks both strong supporters and extreme opponents of Zionism, and, Proskauer said, the AJCommittee cannot adopt official positions on political questions related to Palestine when its own membership is so divided. I refrained from pointing out the inconsistencies in Proskauer's explanation because, in relation to the white paper (a political document par excellence), his practical attitude is so close to our own. Later in our conversation Proskauer questioned me about events in Palestine and suggested that we keep in touch with each other while in San Francisco.

From Proskauer I went to see Ray Brook, one of an army of *New York Times* reporters at the conference and a friend of mine since 1941–42, when I was in Ankara on a mission for the Political Department of the Jewish Agency. Brook was then his paper's correspondent in Turkey and each evening used to broadcast the daily news on the state radio to the *New York Times* in the United States. I used to get pieces of general information in a roundabout way occasionally, especially on the situation of the Jews in a number of European countries under German occupation, but had no idea whether this information was also reaching Jewish centers in the free world or whether, because of strict British military and political censorship, our people in New York knew enough of what was going on in Palestine. I also couldn't be sure that the Turkish censor was allowing such information to be carried by mail from Ankara to the United States. Brook and I therefore agreed that in addition to the news items I periodically fed him on different subjects connected with developments in our part of the world and in Nazi-occupied Europe, which he could use in his paper, he would from time to time include in his program information intended specifically for our New York office and understood only by them. I let Dr. Stephen Wise know of the code we devised for this purpose, and Brook's transmissions were monitored. All this was done without Brook's superiors in New York knowing about the arrangement between us. He realized the importance of the matter for our cause and decided to chance all the risks involved. In order to preserve the secrecy of the arrangement Dr. Wise appointed his daughter, Justine Wise Polier, to receive and decode the messages. By this means I also managed to inform the United States of the call I had received from Jerusalem on the eve of the battle of El Alamein for the arming of the Yishuv in the event of a German invasion of Palestine. Our people in New York made sure that this call received wide coverage in the American press, and Wise made suitable appeals on the subject of arms to President Roosevelt.

Interestingly enough, with Brook in Ankara was Cyrus

Sulzberger, the nephew of Arthur Hays Sulzberger, publisher of the *New York Times*, who was at that time the paper's special correspondent in Turkey. Although I then knew Sulzberger better than I did Brook, I preferred to ask for help from the latter rather than from an assimilated and anti-Zionist Jew, who was a member of the paper's establishment as well.

I met Brook today at his hotel, the Grosvenor. He told me he is one of fifty-five reporters his paper has assigned to San Francisco to gather material for the special edition the *Times* is bringing out in San Francisco during the conference. The operation is expensive but will enhance the paper's prestige in the eyes of the delegates of every country taking part in the conference. In reply to his question about how he might contribute to my mission in San Francisco, I explained to him that we are particularly interested in knowing what is happening in the delegations of Middle East states—Turkey, Iran, and the Arab countries—and he promised to help. He told me that the Great Powers have already reached agreement among themselves on most subjects being discussed at the conference, but that among the delegations of the smaller countries there is considerable unrest. The latter do not want simply to be dragged along by decisions of the Great Powers and have no say in matters. There has already been clear expression of this ferment, especially by the Latin Americans. I also heard from Brook that there are a conspicuously large number of delegates from the Arab countries. The speech before the plenary session of the conference a few days ago by the chairman of the Syrian delegation and prime minister of his country, Faris al-Khouri,[27] received a tumul-

_____

[27]Faris al-Khouri (1877–1962); Syrian Christian; member of Faisal's Damascus government (1920); participated in the Syrian Druze rebellion and was exiled to Lebanon; leader of Syria's National Bloc and came into power with it, becoming

tuous reception when he referred to the rights of "the en-
slaved colonial peoples." The Turks have brought some of
their best men to San Francisco: they want to appear as the
leading voice of the Middle East rather than the Arabs or the
Iranians.

Later, at the morning gathering of Jewish organizations,
Dr. Wise spoke about his conversation with Miss Wu Yi-
fang, a member of the Chinese delegation who is one of her
country's leading educators. Miss Wu sits on China's People's Political Council and has great influence in political
matters. She had asked Dr. Wise whether Jews are Catholic
or Protestant and added that, as a Christian, she had prayed
to the Holy Mother before meeting Wise to help her to be
useful in the matter coming before her! Looking at and listening to Dr. Wise, I was not surprised that his distinguished
appearance and ecclesiastical tone of voice had made the
Chinese lady think she was talking to a Christian dignitary
such as some of the American missionaries in her own country. We were amused, of course, by Dr. Wise's story, but
there is a grim warning in what he related: we should not
take for granted that our problems and aspirations are understood by or even familiar to all or most of the conference
delegates. Many of them have probably heard nothing about
the Balfour Declaration, the white paper, or the Jewish national home and know next to nothing about Jews or Judaism.

I told Louis Lipsky at lunch of the concern that President
Roosevelt's statement to Congress about his conversation
with King ibn-Saud had caused in Palestine. Lipsky spoke

---

president of parliament (1936–39, 1943, 1945–49); foreign and
finance minister (1939); prime minister (1944–45, 1954–55).
At the United Nations General Assembly in 1947 he led the
Arab opposition to the partition plan and to any solution
that might lead to the creation of a Jewish state in Palestine.

critically of the late president's character and pointed to the insincerity of his public statements on Jewish affairs. A fortnight after his talk with King ibn-Saud, Roosevelt repeated to Wise his faithful adherence to his formal promises to the Zionists, and the gist of his remarks was published in the press. But the damage done, said Lipsky, has been only partly corrected, and there is still reason for Jewish concern. I asked Lipsky what he knows of the new president's attitude to Zionism, and he told me that in 1944, while a senator from Missouri, Truman joined the American Palestine Committee supporting Zionist aspirations. Also, Truman's many Jewish friends speak well of his personal integrity, sense of justice, and feelings of friendship and sympathy toward the Jewish people.

We discussed the political activity of the Jewish Agency and of the different American Jewish organizations and institutions. It is clear to me that Lipsky does not approve of Wise's methods, which he feels are more concerned with public relations than with hard work on the vital issues. Lipsky thinks the agency lacks a well-trained, experienced team for political work and that it is not doing enough in organizing and coordinating the efforts of the numerous Zionist bodies and apportioning the work among them. He asked me, by the way, what I know of the United States and what American literature I have read—in his young days he was a literary and theater critic. There is still a bohemian air about him, and his features remind me of a Wild West hero of the old silent films.

In the afternoon I chatted with Hashim Jawad, secretary in the Iraqi Ministry for Foreign Affairs and member of his country's delegation. We have known each other since my student days at the American University of Beirut (1931–34). I first came to know him when he lectured to a socialist group that some university students and a few young staff members formed, which met privately. I was among those responsible for setting up the group and was its only Jewish member. We were encouraged in the venture by Professor Roger Henry Soltau, a former teacher at the London School of Economics who was a friend and admirer of Professor Harold Laski's. Some of the group's members later joined the Syrian National party, an organization following authoritarian and fascist lines that was founded and led by Antoun Sa'ade,[28] and were imprisoned by the French authorities on the eve of World War II. The group's existence did not continue after its original members completed their studies and left the university.

Like most of his delegation, my Iraqi friend is staying at the St. Francis Hotel. Over afternoon tea in his room, he told me that his main job is to prepare material for Arshad al-Omari, minister for foreign affairs and chairman of the delegation, and to write his speeches and those of other delegates. He mentioned that his country passed through a difficult time in the war and that things are still confused. Communal divisions between town dwellers and bedouin tribes, between Sunni and Shi'ite and Arab and Kurd, have led to many crises in recent years. Iraq was the first Arab country to graduate from mandate rule to political independence, and he wants it to set an example to other Arab states in economic and cultural progress as the basis for political stability. But Iraq is failing in its mission because most of its administrators lack creative initiative and practical knowledge in facing social and economic problems. He added that

[28]Antoun Sa'ade (1912–49) taught German at the American University of Beirut. His demands for independence from France and its eviction from Syria ultimately, after his party was banned, cost him his life: he was sentenced to death by a Lebanese military court and executed.

there is a warning here for both Syria and Lebanon, whose many problems closely resemble those of Iraq. He claimed that even before the establishment of the Arab League there was plenty of scope for close ties and constructive cooperation among the Arab countries. These will possibly be widened with the league's assistance if Nahas Pasha, whom he described as "a British tool," does not try to dominate the league so as to strengthen British influence in the Arab camp instead of serving Arab needs. I asked Jawad his views on relations between Arabs and ourselves. He answered that we must first reach an understanding with the Palestinian Arabs before we can hope for one with Arabs and Muslims in general.

I later met with another Arab friend, the Lebanese Dr. Charles Habib Malik,[29] his country's minister in Washington. After finishing his studies at the American University of Beirut, Malik went on to study in the United States, and later became professor of philosophy at his alma mater in Beirut. I first met him through a mutual friend, Brigadier Iltyd N. Clayton, adviser on Arab affairs to the British army command in Cairo during the war. A devout Catholic, Clayton spent his free time reading Thomas Aquinas and other Catholic theologians and loved to discuss religious and philosophical subjects, even in the fateful days before El Alamein, when the danger of a German invasion threatened the entire area. He was an enthusiastic disciple of Jacques Maritain's and used to press Maritain's books on his friends. He once told me he had corresponded with Henri Bergson on the

[29]Charles H. Malik (1906–   ); born in Lebanon; occupied a variety of political and diplomatic posts; member of the Lebanese parliament and foreign minister in several Lebanese governments; president of the thirteenth General Assembly of the United Nations (1958–59); on retiring from active political life he returned to the Philosophy Department of the American University of Beirut.

philosopher's concept of élan vital and spoke of the admiration he had for this thinker, who had opened up to him new horizons in philosophy and in social and personal ethics. As I came to know him better he seemed to me like a crusader prince, with cross in one hand and sword in the other— zealous in everything he did. Clayton saw in Malik spiritual and intellectual qualities that were rare, in his opinion, in the younger Arab generation and prophesied great things for him as a public leader.

In our talks Malik always impresses me with his tolerant opinions on religion and society. He is a gallant opponent, and his attitude to those with whom he has ideological differences is one of moderation and respect. This includes those with whom he differs on the Palestine issue. In Beirut people used to say that he worshiped Socrates, whose bust occupied the place of an icon in his house and had a candle always burning at its side!

I told him of my surprise when I heard that he had left the academic world for diplomacy, although he could serve as an excellent example of Plato's ideal of a philosopher-statesman in the area of human affairs. I avoided adding, however, that in the complexities of Lebanese political life it is hard to see him as suitably representing either the ruling caste of his country or the personal and sectarian intrigues of a society with ancient Levantine traditions and habits. "National duty," replied Malik rather evasively. We did not have much time together, for he was hurrying off to the conference. We agreed to meet shortly for a longer talk.

A reception was held this evening at the home of Mrs. Adele Harris, the widow of a Zionist leader in San Francisco. I learned from some of the Zionists I saw at the gathering that the city is a stronghold of the American Council for Judaism, which considers its main and sacred duty to be the combating of Zionism. Among those active in the council's work are some of the rich and influential members of the community, many suffering from an incurable inferiority complex as Jews. The council, I have been told, cooperates with haters of Zion of every complexion, including the worst anti-Semites and Arab organizations in the country.

Saturday, May 5

The day after I left Cairo an urgent request was sent from Moshe Shertok, asking me to cancel my American trip and proceed immediately to Ankara on an important mission. The plan was abandoned when it was learned that I had already left Cairo. If Agronsky had not had contacts in the American embassy in Cairo who helped us expedite our departure for the United States, I would certainly now be in Ankara or Istanbul, looking after some completely different matters. I would also have missed the chance of visiting America, because the San Francisco conference would no doubt have ended in the meantime.

I was reminded of something similar that once happened to me, in which a few hours' difference changed the course of my life. Late in 1922, when I was still in Russia, I was elected to the Central Committee of Hehalutz (the Zionist pioneers' organization), which had been declared counter-revolutionary by the Soviet authorities and consequently carried on its activities underground. From time to time I used to travel from my home in Minsk to the organization's headquarters in Moscow. On those occasions I would stay in the private apartment of Dr. Aryeh Abramowitz, himself an underground Zionist worker. Since a doctor's apartment seemed to us relatively secure from the inquisitive eyes of the GPU, a few other members of our organization occasionally found shelter there too. Early in 1923, at a meeting of the Central Committee, it was decided that I should travel to the Latvian border to look into the possibility of arranging a clandestine escape from the Soviet Union for our members, with the intention of their ultimately reaching Palestine. At that time there was practically no chance of obtaining a permit for a legal departure from the Soviet Union. I began preparations for the journey at once. My plan was to cross the border and proceed to Riga, where I could get in touch with the Zionist headquarters in London and obtain the necessary support for our undertaking. It was winter in Moscow and there was a heavy snow on the night I was due to board the train to the Latvian border. Dr. Abramowitz suggested that I put off my departure until the weather improved a little, but I turned down his suggestion and we parted with the hope that we should meet one day in Palestine.

A few hours after I left him, in the middle of the night, agents burst into his apartment, arrested Dr. Abramowitz, and deported him to Siberia. After five years in Siberia he was released from imprisonment and expelled to Palestine. It was only then that I learned from him about my narrow escape that fateful night in Moscow. Incidentally, on the way to the Latvian frontier I myself was almost caught by the GPU at Vitebsk, and it was only by good luck that I escaped their clutches and crossed the border safely. After fulfilling my mission in arranging the passage through Latvia of groups selected for immigration to Palestine, and in setting up a plan to use the same illegal means for smuggling Zionist literature to our organization in Russia, I went to Palestine myself.

This morning Jacob Robinson filled me in on the latest developments at the conference, as far as they concern us, and underlined the objectives we should keep in mind. The material prepared by the Great Powers at Dumbarton Oaks for the San Francisco conference contained no proposals for the disposal of former mandated territories. But the Jewish Agency, aware that a decision to this effect was made in principle at the Yalta conference, still has to be ready should the subject be raised in any form at the UNCIO proceedings in the formulation of the United Nations Charter. With this in mind the agency has submitted to each delegation a memorandum signed by Dr. Chaim Weizmann, explaining the background of the Palestine Mandate, stressing the historic rights of the Jewish people in Palestine as recognized by the Balfour Declaration, and asserting the responsibility of the British government to fulfill their obligation to the Jewish national home as laid down in the terms of the Mandate.

Paragraph 12 of that memorandum states that it is "imperative that effective safeguards be provided to assure and preserve Jewish rights pending action in fulfillment of the obligation to establish Jewish nationhood in Palestine." To that end it suggests: "In view of the unique character of the Palestine Mandate and the special rights of the Jewish people thereunder, no action should be taken at the San Francisco conference which would be inconsistent with or prejudicial to the special rights of the Jewish people under the Balfour Declaration and the Palestine Mandate, and all such rights shall be expressly reserved and safeguarded."

One of the requests in the memorandum is that the Jewish Agency should have an opportunity to explain our grievances and problems to the Trusteeship Committee. However, as the conference is not discussing matters relating specifically to particular mandated territories, it is thought that there may not be a chance of the agency's request to appear before any conference forum, including the Trusteeship

Committee, being granted. This naturally causes us much concern, because Arab delegates can operate against us in that committee while we will have no opportunity to speak out in defense of our rights.

Robinson mentioned that although the Jewish Agency memorandum did not refer to the Biltmore Program by name, the wording in paragraph 12 of the memorandum obviously stated its objective.[30]

He believes that the overriding objective of the Jewish Agency at San Francisco should be to ensure that neither the Trusteeship Committee nor the conference itself takes any decision contrary to the spirit and letter of the Palestine Mandate, or proposes anything likely to affect adversely our vital interests as far as the national home or our political efforts toward the fulfillment of the Biltmore Program are concerned.

Robinson then explained that when the conference began, the Jewish Agency had difficulty in deciding on a clear line of action before it knew the position of the Great Powers, especially that of Great Britain, on the future of the mandates system. Now that the British, American, and Australian delegations have published their proposals, the agency can consider how best to maneuver. In the next few days a new memorandum will be submitted to the delegates of the conference, setting out the position of the Jewish Agency on these three delegations' proposals. Their serious defect, in Robinson's view, is that they do not spell out the principle of preserving the existing mandates' integrity— their basic substance and their original objectives—under the

[30]"In line with the original intention of the Mandate and of present-day needs the following steps must now be undertaken: *a*. The immediate announcement of a determination by the responsible powers that Palestine is to be established as a free democratic Jewish commonwealth."

new trusteeship status. The British memorandum proposes that the existing rights of the power holding the mandate be preserved, but says nothing of ensuring the rights of the Jewish people, nor does it speak of the national home—points that were specifically embodied in the Palestine Mandate, the only remaining "A" Mandate after Syria and Lebanon became independent states. The American and Australian proposals are even hazier than the British in this matter, and all of them contain clauses with many pitfalls for us as long as Palestine remains under a mandate or trusteeship system.

The Jewish Agency's supplementary memorandum now being prepared for the delegates of the United Nations conference will therefore deal explicitly with the proposals of the three delegations and suggest amendments designed to guarantee our rights, as defined in the Palestine Mandate. Robinson thinks we should go all out for the duration of the conference to win support from members of the various delegations on whose sympathy and understanding we can rely, and tackle the dangers we face—especially from the Arab delegations, who, as it were, sit in the best seats while we are bound to beg for favors outside the conference forum.

I was greatly impressed by Robinson's lucidity and the breadth of his legal analysis and political assessment of the situation. He is a great asset to our delegation and his views carry, as I have observed, much authority with all the participants at the morning meetings.

———————————

Arthur Lourie and I visited Stojan Gavrilovic, the Yugoslav undersecretary of state for foreign affairs and a member of his country's delegation to the conference. I first met him in Cairo in the war years, when he was a refugee from the German occupation of his country. We asked him to arrange a meeting at which we can explain our problems and seek his delegation's help in safeguarding our rights when the future of the mandates system is dealt with by the conference. His questions showed that he is no stranger to the subject, and he expressed sympathetic understanding of our political struggle in Palestine. I went on to ask him what his government's intentions are concerning the arrest of war criminals who operated in Yugoslavia, including the former mufti of Jerusalem, Haj Amin el-Husseini.[31] He assured us that his country will do everything required of it with regard to all war criminals, but regarding the mufti, it is up to the British authorities to act first in the matter, because it affects a citizen of a country under their jurisdiction. Gavrilovic added that the mufti's role in Yugoslavia was only a tiny element in the overall plans of Fascist Italy and Nazi Germany and said that the mufti's ties with Hitler and Mussolini preceded his arrival in Yugoslavia. We do not find much encouragement regarding Yugoslav intentions in a matter of such moral and practical concern to us as the future of the mufti.

Reuven and I met a delegation of Assyrians who have come to San Francisco to put before the United Nations conference complaints on the suffering inflicted on their brethren in Iraq and Syria. Yosef Durna, now living in New York City, and Samuel Aslan, of Yonkers, N.Y., spoke bitterly about the lack of understanding the British and French delegations showed when approached for guidance and assistance. The American delegation was no more helpful, simply hearing what they had to say and referring them to the

[31]Haj Amin el-Husseini (died 1974); headed anti-Jewish demonstration (1920); was sentenced, then pardoned by the British; appointed mufti by the British high commissioner; after 1929 riots, became the most important leader of Palestine Arabs; president of the Arab Higher Committee (from 1936); fomented the riots and terror of 1936 and 1937; escaped via Syria and Iraq to Italy and Nazi Germany; served as a pro-Nazi propagandist; escaped arrest after World War II and conducted the struggle against partition.

British and French experts on the Assyrian problem because of their previous experience in the matter. Telling us about their meetings and frustrations, the two Assyrians added that "we ourselves have had enough experience—experience has brought about the almost total annihilation of our brothers in Iraq and in the French-controlled Jezireh region. What we need is not advice but deeds to save what remains of our people." The two representatives of the Assyrian community in America asked whether we can do anything for them. We promised to raise the question with Dr. Henry Atkinson, president of the American Christian Palestine Committee, an organization of Christian friends of Jewish Palestine. A person of high standing and influence, Dr. Atkinson serves as adviser to the American delegation, representing Christian religious bodies in the United States.

Dr. Fadhil al-Jamali,[32] a member of the Iraqi delegation and the director general of the Iraqi Ministry of Foreign Affairs, invited me to lunch with him. In the late 1930s we corresponded on the problems of the bedouin in Iraq, a subject on which al-Jamali published a book while studying at Columbia University. I was then writing a book on the life and customs of the bedouin, and al-Jamali helped me a great deal. On one of my visits to Baghdad I got to know him personally, and when his (American) wife came to Jerusalem for medical treatment for her son, my wife and I helped her as best we could. After this we kept in close touch, so I called him to say I was in San Francisco.

[32]Fadhil al-Jamali was foreign minister and later prime minister of Iraq. After the revolution of July 14, 1958, he was imprisoned and sentenced to death, but the sentence was commuted to expulsion from Iraq. Al-Jamali found refuge in Tunisia and is now a professor at the University of Tunis.

We were joined at lunch by Ali Jawdat Pasha al-Ayubi,[33] the Iraqi minister in the United States, and Dr. Farid Zeineddine,[34] an adviser to the Syrian delegation. I knew Zeineddine, a Druze from Lebanon, during my student days in Beirut. Later we used to meet in Palestine when he was headmaster of the Al-Najjah School in Nablus, which was known for its extreme Arab nationalism. Ali Jawdat Pasha was an Arab officer in the Turkish army in World War I, when he joined the forces of Emir Feisal. (Also in the group were Nuri Pasha al-Said[35] and his brother-in-law Ja'afar Pasha al-Askari,[36] who were later among the founders and builders of the young state of Iraq.) Ali Pasha was prime minister of Iraq and minister in several of its governments. Zeineddine, his junior, entered Syria's diplomatic service when the country became independent. Zeineddine's stepfather was Suleiman Abu-Izzedine, a noted Druze scholar in Lebanon. Zeineddine is a pan-Arabist and makes no secret of

[33]Ali Jawdat Pasha al-Ayubi (1886–1969); Iraqi minister of the interior (1923–24); minister of finance (1930–33); chief of the royal household and private secretary to Emir Feisal (1933); prime minister (1934–35, 1949–50, 1957); foreign minister (1939–40); minister in Washington (1944–49); pro-British and pro-Hashemite.
[34]Farid Zeineddine (1907–   ); deputy minister of foreign affairs in independent Syria (1946); head of the Syrian delegation to the UN (1946–54); ambassador to the USSR (1947–51) and to the U.S. (1957); author of works in Arabic on historical and political aspects of the Arab nationalist movement.
[35]Nuri Pasha al-Said (1888–1958); fourteen times prime minister of Iraq (1930–58); prime minister of the federation of Jordan and Iraq; on July 14, 1958, he was killed along with all the members of the Iraqi royal family.
[36]Ja'afar al-Askari was murdered in October 1936, during the Baghdad uprising that temporarily seized the reins of government from the hands of Nuri Pasha al-Said and his associates and gave power to Bakr Sidqi, a Kurd and professional soldier, and Hikmat Suleiman, an anglophobe of Turkish extraction; the regime did not last long, and Bakr Sidqi's fall brought back a government loyal to Great Britain.

his out-and-out opposition to Zionism. He knows a great deal about the history of Zionism and has written articles on the subject for Arab newspapers. He studied in Germany and France and also has a good command of English. Al-Jamali and Zeineddine both studied at the American University of Beirut, but he graduated before I did.

Our host told me that more than two dozen key positions in the five Arab delegations to the conference are held by graduates of the American University of Beirut. So George Antonius[37] hardly exaggerated when he made so much in his book, *The Arab Awakening,* of the university's major contribution to Arab nationalism from its earliest days. A large number of Arab nationalists studied there, and no one stopped them from expressing their feelings freely—whether they were teachers or students—which was not generally true of other Lebanese institutions of learning, especially those under French influence and guidance.

During the meal Zeineddine told the story of how he had nearly been dismissed from the headmastership of the Al-Najjah School when the trustees learned that I had once visited him. I remember the incident well: the Jewish driver who took me to Nablus, and was waiting for me in the school courtyard while I was having tea with Zeineddine inside, was attacked by the Arab pupils who saw him reading a Hebrew paper. "You forget you are in Nablus, not in Jaffa," the boys shouted threateningly. Hearing the commotion, Zeineddine rushed out and brought the frightened driver inside. On the return journey to Jerusalem I thought to myself that this scuffle must have been the only time Zeineddine ever found

[37]George Antonius (1892–1942); born in Egypt; moved to Palestine (1921), where he served in the Department of Education (1921–30); appeared before the Palestine Commission (1936–37); primarily known for his writings on Arab nationalism.

himself defending a Jew—and a Zionist. But the traditional demands of hospitality apparently proved stronger than my host's anti-Zionist opinions; he had followed the much-praised Arab custom of ensuring the safety of a guest in his tent or under his roof.

At today's lunch al-Jamali and his colleagues asked me many questions about how we Zionists see the political future of Palestine. When I mentioned the Biltmore Program, now the basis of our policy, al-Jamali and Zeineddine stressed again and again that there can be no understanding between Jew and Arab based on the principles and objectives of that program. They declared that Arabs will never agree to a "foreign body" with its own political aspirations in their midst, and said that the congress of the Arab League had purposely decided to admit to the membership of its council a Palestinian Arab representative to demonstrate that Palestine is an inseparable part of the Arab world. Perhaps in the past, they went on to say, there was some wavering in the attitude of the Arab states toward the conflict between the Arabs in Palestine and Zionism, but, Zeineddine and al-Jamali stressed, with the establishment of the Arab League a historic decision has been made compelling all its seven members to fulfill without reservation their solemn obligations toward their brethren in Palestine. Now more than ever Zionists should realize that they have as their determined opponents both the Palestinian Arabs and all the millions of Arabs represented by the Arab League. "What chance do the Jews have to come out on top in any struggle with the Arabs," al-Jamali asked me, "even if some of the Great Powers should support the Jews for their own dubious motives?" Al-Jamali remarked half seriously, half jokingly that "even God Himself is on the Arab side." His evidence: the recent rich oil discoveries in Arab countries, an economic and political event of decisive importance because the British and

Americans will now have to depend on the goodwill and cooperation of Arabs, instead of the other way around as hitherto.

Zeineddine contended that the Arabs find it hard to understand how Jews, who are known for their intelligence and shrewdness, can possibly believe they will overcome both Arab hostility and the enormous power and political influence of the international oil companies with interests in Arab countries, to set up a Jewish state in a region where all the factors that count are opposed to Zionist objectives. Better, Zeineddine stated, that we be practical and realistic and use the opportunity—perhaps the last coming to us—to reach an accommodation with the Arabs of Palestine that will ensure our existence and our future in a Palestinian Arab state.

Ali Jawdat Pasha hardly took part in the conversation, only nodding occasionally to express his agreement with his colleagues. There was some tension in the air after al-Jamali's and Zeineddine's statements. However, although not hiding their hostility to Zionism and to our struggle in Palestine, both al-Jamali and Zeineddine tried not to go beyond the limits of "friendly discussion" and at the end of the meal expressed their desire for all of us to meet again soon.

For a change of pace this afternoon I attended a concert by the San Francisco symphony orchestra. Bruno Walter conducted Beethoven's Sixth, and I was enchanted by both the playing and the superb acoustics of the concert hall, which is simple but splendid. I thought of our own orchestra's concerts in the Edison Cinema in Jerusalem. Would we, and Toscanini, one day have a building worthy of the standard of our orchestra's playing, of our maestro, and of the enthusiastic music-loving public of our country?

Anne O'Hare McCormick, the well-known political commentator of the *New York Times* and an acknowledged expert in the intricacies of American foreign policy, was my dinner companion. I first met her a few months ago when she visited Palestine. After her trip she published a series of rather unfriendly articles. No doubt she was influenced by her talks with highly placed British officials she met in Palestine and Egypt and with American representatives in the Middle East. It was not hard to discern the Christian undertone to her outlook in her descriptions of Palestine, and especially Jerusalem, as holy to Christians and Muslims and not to Jews alone. As a devout Catholic, it seems, it is hard for her to accept the possibility of a Jewish state being set up in Palestine, as the Peel Royal Commission proposed in 1937 and as the Zionist movement has determined to work for in the Biltmore Program.

During our lengthy conversation Mrs. McCormick outlined for my benefit what she regards as the new realities of the postwar world, a world in which the United States will be active in practically every corner of the globe—something it has never done in peacetime since attaining independence. Roosevelt, she said, brought about a revolution in America's relations with foreign countries, and in her opinion Truman will be compelled to follow the path on which his predecessor embarked. This policy flows from the very heavy responsibilities and burdens that have fallen on American strength in the face of the world's many unsolved problems. The Middle East is important to the United States because it contains oil reserves greater than those in any other part of the world, and the rights American companies possess to exploit oil in Arab countries are important on both strategic and economic grounds. The United States must for its own interests preserve the military power of its British ally in so strategically important an area as the Middle East, in order to achieve a balance of power and influence among the Great

Powers on the international scene, and also to protect the oil fields and transit routes through which oil is carried—a matter vital to both Great Britain and the United States. These factors, Mrs. McCormick believes, will have decisive weight on any American government policy for the region in its relations with other states, especially Great Britain, and the Middle East countries themselves.

On her visit to Palestine she saw our work and achievements at first hand and was greatly impressed. She was surprised, however, by the fact that our leaders were apparently unaware of the ferment in Arab countries, which more and more was influencing the standing of the Arab world in international affairs. The founding of the Arab League was a good example of this trend. In Mrs. McCormick's view, we should settle with the Arabs quickly before they grow even stronger. It will also be to our advantage if the United States does not have to choose between us and the Arabs in the Palestine controversy. She remarked that, in the event of such a choice, a position adopted by an American government in our favor could easily lead to a wave of anti-Semitism in the United States and cause many American Jews to hold back from helping us. She went on to say that she is sorry that Dr. Judah Magnes[38] has no voice in determining Zionist policies. She regards him as a prophet who sees far into the future.

She listened attentively to my remarks on the different points she mentioned in our conversation, but I doubt whether I moved her to change her views, which take into

[38]Judah Leon Magnes (1877–1948); American Reform rabbi; went to live in Palestine (1922); became president of Hebrew University (1925); advocated binationalism within a Middle East federation, as opposed to the official Zionist policy; organized Ihud Association (1942) to forward his idea.

account only those power factors that in her eyes have already crystallized and the adjusting of United States interests —as she sees them—to the picture she painted. I know, however, that disregarding her views will not make my task in San Francisco practical or constructive. I have learned by now that most powerful and influential American groups hostile to Zionism are working as hard as they can and will continue to try to nullify our efforts—both at the conference and in the country generally—to create a public opinion favorable to our cause and win the support of the American government for our struggle. As for the oil companies and their ability to influence the politics of the American government, I thought about what I had learned on the subject from my Arab friends only a few hours earlier.

Sunday, May 6

Early this morning I studied the large quantity of material I have amassed since arriving here, including the memorandums prepared for the United Nations conference by such Jewish organizations as the World Jewish Congress, the American Jewish Committee, the Jewish Labor Committee, the American Jewish Congress, the Synagogue Council of America, and the British Board of Deputies. All these memorandums deal with the plight of the survivors of the Holocaust in Europe, and all, without exception, castigate the white paper when discussing the Palestine problem. In its analysis of the subjects covered in its memorandums, the most comprehensive and thorough treatment seems to me to be that of the American Jewish Committee. It is the result of a great deal of research and has been expertly edited.

Breakfasted today with Husseyin Cahit Yalçin[39] at the St. Francis Hotel, where he and the other Turkish delegates to the conference are staying. Yalçin used to belong to the Union and Progress party and took part in the Young Turks' revolution against Sultan Abd al-Hamid. He was among Kemal Atatürk's right-hand men at the start of the national revolution, assisting him in his struggle to liberate Turkey from foreign rule and to change the structure and character of Turkish society. After victory, however, they parted company following a disagreement on the internal political structure of the new regime, and Yalçin was imprisoned for some time, along with other early supporters of Atatürk who thought as he did. While in jail he translated John Stuart Mill's *On Liberty* into Turkish.

I met Yalçin in Istanbul during the war, when he was the chief editor of *Yeni Sabah,* a widely read and influential newspaper. Even in the '30s he was already warning in this periodical of the dangers to world peace posed by Fascism and Nazism, and with the outbreak of World War II he supported the struggle of Great Britain and her allies for freedom and democracy in the world. At that time I found Yalçin sympathetic to Zionism and a stout supporter of our political aspirations in Palestine. He introduced me to several influential people in Ankara, who assisted me at various times in my contacts with the Turkish authorities on political and economic matters of interest to the Jewish Agency.

[39]Husseyin Cahit Yalçin (1875–1957); editor and writer; represented Turkey on the United Nations Conciliation Commission for Palestine set up by the General Assembly in December 1948.

Yalçin has aged considerably since our last meeting in 1943, but his alertness and attentiveness are unimpaired. He is one of three representatives of the Turkish press attached to his country's delegation to the conference and serves also as a political adviser to the chairman of the delegation, Hasan Saka, minister for foreign affairs. He is not optimistic about the world situation. Hitler and Mussolini are dead, but Stalin, he observed, is no improvement—he is a persistent threat to democracy in Europe and indeed the entire world. For generations, said Yalçin, Turkey has lived under the shadow of Russia's ambitions, whatever its form of government. The Soviet threat to his country and to others—especially those bordering the USSR—exists, and will continue to exist until the world realizes that Stalin is nothing but a latter-day Peter the Great hiding behind the mask of Marx and Lenin. To Yalçin's regret, the Americans are not sufficiently experienced in world affairs and Britain is too weak to prevent the Soviet Union from undermining the independence of its neighbors in Europe and Asia.[40] He believes the time will come when Anthony Eden and the British Foreign Office,

[40]It is possible that information reached Turkey during World War II of the secret November 1940 discussions between Molotov, Hitler, and Ribbentrop, on the special rights of the Soviet Union in the Middle East, including Turkey. The full details of these negotiations were released in Washington only in 1948. However, Yalçin and his colleagues probably already sensed the coming storm at the time of our conversation because a few weeks later, at the end of June 1945, Stalin claimed from Turkey the territories in the Kars and Ardahan regions (which had belonged to Turkey until 1878, were then annexed by czarist Russia, and reverted to Turkey in the final stages of World War I). The claim was pressed further when the Soviet republics of Georgia and Armenia, obviously at Moscow's prodding, claimed additional large tracts of Turkish territory. The 1947 Truman Doctrine was a direct result of the aggressive designs of Stalin toward Turkey, Iran, and Greece and was intended to defend the territorial integrity and independence of these states against the Soviet Union.

who helped found the Arab League, will realize their mistake.

The Turks have had centuries of experience in dealing with the Arabs and have a good idea of their unstable character. Eden cannot for long rely on the Arabs remaining loyal to Great Britain. Yalçin considers that Arab prestige in international affairs has risen with the foundation of the Arab League. Arab delegates constitute one-tenth of the total number attending the conference, which enhances their bargaining power with other delegations on matters of interest to them. Even the Turkish delegation has to take into account the five Arab delegations every time Turkey needs the support of a majority of the conference.

In answer to my inquiry, Yalçin replied that the question of Turkey's tense relations with the USSR and with Greece may be, in one way or another, raised at the conference. The Turkish delegation, however, will not initiate a formal debate on the subject until they can gauge the likelihood of achieving their objectives; he did not explain what Turkey's real aims are in the matter.

Yalçin went on to express his support for our struggle. In his view, the fulfillment of the Zionist ideal would strengthen democratic forces in the Middle East and would enhance Turkey's own security as a modern, progressive state in the area, with aspirations in many fields akin to those of the Yishuv. However, the Turkish government must be wary in its handling of the delicate and explosive Palestine problem, so as not to put ammunition into the hands of its enemies in an Arab world where many have not yet been reconciled to Atatürk's reforms, particularly in religious matters, and where many aspire to diminish if not eradicate entirely Turkish influence on the world scene and in the Middle East particularly. I detected in Yalçin's reference to the Arabs at the conference a clear warning that we cannot rely on Turkey's open support, at any rate, for our political claims in world forums.

After my meeting with Yalçin I went to nearby Oakland, California, for the opening of the International Conference of Labor Organizations, attended by delegates from thirty-five countries and representing sixty million members of 235 trade unions. I had no difficulty in obtaining an entry permit to the conference on the strength of my card as a correspondent of Palcor and *Davar.* On the rostrum of the large conference hall were seated Sidney Hillman and Philip Murray, the leaders of the CIO, Sir Walter Citrine and John Edwards of the British Trade Unions Congress, V. V. Kuznetsov and P. Tarassov from the USSR (the former is chairman of the Trade Unions Council of the Soviet Union), Li Ping-heng from China, Vicente Toledano from Mexico, and Leo Pressman of the International Labor Office. Conspicuously absent were William Green, president, and other representatives of the AFL, who boycotted the conference because of the Soviet Union's attendance.

After the gala opening, in which every speaker stressed the need for unity, cooperation, and solidarity in the world labor camp, the journalists present were invited to a question-and-answer session with members of the conference executive. Kuznetsov made much of the freedom enjoyed by trade unions in the Soviet Union. "If you don't believe me," he declared, "come and see!" "Strikes? There are no strikes in the Soviet Union. Our workers are contented and have no need to strike." A reporter from the New York Yiddish newspaper *Der Morgen Journal* asked Philip Murray about the attitude of the conference toward the idea of a Jewish state in Palestine. He replied that the conference was convened to discuss matters affecting workers and did not concern itself with political issues outside that field. An Indian journalist asked him why the conference did not speak out against the brutality of the British authorities in India and Palestine, and why it did not demand the granting of independence to the peoples of these countries. This time Murray answered that the conference executive would examine the matter. I did not manage to speak to the Indian questioner to discover the reason for his interest in Palestine.

The press conference was brief. The general consensus of the assembled journalists was that the labor conference was more for show than for initiating binding decisions, since it had no illusion about the futility of achieving genuine understanding or any kind of fruitful cooperation between the workers of democratic countries and those of the Soviet Union.

I returned to San Francisco and reported the substance of my various conversations of the past few days to Goldmann. He told me about the strong influence wielded by pro-Arab circles within the United States delegation and said that we should therefore direct increased efforts at it, especially the members concerned with the Middle East. The American representative on the Trusteeship Committee is Commander Harold Stassen,[41] who has considerable influence on the course of the committee's work and a fair understanding of our problems and interests. What we know of the personal attitude of Edward Stettinius,[42] secretary of state and chair-

[41]Harold E. Stassen (1907–); prior to enlistment in the U.S. Navy was governor of Minnesota; president of the University of Pennsylvania (1948–53); advocate of Christian-Jewish friendship and cooperation in the United States; unsuccessful in attempts to win the Republican party's nomination for the presidency of the United States.

[42]Edward R. Stettinius, Jr. (1900–49); secretary of state (1944–45); president of General Motors and U.S. Steel; after his resignation from the government until his death was president of the

man of the United States delegation, is rather discouraging. Dr. Wise will be meeting him in the next few days. Meanwhile our memorandums have been sent to him, accompanied by a summary of the different expressions of sympathetic attitude toward Zionism and the Jewish national home by practically every U.S. administration, together with the wish that this attitude will continue. Similar material was also sent to Stassen.

Sol Bloom (a Jew), chairman of the House of Representatives Foreign Affairs Committee and an active member of the American delegation, is rather reserved on matters concerning Palestine, and our people do not bother with him much. There are two senators in the delegation: Tom Connally, a Democrat, and Arthur Vandenberg, a Republican; Vandenberg's attitude to our cause is more sympathetic than that of his Democratic colleague. One member, Virginia Gildersleeve, is well known for her hostility to Zionism, and we can be sure she will lose no opportunity to harm our cause. Of the influential advisers to the delegation from the State Department, Professor Isaiah Bowman (a non-Jew), a member of the Advisory Committee on Post-War Foreign Affairs, founded after Pearl Harbor, is known for his negative feelings toward Zionism, but another adviser, Charles Taussig, has gone out of his way to be helpful to the representatives of the American Jewish Conference on the advisory body to the American delegation, and Herman Shulman is in con-

---

University of Virginia. As undersecretary of state he led a policy-planning mission to London (April 1944). Stettinius later admitted his ignorance of affairs in Palestine, the fact that he found himself entirely in the hands of his advisers from the Near Eastern Division of the Department of State, and his advocacy, when discussing with the British the future of Palestine, of a trusteeship system of government and, in reality, the retention for the time being of the white paper regime (memorandum by Evan Wilson in *Foreign Relations of the United States, 1944,* 5:592–95).

stant touch with him. Goldmann has good personal relations with Alger Hiss,[43] the secretary-general of the conference. Hiss is still on the staff of the State Department, as the position he holds is a temporary one until a permanent secretary-general of the United Nations Organization is chosen.

Monday, May 7

In the morning I met Henry Villard and Foy Kohler[44] of the United States delegation, who are the delegation's State Department advisers on Near Eastern and African affairs. Villard is the chief of the Division of African Affairs in the State Department, and Kohler is assistant chief of the Division of Near Eastern Affairs. These two divisions are incorporated within a single Office of Near Eastern and African Affairs of the State Department, which deals with U.S. relations with some of the largest areas on the world map. Before leaving Palestine I was given a letter of introduction to the Division of Near Eastern Affairs by Joseph Satterthwait, counselor in

[43]Alger Hiss (1904–   ); later accused of handing over secret information to the USSR, convicted of perjury, and sentenced to imprisonment; before serving as secretary-general of the San Francisco conference had held several important positions in the State Department, including that of director of the Office of Special Political Affairs.

[44]Foy D. Kohler (1908–   ); American ambassador to Soviet Union (1962–66); in his thirty-six years of service in the State Department occupied high posts in various parts of the world and was head of the office of Special Political Affairs; on his retirement in 1966 was appointed professor of international relations at the University of Miami, Florida.

the United States embassy in Ankara. I had come to know him in 1941 when Eliezer Kaplan and I were in Turkey to inquire about the possibility of a larger number of refugees from German-occupied Europe getting to Palestine via Turkey. It was necessary for the Turkish authorities to grant transit visas to these people, to whom it was a matter of life and death. Among people of influence in Ankara, we had asked the American ambassador, Lawrence Steinhart, to intervene in our behalf at the Turkish Ministry for Foreign Affairs. The ambassador appointed Satterthwait to deal with our request, which he carried out efficiently and with dedication, although the results were disappointing.

Villard and Kohler quizzed me closely on the situation in Palestine and our relations with the Arabs, both in Palestine and in neighboring countries. Villard wanted to know our attitude toward the Arab League and wondered if we had had prior knowledge of the Annex Regarding Palestine in the pact adopted by the Arab states at their Cairo congress. Kohler, who appeared well versed in Soviet affairs and its activities in the Middle East, asked what we thought its aims were in relation to the Yishuv.

The conversation lasted about two hours. It appeared that both Villard and Kohler had some prior knowledge about my activities in the Jewish Agency's Political Department, my studies at the American University of Beirut, and my contacts with Arab leaders in neighboring countries. When our meeting broke up Villard mentioned that he must return to Washington in a few days and suggested that Kohler keep in touch with me. He invited me to call on him at his office when I am in Washington.

During our talk I was struck by the apparent paucity of the contact between Zionist bodies in the United States and the State Department's Division of Near Eastern Affairs. It seems there is no regular contact between us and those responsible for Near Eastern affairs and, some say, for framing American policy in our part of the world. Villard and Kohler, judging by their rank in the State Department, do not decide matters of major policy and are mainly concerned with implementing it. They undoubtedly play an important part in elaborating the different stages of that policy, however, as American interests in the Middle East are defined against the background of changing conditions and current developments in the area. To reach an effective and working relationship with people like Villard and Kohler one has to possess firsthand knowledge and personal experience in the fields they deal with. As a matter of fact, in all the American Zionist bodies represented here I have not yet met a single person with the requisite level of either background knowledge or practical experience in Arab or Middle Eastern affairs.

Replying yesterday to a journalist's question, Secretary of State Edward Stettinius said the conference will only discuss the administration of trusteeship territories in general, and will not deal with the future of specific territories that will become the responsibility of the United Nations. This was the first public statement by the United States delegation on the subject as it was agreed on at the Dumbarton Oaks conference. Churchill's statement in Parliament on February 27, 1945, had already made it clear that Palestine would not be on the agenda of the conference.

I met over lunch with a Lebanese friend who holds an important position in his government's service. He spoke about the challenge Lebanon is facing in using its national independence to hasten economic development and social progress. It is in these fields, he said, that the creative capacity and political maturity of the newly independent Arab states will ultimately be judged. Under the new political conditions neither Lebanon nor Syria will be able to blame the French, as in the past, for their failures or for the difficulties they encounter. They have to develop a sense of responsibility for their actions. He went on to say that the true criterion of a young state's maturity is bound to be how much its leaders aspire to base the political independence of their people on solid social and economic as well as spiritual foundations. Arab society, both Muslim and Christian, has always rested on religious values. The oriental Jewish communities, he said, are no different from their neighbors in this respect. Nevertheless, although the spiritual values and rights of each community should be fully and carefully protected, the leaders of Lebanon and Syria will have to cut back the religious institutions' dominating influence on the social and political life of their countries, so that antagonisms and divisions between communities do not deepen further and undermine the democratic character of the society and the rights of the individual. These divisions have cost both states dearly in the past, and in the new circumstances communal rivalry is likely to become even more dangerous.

In answer to a question my friend expressed concern, in carefully measured terms, that in the hands of its Muslim members the Arab League may become an instrument that can be turned against Lebanon, with its historic Christian character and distinct cultural and social structure. To hear this assessment from a Maronite would not have surprised me, but the Greek Orthodox community to which my friend belongs has always been flexible in its relations with Muslims and has for the most part supported nationalist tendencies in neighboring Arab countries. True, it has been easier for Maronites, who are concentrated in Lebanon, to take an independent position than for the Greek Orthodox or the Greek Catholics, who are scattered throughout the territory of the former French Mandate and are less numerous in Lebanon than the Maronites.

On the Palestine question my friend's views were more moderate than I have been used to hearing from Arab leaders in Palestine or in neighboring countries, but he, too, would not admit our claim to Jewish statehood. Zionism, he argued, has come too late in historical terms to bring about revolutionary change in the political destiny of Palestine. The British no longer have the power—to say nothing of the will—to help establish a Jewish state in even *part* of Palestine in the teeth of united Arab opposition. He doubts whether it is realistic to expect American support for the Biltmore Program; in his view oil has become too important a factor in American thinking and considerations on the Middle East.

He thinks that in the present circumstances the Middle East is wide open for the entry of Americans into its affairs and that their prospects are most promising. But America will have to learn from Britain's mistakes. They first have to forget Kipling's dictum, "East is East and West is West, and never the twain shall meet," and pursue a course opposite to that despairing philosophy enunciated by the prophet of British imperialism.

We agreed to meet again soon.

I took part in talks between Wise, Marcial Mora, the Chilean ambassador in Washington who is a delegate to the conference, and Guillermo Belt Ramirez, the Cuban ambassador in Washington and the chairman of his country's delegation. Mora is prepared to support the claims outlined in our memorandum, which he had in his hands during our meeting. Belt was reserved and confined himself to noncommital courtesies.

I went to Molotov's press conference, called by the Soviet delegation at the St. Francis Hotel. V. M. Molotov, chairman of his country's delegation at the conference, entered the room with a large entourage, including bodyguards. Molotov remained standing throughout the press conference, as did the other members of the Soviet delegation who stood at his side—Chairman Kuznetsov of the Trade Unions Council of the Soviet Union, A. I. Lavrentiev, a member of the government of the Russian Soviet Federated Socialist Republic, A. A. Gromyko, the Soviet ambassador in Washington, and Rear Admiral K. K. Rodionov, a military member on the delegation. Only Molotov spoke. He read a prepared statement, repeating almost verbatim what he said a few days ago to the plenary session of the General Assembly. The large number of newsmen bombarded him with questions, some not at all friendly to the Soviet Union. Molotov replied to two questions only and then abruptly left the hall followed by his entourage, the cameramen who darted around him, and some persistent journalists who pressed him to answer further questions and to whom he made no reply.

A. Jouve, the chief representative of de Gaulle's Free French in Turkey during the war, introduced me to Georges Gorse,[45] a member of the French Consultative Assembly and an adviser on Middle Eastern affairs to the French delegation. I had gotten to know Jouve when I was in Turkey during the war and had found him to be an enthusiastic supporter of Zionism. He has come to San Francisco on an assignment for a

[45]Georges Gorse (1915–   ); was a member of the French government, a de Gaulle loyalist, and one of his advisers on Middle East affairs; strove to maintain French influence in the region, working through his many friendships in Arab countries; has been the ambassador to Algeria and Tunisia and the French representative to the United Nations.

Paris newspaper and also serves as an unofficial adviser to René Pléven, the French minister of both finance and national economy, who is a member of the conference delegation. I am sure we can count on him in our effort to win French help for our cause.

It didn't take me long to discover that Gorse's hostility to England far surpasses his sympathy for Zionism. The mention of Major General Sir Edward Spears's name was enough to anger him. In his view the British are two-faced in everything they do, deceiving in turn the Arabs, the Jews, and the French, and are now building up the Arab League in order to achieve total mastery in the region. In 1918 the British had no choice but to submit to Clemenceau's demands in the Middle East. Now they are exploring France's weakness and attempting to supplant them in Syria and Lebanon. The real purpose of granting independence to these countries was, in his opinion, to eradicate French influence there. He and his colleagues are glad that the Jews have at last unmasked the true face of their British "friends," who promised a national home to the Jewish people in Palestine. Now it is the turn of the Arabs—they too will see what lies behind the British chimera called the Arab League.

I found that Gorse knows Egypt well. He taught at the Fuad University in Cairo in 1940 and is well versed in the problems of the Middle East. From what he said I gathered that despite its many domestic and international problems the French government has not given up the idea of playing a role in our area. The Middle East, he said, is on the eastern shores of the Mediterranean, "France's sea." Generations of tradition cannot be erased by a passing sequence of events, he asserted. France has deep roots in Syria and Lebanon, and its cultural influence encompasses most of the Middle East, including Egypt.

Gorse told me that Paul-Émile Naggiar,[46] formerly French ambassador to China and the Soviet Union, is his delegation's representative on the Trusteeship Committee and is greatly esteemed by both Jouve and Gorse. He asked me about recent developments in Palestine, particularly about underground activities. We agreed to meet again.

Later today I had a talk with a member of the Turkish delegation, a highly regarded and influential person in his country whom I came to know during my stay in Turkey. He is a well-educated man and has a pleasant way about him. Like his colleague Yalçin, he stressed the imminent Soviet danger to the free world if the Western powers do not wake up and frustrate Stalin's aggressive designs in Europe, Asia, and anywhere else the Soviet dictator sees an opening. The threat of direct Russian attack is greatest to those states bordering the Soviet Union: Turkey, Iran, and Iraq. In his view the tragedy is that the U.S., the only Great Power able to arrest Soviet expansion, still regards the Soviet Union as an ally and does not understand Stalin's true intentions. The British, who have had generations of experience in dealing with the Russians, understand the position better than the Americans and see the need to strengthen the ability of Russia's Middle East neighbors to resist being overrun by the Soviet Union. Great Britain realizes that a Soviet advance will endanger Britain's own vital interests and its whole position in the area.

He was more restrained than Yalçin when I raised the

[46]Paul-Émile Naggiar (1883–1962); most of his life was spent in diplomatic service in the Far East; ambassador to China (1918) and then to the Soviet Union (until 1940); French representative at international gatherings, including the UN.

question of Turkey's attitude to the problems of the Middle East and simply replied that Turkey's policy will be "cautious and realistic." He added that Turkey values our achievements in Palestine and certainly wishes us well in all our endeavors. However, he says, we have to realize the grave problems Turkey is facing at present and to understand its delicate position every time our interests are involved, or those of the Arab states or of Great Britain. He has no great faith in the Arab League's ability to set up a united Arab front, certainly not to maintain one for any length of time. As for Turkey's relations with the league, Arab history is one long tale of quarrels and enmity with the Turks. Political changes do not alter a people's character. The creation of the Arab League was more the result of a conjunction of expedient political interests than any natural historical process. Only time will tell whether it leads to a strengthening of the fabric of Arab society and responsible politics or proves a total failure.

Later in the conversation he mentioned the delicate situation Turkey finds itself each time it has to take a position with regard to the mandated territories formerly part of the Ottoman Empire, which were lost after World War I. I again had the feeling I experienced after my talk with Yalçin, that we cannot count on Turkey's help at the conference. We will be doing well if the Turkish delegation does not side with our opponents and merely remains neutral on the Palestine issue. I reported the substance of the meeting to Goldmann.

Tuesday, May 8 (V-E Day)

At this morning's joint meeting of Jewish organizations we discussed the activities that must follow the supplementary memorandum we are submitting today to each conference delegation. The memorandum contains our reaction to the proposals of the British, American, and Australian delegations on the future administration of League of Nations mandates within the new framework of the United Nations. Our demands in the supplementary memorandum for the preservation of the rights of the Jewish people with regard to Palestine follow a critical analysis of American and British proposals, and have been reiterated as follows:

Neither the American nor the British proposals make comprehensive provision for the preservation of existing rights and privileges under the Mandate of the League of Nations. Such a clause would be in accordance not only with the demands of justice and the theory of acquired rights, but also with the century-old tradition of European and American history in accordance with which even war cannot be allowed to impair such vested rights and interests. The need for such a safeguarding provision is the more imperative by reason of the fact that the definition of the purposes of the trusteeship must necessarily be couched in terms too general to allow adequately for the unique character of the Palestine Mandate, with its dynamics in matter of population and its objective of creating a national home for a people to come to the country. It is therefore suggested that whatever the final text of the chapter on trusteeship, the following safeguarding clause should be included:

No trusteeship arrangement shall deprive any people or nation of any rights or benefits acquired or impair any obligations assumed under existing mandates held by members of the United Nations.

In our discussion there was more criticism of the three memorandums (British, American, and Australian) for not containing the explicit promise that the rights and privileges conferred by the League of Nations mandates on *all* parties concerned should be preserved and protected, and not simply those of the Mandatory Power. It was emphasized that the British memorandum took pains to ensure the safeguarding of Great Britain's rights as the holder of the Palestine Mandate, but did not refer to the rights of the Jewish people or to the national home, which had equally formed part of the terms of the Mandate.

In summarizing the analysis and notes on the contents of the British, American, and Australian proposals, the supplementary memorandum to the United Nations contained demands to:

(1) Include in the chapter of the Charter of the United Nations dealing with international trusteeship a clause designed to preserve existing Jewish rights acquired under the mandate system of the League of Nations.

(2) Center responsibility for the transfer of League of Nations mandates to the authority of the United Nations in the hands of the permanent member of the Security Council. In the case of any particular territory held under mandate by a United Nation not a member of the Security Council, the responsibility would be shared by the nation holding such a mandate.

(3) Define the beneficiaries of the trusteeship system so as to take into account the rights of the Jewish people as a whole to Jewish immigration and settlement in Palestine.

(4) Qualify provisions for nondiscrimination or the "open door" in regard to trusteeship areas by imposing requirements of reciprocity.

(5) Vest the General Assembly and the Social and Economic Council with power sufficient to enable them to carry out their supervisory functions in regard to trusteeship areas; and to create a Trusteeship Council of such a character as to command confidence and authority, and such as would be capable further of developing a comprehensive and consistent system of trusteeship law. The establishment of such a system would indeed be among the most promising and challenging experiments in modern international relations.

We have decided to increase our information activity aimed at every delegation and to give the widest possible publicity to our case. Kenen mentioned the enormous sums of money being spent by the American oil companies with concessions in Saudi Arabia to finance Arab propaganda. Senior personnel of the companies have been assigned to the Saudi Arabian delegation for public-relations work and also to assist other Arab delegations in their anti-Zionist activities among fellow delegates and journalists.

Agronsky reported on his contacts with leading American journalists and said that he will continue to enlighten his press colleagues on our problems and demands. Monsky is optimistic about our prospects at the conference: we have influential friends in the United States delegation who are ready to help us. One of our major channels of influence is the United States Congress. Several congressmen of both houses are here in San Francisco and have been in touch with the American delegation. Goldmann and Monsky mentioned that the Russian position is unclear; their representatives at the conference are saying nothing, although all proposals laid before the Trusteeship Committee are in the name of the five Great Powers, which includes the Soviet Union. Lipsky emphasized the importance of the many Latin American delegations; together they carry great weight at the conference. Wise complained of the confusion and the lack of clarity in the exposition and presentation of our case because there is no coordination among the numerous Jewish bodies at the conference. He again stressed the great damage this does to our cause and the embarrassment it causes our friends. Wise and others contrasted our plight with the position of the Arab states, which, on the Palestine question, act and work as one united group. If we do not manage to organize our efforts more efficiently we will jeopardize any prospect of success. However, those to whom Wise was referring were not present to hear him.

I had a second talk with Proskauer. He again told me about his efforts to have the white paper of 1939 canceled, together with its restrictions on immigration to Palestine, especially since he does not believe that immigration to America will be open to a large number of Jewish survivors of the Holocaust. I gathered that this is one of the weighty considerations behind the American Jewish Committee's efforts to abolish the existing laws restricting immigration to Palestine. Proskauer explained that the AJCommittee is actively involved in every initiative to promote the entry of Jews into Palestine. That is the declared policy of the AJCommittee, and it has been made known to both the American and British governments. He repeated his opinion that the struggle against the white paper should not fall only on the shoulders of the Jewish Agency and the World Zionist Organization. If that should happen, the British government would represent the campaign against the white paper as being entirely politically motivated and as concerning only those Jews who accept the leadership of Weizmann and Ben-Gurion.

I explained to Proskauer that without favorable political conditions in Palestine we cannot deal properly and effectively with the problems posed by immigration. I pointed out that it is not enough simply to bring immigrants into the

Eliyahu Elath (Epstein)

Nahum Goldmann

Abba Hillel Silver

Israel Goldstein

Moshe Sharett (Shertok)

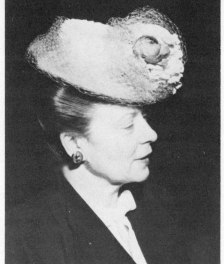

Rose Halprin

Morris Rothenberg

Isaiah Kenen

Eliezer Kaplan

Louis Lipsky

Emanuel Neumann

Rebecca Shulman

Stephen S. Wise

Arthur Lourie

Hayim Greenberg

country: we must see to their absorption and ensure their future in the land. We can do this only when we become our own masters. The Biltmore Program is more than a natural and logical step toward the fulfillment of the Zionist dream —it is the tangible expression of what is required for our very existence as a people. Proskauer disagreed and tried to explain the great harm he felt the program has done to the unity of American Jewry.

Despite his sharp criticism of Zionist policies and tactics it is clear to me that we may rely on Proskauer's help in a number of ways. There is indeed good public relations value in the assistance of a non-Zionist body as prominent as the American Jewish Committee, however qualified and partial that assistance may be. It seems to me that it will make things easier for Proskauer if we, the Palestinian members of our delegation, rather than the American Zionist leadership, keep in touch with him; with the latter he has personal and public scores to settle going back many years, which have a direct bearing on his behavior. It is easy to see, judging by some of his remarks, that there is little love lost between Proskauer and Wise; from our point of view the less that personal animosities among Jewish leadership in this country —Zionist and non-Zionist—bear on our affairs, the better off we will be. I must therefore watch my step in order not to become involved in local quarrels and personal intrigues.

In a long talk we had on the American administration's position on the Palestine question, Morris Rothenberg cautioned against Wise's optimism. He feels that Wise did not realize the late president's true character and that Roosevelt did not always keep the promises he made to Wise or, indeed, to other Jewish and Zionist leaders. Wise was too often satisfied by extracting a declaration from Roosevelt, whose practical value Wise did not scrutinize enough when it came out or examine in the light of other, often conflicting, declarations or acts by the president himself or members of his administration. Rothenberg says that we should begin our assessment of United States foreign policy in the Middle East by analyzing the background of overall American interests throughout the world, including the Middle East; if we do not do this we cannot expect to understand the ultimate objectives of that policy or policies, or forestall the dangers that might, as a result, await us.

I later heard a similar assessment from Herman Shulman, who thinks our chief danger is the State Department. He believes its staff is backing the oil companies and will do everything it can to deny support for any of our claims that encounter Arab opposition. Shulman feels that American Zionists should quickly embark on an active and high-powered political and public-relations campaign.

Goldmann and I visited the conference building. He was about to meet the chairman of the Czechoslovak delegation, Minister for Foreign Affairs Jan Masaryk. Goldmann introduced me to Masaryk, who asked about the situation in Palestine and expressed his concern regarding the growing tension in the country. He recalled his father's visit to Palestine before the war and remembered how greatly impressed his father had been by our agricultural settlements. The visit had deepened the elder Masaryk's Zionist sympathies and influenced his colleagues in the Czechoslovak government in the same direction. Goldmann suggested to Masaryk that, in countries that had been under Nazi occupation, the property of Jews who were annihilated leaving no heirs should be used for the absorption of those who survived and would emigrate to Palestine. Masaryk favored the proposal and promised to recommend its acceptance to his government. Goldmann added that he has made a similar suggestion to the representative of the Yugoslav government, who had also favored the idea.[47]

In the conference building I came across Mahmoud Abul Fath, the well-known Egyptian senator and journalist. I used to meet him when I was in Cairo on Political Department business. He told me he is in San Francisco as an adviser to the Egyptian delegation on press and publicity matters.

I asked him how it feels to be an Egyptian in the Arab League. "I was and still am an Egyptian," he replied, "and this changes nothing either for me or for those who, like me, see Egypt's joining the league as an important achievement. Undoubtedly Egypt will play a central role in the league and guide its activities. It will enhance Egypt's prestige in international affairs and will fill a need on the world scene and in the community of Muslim and Arab states. We will play the part in the Arab League that Britain does in the British Commonwealth."

He inquired if I was interested in listening to the proceedings of the conference. I thanked him for his kindness, and he returned a few minutes later with a valid entry pass to the guests' gallery. After I had heard two speeches and satisfied my curiosity, I left the hall to meet a journalist from the *Christian Science Monitor.* The meeting had been arranged by Si Kenen.

---

[47]None of these appeals—to the Czechoslovak, Yugoslav, or Greek governments—bore fruit, however, or won substantial support in the capitals of the countries concerned.

When I met Judge Rothenberg again this evening, I told him that I had gained admission to the conference through the help of an Arab friend and that since coming to San Francisco I have met with more Arab friends and acquaintances than with Jews or Zionists! Rothenberg consoled me by saying that the day will come when we will sit in the United Nations and have no need of favors by friends to enter the conferences of that organization.

Wednesday, May 9

Ambassador John Politis, a member of the Greek delegation whom I knew in Cairo during the war, arranged for me to be received by John Sofianopoulos, the Greek minister for foreign affairs, who is chairman of his country's delegation. Politis is a man of broad education and rich political experience and is one of the prominent Greek political leaders who found refuge in Egypt during the Nazi occupation of their country. I learned a lot from him about Greek politics and public affairs, which have always been rather complicated.

I explained to Sofianopoulos our appeal for safeguarding our rights as laid down in the terms of the Palestine Mandate. The minister replied that he had received our memorandum but had not yet had time to study it properly. He asked me what the British position is on the matters I raised and how the United States reacted to our appeal. "You will certainly have sought their assistance," he remarked. I asked him about the position of the Jews in Greece who had managed to stay alive. He dwelt on the help Jews received from the Greek public during the German occupation, adding that many people endangered their own lives in order to save their Jewish neighbors. He spoke in glowing terms of the personal contribution of Archbishop Damaskinos, the head of the Greek Orthodox Church, who did all he could to help Jews. His government is presently engaged in gathering material on the subject, which will be examined from every angle. I remarked on Moshe Shertok's recent visit to Greece and the friendly reception accorded him by the regent, Damaskinos, and Premier Bulgaris.

When I tried to probe his views on the Palestine question, he quickly brought our conversation to an end. I realized that Greece, like Turkey, is interested in winning Arab support in their present conflict and that both therefore do not wish to alienate the Arabs. These two countries will be careful not to support us, openly at any rate, on the Palestine question. The Greek government has a reason for not incurring Arab enmity: there are many Greek nationals in Arab countries, especially in Egypt, which has a large and wealthy Greek community. I later reported the substance of the meeting with Sofianopoulos to Goldmann.

I spoke by telephone with Eliezer Kaplan, who is in New York on Jewish Agency finance business, and told him about the urgent requests for funds coming to Jerusalem from refugee camps liberated in Europe. Yitzhak Gruenbaum[48] has asked for an immediate £15,000 to forward to Bergen-Belsen

[48]Yitzhak Gruenbaum (1879–1970); Zionist and Jewish leader in Poland; publicist, historian, and minister of the interior in Israel's first cabinet; early leader of Radical Zionists, opposing the expansion of the Jewish Agency; elected to the Jewish Agency executive (1933) and settled in Palestine; headed the agency's Absorption and Labor Departments and, during World War II was chairman of the agency's Rescue Committee; initiated negotiations for cooperation between Haganah and Irgun Tzvai Leumi (1947–48).

and £5,000 for children rescued in France. Ze'ev Schind[49] needs money to complete the purchase of the Turkish ship *Asia,* for which he has already paid £15,000. There are good chances of buying vessels in France and Italy to transport immigrants to Palestine, but at least £20,000 is needed. The Joint Distribution Committee is cooperating with us in a number of activities but will not bear the entire cost of the immigration from Europe. I informed Kaplan of the decision taken in Jerusalem to send fifteen emissaries to the United States and Canada to prepare young people for *aliya* to Palestine, but the Zionist organizations of these countries have to participate in the operation by paying for maintaining them.

While I was listing the sums of money needed for such urgent tasks, I sensed that Kaplan was becoming increasingly tense. He answered that he is doing his utmost to return to Palestine with funds that will meet at least some of the needs that cannot possibly be postponed. He told me that his discussions with the Joint Distribution Committee have not finished and that there are still problems which he hopes can be overcome.

I met Kohler and Philip Ireland,[50] special assistant to the director of the Office of Near Eastern and African Affairs of the State Department. Ireland has served in several Arab countries and knows Iraq especially well. He doubts if the

[49]Ze'ev Schind (1909–53); born in Lithuania; moved to Palestine (1929); went to Paris (1937) to help direct the illegal immigration movement; later operated from Turkey and then the U.S.; became one of the top three Mossad operatives, a specialist in shipping; among the many ships he secured for Aliya Bet, was the *President Warfield* (renamed *Exodus 1947*).

[50]Philip Ireland published a book on the history and problems of Iraq since its foundation, *Iraq: A Study in Political Development* (New York: Atheneum, 1970).

Arab League can promote fruitful cooperation among its members. He considers Iraq to be nothing more than an artificial conglomeration of numerous religious sects and national groups like the Kurds, with conflicting social, economic, and political interests. Iraq needs, in his opinion, many years to grow into a single nation. In Syria and Lebanon the situation is not much different, and he doubts whether the recently acquired political independence of those countries will foster unity or understanding between their various communities. It is even possible that these countries' internal divisions will deepen under the new circumstances.

Kohler does not fully share Ireland's views and seems more optimistic about the Arab League's prospects of success. Both agree, however, that the Middle East is becoming increasingly important in world affairs, because of the changes taking place in the region and because of the Soviet Union's growing activity in the area, particularly in the countries it borders—Iran and Turkey.

When the conversation turned to the Palestine question, I recognized at once the British influence on them both. Each emphasized that the United States can follow no course in the Middle East without full coordination with its British ally. While the United States has its own legitimate interests in the Middle East, which do not always exactly mesh with those of Great Britain, the present international conditions require understanding and close cooperation between the two democratic powers; if at all possible, disagreements between them on fundamental issues of policy must be prevented, and their activities on the international scene and specifically in our part of the world must corelate. Although neither Kohler nor Ireland mentioned the word "oil," it was perfectly clear what was meant by the "legitimate interests" of the United States in the Middle East.

Dr. A. Fastlicht,[51] a Mexican Zionist leader, introduced Agronsky, Reuven Zaslani, and me to a number of Latin American journalists. From their questions and the opinions they expressed, we sensed their friendly attitude to us on the Palestine question. We can rely, they believe, on the understanding and assistance of Latin America. The Holocaust in Europe has shocked public opinion in their countries, and they understand our struggle for free Jewish immigration to Palestine and the achievement of political independence.

Thursday, May 10

Agronsky assembled a number of distinguished American journalists at breakfast. It is apparently the practice in this country to use every possible moment for "business," starting with breakfast, and we have used almost every meal for meetings. Agronsky, Reuven, and I dealt with their many questions across oceans of coffee. Replying to a question by a Jewish member of the *New York Times* staff, Agronsky explained what had led him to leave the wealthy and prosperous U.S. for a poor country at the other end of the earth. His reply seemed to make a greater impression on the non-Jews there than on the questioner!

Also present was the well-known Indian journalist J.J. Singh, who has been sent to cover the United Nations con-

[51]Dr. Adolfo Fastlicht (1905–64); president of the Zionist Federation and of the B'nai B'rith in Mexico; served as first honorary Israeli consul in Mexico; organizer and vice-president of the Instituto Mexico-Israel.

ference by the *Hindustan Times* of New Delhi, and has been active in the movement in the United States for an independent India. He asked me several pointed questions on conditions in Palestine and spoke fervently about his total support for Zionism. He did not miss the opportunity to criticize Muslim communal leaders in India for undermining the unity and future of the people of India. Mohammed Ali Jinnah and the former mufti of Jerusalem, he argued, have turned Islam into a reactionary political force that is jeopardizing the progress of Asian peoples. Singh, who is a Sikh, painted Islam's fanaticism and intolerant attitude toward other faiths in the blackest terms. He ended by appealing for support of movements in Asia that strive to build progressive, democratic societies in a politically independent framework.

I had a long chat with a member of a respected Jerusalem Muslim family, whom I met by chance in the conference building. At one time we both attended the lectures of Professor Assad Rustum at the American University of Beirut and prepared a joint seminar paper on the Young Turks revolution. He is a translator for a number of Arab delegations at the conference and also has the job of distributing Arab League material on the Palestine question to delegates. We met as old friends. In Beirut, when I had no money to buy textbooks he used to lend me any book I needed, sometimes even before he had read it himself; he was never short of funds. He differed from many other students from Palestine in his moderation in debating political subjects and in the good relations he enjoyed with his Jewish friends.

I asked him how he feels in his present assignment. He replied that if it were not for "you Zionists," instead of being a translator he would be a member of a full delegation to the conference from an independent Palestine. "Are the Arabs of

Palestine," he asked bitterly, "more backward in their education, social development, and political awareness than the Saudis or the Syrians next door, that they are denied the right to representation at the San Francisco conference because a certain British foreign secretary [Balfour] decided for his own selfish imperialist reasons to promise to one people [the Jews] a land inhabited by another [the Arabs]?" I countered that if the Arab leadership had accepted the partition plan of the Peel Royal Commission, neither he nor I would be working in San Francisco as citizens of mandated Palestine with no official standing at the United Nations conference, but would be attending as the representatives of two independent states, Jewish and Arab. He answered that Arab leaders did not agree to the treacherous division of their homeland because every Arab rejects the Jewish claim to a separate independent state, even in the tiniest corner of their land, and rejects just as vehemently the right of the British to decide their future.

I went on to dispute the points he made, denying that ties between the Jews and their homeland have ever been broken and explaining that Jewish settlement in Palestine never ceased in all the years of Jewish exile. I mentioned that Arab immigration to Palestine has itself been stimulated by Jewish immigration and that many Arabs have lived there for much less time than, for instance, the Jewish family of Zinati in the Galilee village of Peki'in. Arab family histories purporting to verify claims of residence in Palestine for thirteen hundred years are entirely unfounded when applied, say, to families such as the Husseinis, Nashashibis, and Tuqans, to name only a few. To my astonishment he agreed that the three families I cited are indeed "new immigrants" to Arab society in Palestine compared with his own, "whose connection with Palestine dates back to the Muslim conquest," and said that no family could rival his in nobility of origin or in its contribution to the Muslim Arab cause.

It was interesting to see how the narrow family pride of this young university-educated man with modern, nationalist views exposed the whole falsity of the "Arab character" of Palestine—when the origin of Arab families in Palestine was mentioned, he was more concerned about debunking other Arabs' claims than about upholding an ideological position.

In the course of our conversation my friend took from his briefcase two books that apparently are helping him in his work, George Antonius's *The Arab Awakening* and Hans Kohn's *Nationalism and Imperialism in the East,* and we began to argue the scientific value of the two works. I said that considering the propagandistic nature of his book, Antonius has done quite a lot of serious research, but to picture the Arab national awakening as a politically organized process from the appearance of Wahhabism to the present day is nothing but a distortion of the truth. He employs the criteria applied to nationalist movements in Europe in the nineteenth century, which are no guide to the reality of the Arab situation and to their social and political aspirations during the same period.

I did not dwell on Hans Kohn's book, saying only that it is a sincere attempt to describe the Orient and its problems from a Western viewpoint, but that the author does not know the world he is describing—the foundation of its life, the traditions of its peoples, the languages they speak, the relations among the various communities of the area, and the relations between its people and the world outside. Nevertheless, I said, the fact that Hans Kohn was once a Zionist but is now contributing so greatly to vindicating the Arab cause to Western readers might be in our favor when the time comes for Jews and Arabs to reach an understanding and a peace settlement. Meanwhile, I commented, the history and problems of Arab nationalism still await serious scientific research. Works of propaganda lacking truth and objectivity do not always help the Arab case on Palestine or other problems of importance to the Arab world generally.

We parted on friendly terms and hope to meet again while we are in San Francisco.

At Goldmann's request I met Stanoje Simic, the Yugoslav ambassador in Washington, who is his country's representative on the Trusteeship Committee. I gave him the memorandums we prepared for the conference and added a few words of explanation. He asked me about the situation in Palestine and our relations with the Mandatory government and the Arabs. He expressed his sorrow at the heavy suffering of Yugoslav Jewry under the Nazi occupation, mentioned the help the Serbian population has provided for the survivors, and said his government is concerned about reviving Jewish life in Yugoslavia and is ready to help those who wish to join their relatives in Palestine. He added that those Jews who want to emigrate to Palestine "of course" must have the agreement of the British authorities and possess valid entry certificates to the country.

I talked with a prominent member of the Iranian delegation. I got to know him when I was in Teheran in 1937 to ascertain for the Political Department the position of government leaders and, in particular, their attitude to the partition plan of the Peel Royal Commission. He is a cultured man with a broad Western education who has done much to further the spread of education in Iran. He visited Palestine before the war and was impressed by our achievements.

He praised the Jewish contribution to the general progress of Palestine and criticized Arab leadership for refusing to reach a settlement with us. His view is that the Arabs lack leaders of caliber who can see the advantages of having Jews, with their energy and creative initiative, as neighbors. The Arab League he regards simply as a British device to enhance their own influence in the Arab countries. He mentioned that neither Turkey nor Iran is prepared to accept an Arab claim to represent the entire region just because of the number of votes they control at the United Nations. The arithmetical approach is no aid to a correct appreciation of the balance of forces in the Middle East; and the fact that the United Nations conference accords one vote to each member, one to the United States and one to Lebanon, is hardly likely to contribute to the stability or prestige of the organization. The principle of the equality of members is just, but in the end—despite what the Charter may say—effective power in international affairs will remain with the Great Powers.

In reply to my question about events in Iran, he expressed concern over developments in the north of his country, where subversive Soviet activity is on the increase and is awakening separatist tendencies. When I tried to ascertain the stand of the Iranian delegation on the Palestine question, I received no direct answer. He thinks that because of its serious difficulties Iran has to take "great care" of its ties with Great Britain and its relations with the Arabs. I parted from him with my feelings strengthened that Turkey, Greece, and Iran are unlikely to do anything to incur Arab disfavor or anything of substance to our benefit. He gave me to understand that what he said in our conversation was strictly confidential.

––––––––––––

At a meeting of our staff Wise, Monsky, and Goldmann spoke about the need to maintain active contact with delegates and journalists. I replied to questions on the Arabs in Palestine and neighboring countries. Most of the questioners knew next to nothing about the subject. I thought to myself:

how can we expect worthwhile results from their explanations to others?

Later I went to a reception given by San Francisco Zionists for Jewish representatives in the city. The president of the local Zionist organization, Leo Rabinowitz, an attorney, made a passionate speech, followed by addresses by a dozen representatives of different Zionist bodies. Someone greeted me in Hebrew: in 1929 he had been a pupil in the agricultural school of Mikve Israel, and during the riots of that summer he volunteered as a guard in the Galilee and was sent to Sejera. I was in charge of the Haganah in Sejera, and that boy, together with a few other pupils of Mikve Israel, were the core of our military strength in the village. They were given defense jobs and also helped the farmers work the fields and vineyards. This particular young man later left Palestine, reached the United States, and finally settled in San Francisco. He said that he intends to return to Palestine, "after my children finish their studies" (it was unclear whether he meant elementary school, high school, or university studies).

Friday, May 11

This morning I had a long conversation with Sir Firoz Khan Noon, the member responsible for defense on the governor-general's Executive Council in India and a delegate from that country to the conference. I handed him our memorandums and explained the requests they contain. He asked me about events in Palestine and our relations with the Arabs. As a

Muslim he stressed the spiritual ties of his coreligionists to Jerusalem and expressed the view that, despite the former Jerusalem mufti's connections with Hitler, had the Nazis won the war the fate of the Arabs would have been no better than that of other peoples classified by them as "non-Aryan." The Middle East would have been turned into a German or Italian colony with a far worse government than the region has ever known.

As for Palestine, I gathered that neither he nor any other member of the Indian delegation can lift a finger—and certainly will not—without the approval of the British government. I had already heard from the Indian journalist J.J. Singh that the "so-called India delegation" is simply a tool of its British advisers. The representative of the British raj, Edward Brownsdon, undersecretary for external affairs in the Indian government, bears the title of "secretary to the Indian delegation," but according to Singh he actually directs all the delegation's work.

Later Anne O'Hare McCormick invited me to meet with some of her *New York Times* colleagues who are in San Francisco. I found it well worth my while to make the acquaintance of reporters from this influential American newspaper. The *New York Times* has never been known for its support of our cause, and its publisher, Arthur Hays Sulzberger, is an outspoken opponent of Zionism. I learned that his father had been a Zionist and had even been present at the opening of the first Zionist Congress at Basel in 1897, but that his son adopted the hostile attitude of his father-in-law, Adolph Ochs, when he married Ochs's daughter and came into the newspaper.

Ray Brook was there and told me about the extensive activities, both at the conference itself and on its fringes, of the American oil companies that have concessions in Arab countries. They want to strengthen the standing of the Arabs with the American public and with Congress in Washington. The companies' agents have at their disposal a generous budget and experts in public relations. By the way, one agent, the owner of a large public-relations firm in Washington, is a Jew. I was told he receives large sums of money to carry out the pro-Arab propaganda campaign by the oil companies.

I invited Charles Malik to lunch with Goldmann, Lourie, and me at the restaurant of the Sir Francis Drake Hotel. Goldmann explained our position as it is outlined in the memorandums distributed to all conference delegations. He emphasized that prospects for an agreement between the Arabs and ourselves depend more than anything else on Arab readiness to concede the special rights of the Jewish people in Palestine. Goldmann stated our desire to establish friendly relations with Palestinian Arabs and the rest of the Arab world, most especially with our neighboring countries, on the basis of mutual trust, understanding, and cooperation.

Malik listened to what Goldmann said, but was rather reserved when the time came to respond and retreated into philosophical musings on love for one's fellowmen, peace as "the highest goal of contemporary mankind," the humanitarian mission of the United Nations, and so on. He obviously had no desire to enter into a political discussion, but some rapport between Goldmann and him was achieved when the conversation moved on to more concrete philosophical topics, including Bergson's concept of ethics and the modern school of theology in Europe and America. Goldmann was apparently not much struck with Malik's comments on the subjects under discussion.

I was not surprised by Malik's caution in avoiding speaking freely in the company of three members of the Jewish Agency. The mere fact of his meeting us is enough to raise suspicion among his colleagues if the matter becomes known to representatives from the different communities in his own delegation, who do not trust each other and would not hesitate to sabotage each other's position for communal and personal reasons. A liberal person and a deeply religious Christian, Malik undoubtedly feels himself a stranger to the fanatical Saudi Arabian Wahhabis and must, in addition, guard his behavior and his every word from the suspicion and hostile interpretations of his Arab League colleagues. It was an act of courage on his part to meet us in public at all.

I later met Harold Beeley,[52] associate secretary of Committee II/4 (the Trusteeship Committee). I first met him when I went to London in 1937 with Yitzhak and Rachel Ben-Zvi, as official representatives of the Yishuv at the coronation of King George VI. Beeley at that time worked at Chatham House (the Royal Institute for International Affairs) on Middle Eastern matters. I had known of his support for the Arab point of view on the Palestine question for many years. Although his attitude was undoubtedly governed by thoughts of the resulting benefit to Great Britain, his outlook was probably also colored by the romantic pro-Arab atmosphere created in Britain during and after World War I by the military and political exploits and adventures in Arabia of T. E. Lawrence, St. John Philby, Gertrude Bell, and Bertram Thomas, who had breathed new life into the established tradition of C. M. Doughty, R. F. Burton, F. T. Palgrave, and other early British travelers in Arabia. We had met only once, but corresponded whenever I sought publication in London for articles I had written on Middle Eastern topics.

[52]Sir Harold Beeley (1909–   ); secretary of Anglo-American Committee of Inquiry on Palestine; British ambassador to Saudi Arabia and Egypt.

Beeley mentioned that during the war he had worked for Chatham House and had assisted the Foreign Office with research and the preparation of material—including formulating proposals—on Middle East questions. I had heard before that the main centers of his work were London and Cairo; it was in Cairo that most of the material was assembled and analyzed. It was obvious that the material prepared by Beeley and his team was read by interested and influential "outsiders," as well as by Chatham House personnel, and that the Royal Institute clearly wished its output to be used for political guidance by government departments in Whitehall, primarily the Colonial Office and the Foreign Office.

Toward the end of the war Beeley joined the permanent staff of the Foreign Office, although still apparently maintaining his connection with Chatham House. From what he told me I can easily see how close the relations are between the Foreign Office and the Royal Institute for International Affairs, at least in research carried out for Foreign Office use. Knowing Beeley's anti-Zionist views, I assume that the material will not be serving our interests.

I tried now to have him clarify the position of the British members of the Trusteeship Committee on the question of the remaining mandates of the League of Nations, and first and foremost on the only remaining "A" Mandate, that of Palestine. I understand from what he said that they will strive to prevent changes in the terms of the Palestine Mandate. Their concern seems to be due to a fear that any change in the Mandate's integrity could lead to unforeseen results that might damage the existing British position and interests in the country. So far so good.

Saturday, May 12

I breakfasted with Georges Gorse and Raoul Aglion, both members of the French delegation. Aglion (formerly Agion) comes from a well-known Egyptian Jewish family and is a French citizen. He is a lawyer with a complete command of English and serves as a legal adviser in the French embassy in Washington.

I asked them what French aims are in independent Syria and Lebanon and in the new Middle East generally after the war. I also inquired if France intends to have its troops stay in these countries against the wishes of the local governments. Gorse replied that the French forces at present in Syria and Lebanon are part of the Ninth British and Allied Army, and that therefore there is no basis for Syrian complaints against France since the French are not opposed to the presence of British troops on their territory. France also has the unfettered right to decide the size and composition of its army in Syria and Lebanon, whether French or Senegalese (the Syrian press has been full of bitter criticism of the presence of French colonial troops in Damascus). Gorse added that the Syrians would never have dared rise against France if the British and Americans had not been hostile to France in the matter.

As for Lebanon, most Christians there fear Arab nationalism and regard the Arab League as a threat to the independent existence of Lebanon as a refuge for the Christians of the entire region. However, because of a lack of unity among Lebanon's Christians and because the Maronites themselves are split into several groups at odds with one another, the country's Muslims have managed to push Lebanon into the Arab League. The fact is that Lebanon needs France more than ever to protect itself from its aggressive Muslim neighbors. There are even many prominent Muslims in Lebanon who fear the expansionist aspirations of the National Bloc in Damascus, whose aim is to end Lebanon's independence and bring the whole country under Syria's wing. With Lebanon's adherence to the Arab League many communal leaders in that country have fallen into Britain's lap. From the time of Spears's dominating military and political role in Syrian and Lebanese affairs, the British have built up a core of pro-British leaders in Beirut, including Camille Chamoun [later president of Lebanon] and Charles Malik, who look to Britain for guidance. France has to contend with the Americans, who are hostile to de Gaulle, and the British; both seek to usurp France's historic place in the Levant.

Despite Gorse's unqualified opposition to the Arab League, I detected no sign of support for Zionism on his part other than his expressed satisfaction that, like the French, we too now find ourselves opposed to British policy. Aglion hardly took part in the conversation; he promised to meet with me with Ambassador Naggiar, the French representative on the Trusteeship Committee.

I visited the local Reform temple, a stronghold of the rabidly anti-Zionist American Council for Judaism. The temple's spiritual leader is Rabbi Irving F. Reichert, who is also the leader of the local branch of the council. Among his congregants are some of the wealthy Jews of San Francisco. The synagogue is an imposing building with an equally beautiful interior.

This was my first visit to a Reform temple. I was present for the Sabbath morning service, and I heard the rabbi's brief sermon, which was devoted to questions of individual ethics and duties to others. His attire and manner of delivery brought to mind the Protestant clergymen of my acquaintance in the Old City of Jerusalem. Not all Reform rabbis, of course, share Reichert's attitude to Zionism. Both Wise and Abba Hillel Silver[53] belong to the Reform movement, and no doubt help to minimize the poisonous influence of the American Council for Judaism among Reform Jews.

Adele Harris, a friend of Irma Lindheim's,[54] told me that Irma's son Daniel was killed during the last days of the war in Europe. He had been my pupil when the family lived in Palestine in 1928. I am grieved by the news, for I was very fond of the boy and know how great the loss must be to his mother. He is the second son she has lost in recent years.

This evening Judge Rothenberg, Agronsky, and I were speakers at a meeting called by the CIO branch in the city to express their members' solidarity with our cause. Most of those present were non-Jews. Also attending were representatives of fifty-five trade unions in the western part of the

[53]Abba Hillel Silver (1893–1963); Reform rabbi; born in Lithuania; president of the Zionist Organization of America (at various times between 1938–48); chairman of the American Zionist Emergency Council; chairman of the American Section of the Jewish Agency; one of the chief Zionist spokesmen at the Palestine hearings of 1947 before the United Nations.

[54]Irma Levy Lindheim (1886–   ); Zionist leader in the United States and Israel; national vice-president of the Zionist Organization of America (1926–28) and national president of Hadassah; settled in Israel (1933), becoming a member of Kibbutz Mishmar Ha'emek; returned to U.S. on numerous occasions to lecture in behalf of the Jewish National Fund, Hadassah, the League for Labor Palestine, Histadrut, and Hashomer Ha-tza'ir.

U. S. affiliated with the CIO. The well-known seamen's leader, Harry Bridges, chaired the gathering and delivered a passionate speech in support of our fight against British imperialism. He described the socialist society that the Jewish workers' organizations in Palestine are building in the feudal and backward Middle East. Agronsky dealt with the white paper and the British breach of the terms of the Balfour Declaration and the Mandate. Rothenberg called on the United States government to support the Zionist cause. I described the reactionary character of the Arab leadership and its many instances of collaboration with the Nazis and Fascists against the Allies during the war. I also referred to the Histadrut's contribution to the social and economic development of Palestine, including the Arab segment of the country's population.

At the end of the speeches, Bridges read the declaration of the World Conference of Trade Unions held in London in February 1945, which stated that

This world congress is of the opinion, too, that after the war thoroughgoing remedies must be found, through international action, for the wrongs inflicted on the Jewish people. Their protection against oppression, discrimination, and spoliation in any country must be the responsibility of the new international authority. The Jewish people must be enabled to continue the rebuilding of Palestine as their national home, so successfully begun, by immigration, agricultural settlement, and industrial development, respecting the legitimate rights of other national groups and giving equality of rights and opportunities to all its inhabitants (Par. 16 of the Peace Settlement Resolution).

This was received enthusiastically by the meeting, which called on all American workers to support the Yishuv in its struggle against British policy in Palestine.

Monday, May 14

At our meeting this morning there was stress on the need to augment our efforts directed at conference delegates. Reliable information has confirmed increased activity among the Arabs to nullify our attempts to safeguard our rights in the Trusteeship Committee. Arab members of the committee have already drawn up proposals to delete from the Palestine Mandate the international significance of the Balfour Declaration and its implications regarding the Jewish national home and the official status of the Jewish Agency.

Our American colleagues reported on their talks with Harold Stassen, who has promised to maintain a careful watch on matters connected with the Palestine Mandate and to prevent any undermining of our rights. Goldmann and Monsky reported on their contacts with the delegations of South Africa, Holland, and New Zealand, whose chairmen have assured them of their full support. Again the special importance of Peter Fraser's friendly attitude was noted: he is chairman of the New Zealand delegation as well as of the Trusteeship Committee. Monsky said that Fraser had been ready to allow a Jewish delegation to appear before the committee and submit its views and demands on matters that might affect the future of the Palestine Mandate. Fraser had already spoken to several committee members, but when the British member opposed such an invitation to a Jewish delegation Fraser dropped the idea. Goldmann reported that Field Marshal

Jan Smuts,[55] chairman of the South African delegation, has promised to address the General Assembly in our behalf should we have such a need. We can also rely on the active assistance of Eelko N. van Kleffens and Jan Masaryk, both of whom are chairmen of their countries' delegations and are, respectively, ministers for foreign affairs of the Netherlands and Czechoslovakia.

At a press conference this morning attended by more than one hundred reporters of the American and world press, Goldmann explained the Jewish Agency's position on the deliberations in the Trusteeship Committee on the future of the mandates system.

He opened the conference by saying that the Jewish Agency for Palestine, which is internationally recognized under the Palestine Mandate as the guardian of the interests of the Jewish people in all matters relating to Palestine, has presented a supplementary memorandum to the United Nations conference, urging specific amendments to the trusteeship proposals submitted by a number of delegations. We are hopeful, he said, that with the conclusion of the war in Europe, the original purpose of the Balfour Declaration and the Palestine Mandate will now be speedily fulfilled, and that the Jewish people will soon be permitted to reconstitute Palestine as a free and democratic commonwealth. However, he continued, it has been repeatedly stated that the Palestine

[55]Jan Christiaan Smuts (1870–1950); an outstanding South African military leader and statesman; prime minister of the Union of South Africa (1919–24, 1939–48); ardent friend of the Jewish people and of the Zionist cause; actively participated in the framing of the Balfour Declaration and in the efforts to establish the Jewish Legion (while he was a member of the British imperial cabinet).

question will not be on the agenda of this conference because territorial questions are not to be discussed. Nevertheless, the Palestine issue is relevant to the trusteeship question now before the conference, since Palestine is held under the Mandate that was created by the League of Nations after World War I for the benefit of the Jewish people.

He went on to say that we are therefore vitally concerned that any trusteeship scheme that is written into the United Nations Charter shall expressly safeguard the rights of the Jewish people to Palestine and shall place no obstacles or impediments in the way of the exercise of those rights.

Then Goldmann dealt with the trusteeship proposals made to the conference by the British, American, and Australian delegations and said that an examination of these proposals reveals that the definition of the purposes of the trusteeship is couched in general terms. As a result, no adequate allowance is made for the unique character of the Palestine Mandate in matters of population and its objective of creating a national home for a people still to come to the country.

He concluded his statement by explaining the proposals made by the Jewish Agency in its supplementary memorandum to the conference on May 8.

Goldmann faced a barrage of questions on the Palestine question. In his replies he described the tension in the country as a result of British policy based on the white paper and underlined the urgent need for the surviving remnants of European Jewry to gain free entry to Palestine. After him, Monsky spoke of the crucial problems faced at the moment by the Jewish people and demanded the outlawing of every form of anti-Semitism in the world.

I took part in preparing a letter to Alger Hiss, secretary-general of the conference. We learned that the Egyptian delegation has furnished Hiss with a copy of the resolutions taken by the Arab states at their congress held in Cairo in March, and that on May 5, at Egypt's request, the secretary-general distributed the material to all delegations as an official document of the conference. As this document carries the symbol III/4/1, it indicates some bearing on the problem of regional-security arrangements, a detail that causes us special concern.

The Jewish Agency's letter to Hiss begins by taking exception to the official circulation of the Pact of the League of Arab States in the form of an official document, since among the signatories were Transjordan and Yemen, neither of whom are members of the United Nations. On this ground alone, we said, the secretariat should have refused to give official circulation to the Arab League's material. After pointing out the internationally recognized status of the Palestine Mandate, the letter, referring to article 12 of the Mandate, emphasized the sole right of Great Britain, the Mandatory Power, to control the foreign relations of Palestine, and, referring to article 4 of the Mandate, the right of the Jewish Agency to advise and cooperate with the Mandatory Power in all matters affecting the establishment in Palestine of the Jewish national home. The Jewish Agency has recorded its strong objection to the classification of Palestine as an Arab state in the Pact of the League of Arab States and to the attempt of the Arab states to include that country within the sphere of their activity. For the above reasons, the letter states, and since the Pact of the League of Arab States has been officially distributed as a conference document, it is proper and just that the Jewish Agency's objection to the Annex Regarding Palestine, be likewise distributed as a conference document. The letter was drafted by Jacob Robinson and signed by Nahum Goldmann; it will be sent tomorrow.

I received an irate telegram from Israel Mereminsky,[56] now on a mission in New York in behalf of the Histadrut executive, criticizing me for taking part in the meeting organized by the CIO, who, he has been informed, are nothing more than declared or crypto-Communists. The Communist Yiddish newspaper *Morgen Freiheit* reported that I addressed the gathering in the name of the Histadrut, which enraged the AFL, including its president, William Green, and our friends on the Jewish Labor Committee. I replied that I had not spoken in the Histadrut's name or in anyone else's name, and pointed out that when I met the CIO leaders in San Francisco, they had suggested that I address the meeting because of the good they thought it could do our cause. I added that we have to win support in any public circle or organization prepared to help us and that the time has come when we should refrain from being dragged into local quarrels, whether of Jewish or non-Jewish organizations.

[56]Israel Mereminsky (Merom) (1891–   ); active as a Zionist organizer from his youth, helped organize and served as general secretary of the Russian Ze'irei Zion; worked in reorganizing Jewish communal life following the Russian Revolution; settled in Palestine (1924); member of Executive Committee of the Histadrut and served in various capacities in the Histadrut secretariat; representative of the Histadrut to U.S. during World War II; member of the Vaad Leumi (1925–39), and for forty years (from 1920), member of the Greater Actions Committee of the World Zionist Organization.

Tuesday, May 15

Louis Lipsky and I took part in an early morning press conference that was organized by Si Kenen for nearly fifty journalists specializing in labor and industrial questions. About half the reporters were from abroad, including some from Asia. Lipsky spoke of the problems facing the Jewish people in the aftermath of the Holocaust. I dealt with the work of the Histadrut and the part it has played in raising living standards, both social and economic, of the Arabs in Palestine. The host of questions, including some from journalists representing the Communist press, American and foreign, testified to the degree of sympathy there is for our cause.

Samuel Bronfman suggested that I meet Maurice Abraham Cohen, the "Chinese General," a man with many friends in the top leadership of China, including T. V. Soong, minister for foreign affairs, acting president of the Executive Yuan, and chairman of the conference delegation. Cohen was born in London to Orthodox parents who were originally from Poland; he now lives in Montreal. The Canadian Zionists sent him to San Francisco to help us in our approaches to the Chinese delegation.

Cohen gave me a detailed description of the many years he spent in China, first as the bodyguard of Sun Yat-sen, then as an instructor and adviser in the Chinese army, in which he rose to the rank of general. Since leaving China he has kept in touch with many of his friends in the public and political life of the country.

Cohen offered to introduce me to some of his friends in the Chinese delegation, to whom I'll be able to explain our problems. He knows that the Arabs are actively wooing the Chinese delegates; their propaganda stresses Asian solidarity, which "obliges China," so they claim, to support their campaign against Zionism. Cohen doubts whether the majority of the Chinese delegation have even heard of Zionism; even among educated delegates knowledge of Jews and Judaism is very sketchy. He thinks that Arab propaganda can very well succeed if we do not take effective countermeasures.

Cohen himself is doing what he can to explain to his friends the true state of affairs in Palestine, but believes a thorough and continuing program of enlightenment is required because of the important role China will play at the United Nations.

Cohen's memoirs, he told me, are to be published soon in London, and he is interested in having them translated into Hebrew. I cabled Zalman Rubashov[57] asking if *Davar* might be interested in serializing them.

Dr. Henry Atkinson introduced me to John Foster Dulles,[58] State Department political adviser to the American delegation. Dulles has been active in the World Organization of Protestant Churches and has, according to Atkinson, a broad understanding of the international problems that face the

[57]Later Zalman Shazar (1889–1974); third president of Israel; at the time, editor of the Hebrew daily newspaper *Davar,* published in Tel Aviv.
[58]John Foster Dulles (1888–1959); later became U.S. secretary of state (1953) but was forced to resign due to illness (1959).

United States. He has close ties with Republican senator Arthur Vandenberg; the American delegation apparently does nothing without Vandenberg's knowledge and support.

Our conversation took place in one of the suites the American delegation occupies at the Sir Francis Drake Hotel. Dulles asked me about our relations with the Mandatory government and with the Arabs, and wanted details about the absorptive capacity of Palestine. He showed an interest in the internal political structure of the Yishuv, its institutions, and the place of religion in our everyday life. He also wanted to know about our relations with Soviet Russia and our attitude toward Communism. Atkinson's friendly remarks played a useful part in the conversation.

At a meeting with Hadassah leaders, Agronsky and I spoke about the situation in Palestine and the prospects of reaching an agreement with the Arabs. Some of the women incline to the binational views of Dr. Magnes, but most believe the solution to the problem lies in Jewish statehood. We were told that Hadassah has undertaken to raise part of the money required for immigration and the absorption of immigrants from liberated Europe, on the assumption that their numbers will grow and that they will reach Palestine by every possible route. We explained the complex political and economic problems connected with *aliya.*

Foy Kohler introduced me to Paul H. Alling, deputy director of the Office of Near Eastern and African Affairs in the Department of State, who is the senior adviser to the United States delegation on the affairs of Africa and the Middle East. I could tell from Alling's questions that he does not know much about Palestine. When I mentioned the ex-mufti's and other Arab leaders' cooperation with the Nazis, he hardly reacted, saying only that it was for the British in the countries under their jurisdiction to see that all those who helped the enemy during the war are brought to trial. I described our attitude to the Arab League and mentioned in particular our objection to the inclusion of Palestine in the Pact of the League of Arab States.

At our morning meeting a bitter argument broke out between Dr. Wise and Rabbi Herbert Goldstein, the representative of the Rabbinical Assembly of America, over the independent activity of Goldstein and his colleagues at the conference, and the fact that it is not coordinated with that of other Jewish bodies. Wise referred to the important decisions that the conference may make on matters affecting the position and vital interests of the Jewish people, both in the Diaspora and in Palestine, and stressed the moral and public damage caused by the frenzied activity of Jewish representatives, none troubling to inquire and check what the others are doing. His warning was directed primarily at the Jewish organizations in America, whose contacts with the United States delegation are supposed to be carried on through the American Jewish Conference and not independently, as has been the case with Rabbi Goldstein and his friends. It is bad enough, thundered Wise, that the American Jewish Committee works on its own, and so adds to our difficulties at the United Nations conference. An organization of rabbis, he continued angrily, should be the first to uphold the unity of our people and set an example to others. Goldstein replied as best he could in his own defense, but the incident highlighted the lack of unity and internal discipline in American Jewry. Perhaps a central national institution representing all the various organizations and trends of American Jewry might be the answer, something like the British Board of Deputies. However, the pluralism of American life has its roots deep in the country's social structure and public mentality, and the federal form of government has its influence on the tradition and organization of American society. American Jewry has apparently adopted that approach in its own public affairs. After all, *Wie es christelt sich, so jüdelt es sich!*

While traveling by cable car to the conference building this evening to meet Zev Brenner, the Palcor correspondent, I saw the aged Field Marshal Smuts climbing one of the many steep hills in the city, with his young aides struggling to keep up with him. Friends who have spoken to him recently tell me of his outstanding alertness of mind and physical stamina, which have hardly lessened over the years. His prestige and influence are at their peak, and he plays an active part both in the plenary sessions and in the work of the committees concerned with political questions. Every time he meets with Jewish representatives he takes the opportunity to voice his sympathy for Zionism.

Wednesday, May 16

This morning I went to the office of the Greek delegation to see Militiades Delivanis, secretary of the Greek ministry for Foreign Affairs. John Politis had told me that Delivanis has a great deal of influence in the delegation and that he is personally close to the minister for foreign affairs and chairman of the delegation. Delivanis knows something about the Yishuv, has visited the Hebrew University in Jerusalem, and values what we have done in developing the country. He said that on all matters connected with the mandatory regimes of the League of Nations dealt with by the Trusteeship Committee, their delegation is assisted by two advisers: John Spiropoulos, a professor of international law at Athens University, and Constantine Goulimis, a legal counselor of the Ministry for Foreign Affairs. He suggested that we meet both, particularly Professor Spiropoulos, to explain our problem from the legal point of view. When the subject is dealt with in the Trusteeship Committee it may facilitate their representatives to assist us on legal grounds in cases where they find it difficult to do so on the basis of political arguments in our favor. Despite the exquisite courtesy of Delivanis, I cannot help again feeling that we stand little chance of receiving tangible assistance from the Greek delegation: Greece is caught between the British and the Arabs and prefers to do nothing to offend either.

Goldmann and I saw Ambassador Paul-Émile Naggiar, the French representative on the Trusteeship Committee, in his office at the Hotel Clift. Goldmann reviewed all the matters that are giving us concern and particularly mentioned the claims we will be presenting if the authority of the mandate system is transferred to the United Nations.

Naggiar has read our memorandums and knows clearly what we want to achieve at the conference. From what he said it appears that France will make no proposals of its own on the mandates issue and will define its attitude to the proposals of others during the committee's discussions. He thinks that the proposals of the United States, Great Britain, and Australia are rather vague and often unclear and that, although the Trusteeship Committee has been considering the matter, its discussions have not yet reached the practical stage. The Soviet delegates still have not shown their hand,

and even the Arabs seem to be waiting to see how things develop among the Great Powers.

I chatted with Elizabeth MacCallum of the Canadian delegation, who is in charge of the Middle East desk in the Canadian Ministry for External Affairs. She was born to a family of Protestant missionaries in a small town in Turkey's Taurus Mountains and is fluent in both Turkish and Arabic. I discovered that her sister was the librarian at the American University of Beirut when I was a student there. Her views are basically pro-Arab, but she is ready to listen to our point of view and even to agree with some of the arguments I advanced as a basis for a Jewish-Arab settlement. I do not feel she has much to say in the framing of her government's policy in our part of the world.

I dined with Professor Abraham S. Yahuda,[59] who is attending the conference as a correspondent for several newspapers. He also serves as an adviser to the New Zionist Organization, which has circulated a paper prepared by him in reply to the manifesto published by the pro-Arab Institute for Arab-American Affairs. The New Zionist Organization people work independently and do not participate in the sessions of the American Jewish Conference and the associated Zionist bodies.

[59]Abraham Shalom Ezekiel Yahuda (1877–1951); scion of an old Sephardic family; studied and taught in Germany, Spain, England, and the U.S.; attended first Zionist Congress (Basel, 1897); intervened in behalf of the Yishuv with Spanish authorities (during World War I); worked to call the attention of American Jewish leaders to the plight of the Yishuv; ardent Zionist; close follower of Max Nordau, supporter of Zionist-Revisionist leader Vladimir Jabotinsky, and consistent critic of Weizmann.

Yahuda had heard from Professor Nahum Slouschz[60] that I would be coming to America and wanted to speak to me about our common interest, the Arab problem. He told me he has devoted a lifetime to Islamic and Arabic studies and to trying to foster understanding between Arab and Jew. To his regret he has never been encouraged in his task by Zionist leaders, who have turned down every attempt on his part to find ways of promoting cooperation between the two peoples and searching for a political settlement of the problem. In his opinion he is the best-qualified person to win Arab trust because of his background and understanding of Arab mentality and his command of Arabic. Even the most talented and enlightened Zionist leaders are of Western origin and education and will never be able, he said, to evaluate properly the mental attitude and methods of public and political behavior of the Arab leadership. He asked bitterly what hope there is of anything coming from contact between them when the two sides are complete strangers to one another. The British and French were backed up by military power when they became masters of Middle East affairs after World War I, but even they have come to understand that physical strength alone is not a sufficient basis for stability of their power and influence, and they have tried to develop common interests backed by mutual understanding with the local inhabitants. Yahuda cited in this connection Marshal Louis H. Lyautey's fruitful work in North Africa as the French administrator of the area and praised the contribution made by Professor Slouschz, when serving as Lyautey's ad-

[60]Nahum Slouschz (1892–1966); writer, scholar, and Zionist leader; close associate of Herzl's (from 1898); lecturer in modern Hebrew literature; when sent by the French Academy to explore antiquities in North Africa, took special interest in Jewish antiquities and the situation of the Jews of North Africa; later did archaeological exploration in Tiberias and its vicinity; wrote extensively in Hebrew and French and translated French literature into Hebrew.

viser on matters affecting North African Jews, to the improvement of the position of Jews residing there.

Yahuda went on to accuse Dr. Weizmann personally of excessive concentration of his energies in London and Geneva, to the neglect of the painstaking labor that is vitally necessary in Cairo, Damascus, and Baghdad. He argued that after the first encounter with Emir Feisal in Aqaba, Weizmann should have kept in contact with him and his entourage and worked to create new links with other Arab leaders, not necessarily through Lawrence and the British officials, but independently and directly. In any event, nothing was done either by Weizmann himself or by his associates and political assistants, and the feeling grew among Arabs—despite our occasional formal declarations—that we have been coming to the East not to become an integral part of it, but like the European settlers in a British colony in Asia or Africa, to remain a foreign body alien to all trends and purposes of the inhabitants of the region, their customs, and traditions.

Even the Hebrew University, Yahuda thinks, does not nourish an "Eastern consciousness" among its teachers and students, the future leaders in every walk of Yishuv's life. The trouble, in his opinion, is that most of the teaching staff at the university's School of Oriental Studies are not suited to their posts because practically all of them came from Europe, studied there, and have no personal knowledge of or contact with Arabs. By and large those who are familiar with Arab history know practically nothing about the current problems of Arab society and countries. He said that methods of teaching Arabic subjects at the Hebrew University are too academic and mostly detached from reality. The result is that the students are not trained for daily relations with their Arab neighbors. Yahuda remarked bitterly that he had not been invited to join the staff of the university both on personal grounds and because of his opposition to the objectives and methods of instruction, so different from his own, employed by the School of Oriental Studies in Jerusalem.

He is pessimistic about prospects for a Jewish-Arab settlement over Palestine. World War I fragmented the Arab world; World War II has driven them toward unity, and the founding of the Arab League has pushed them further in the same direction, although it was Britain's brainchild, not their own. Hence the neighboring Arab states will now back the Arabs of Palestine even harder than in the past, opposing the creation of an independent non-Arab entity in an area where the majority of the inhabitants are Arab and where a large measure of political sovereignty is already in their hands.

Before we parted, Yahuda presented me with a copy of his book, *The Accuracy of the Bible*. It is a highly controversial work. For his part, Yahuda regards it as one of the most profound and original works of biblical scholarship ever written.

Thursday, May 17

Goldmann and I went to see Sinasi Hisar, a legal counselor to the Turkish delegation and an expert in international law who, we have learned, participates in the deliberations in the Trusteeship Committee. He told us that he has not the slightest doubt that the UN will have the sole and exclusive right to make decisions on the future of mandated territories, and said that no other body possesses the authority to annul or amend the terms of a mandate sanctioned and operated under the authority of the League of Nations. However, he added, in practice, matters in international affairs are never considered from the legal standpoint alone: each delegation has its own approach to any subject on the agenda of the United Nations conference under discussion, and the approach is not always based on legal assumptions or logical reasoning. Hisar believes that mandatory regimes will not last much longer. The Atlantic Charter is having worldwide reverberations at least as strong as those that followed Wilson's Fourteen Points. Although the Atlantic Charter has done much to raise the prestige of the United Kingdom and the U.S. in the world, Britain, more than any other power, will still have to show that its imperialist phase has come to an end and that the world has embarked on a new course for the achievement of national rights by all those to whom they were denied in the past. In these new circumstances, he said, there is no place for mandates, which have served as a cloak for alien rule. He hinted that the USSR hungers more than any other power for more territory; to prevent its expansion, the democratic powers themselves have to act liberally toward the peoples they once ruled and toward those still under their domination.

Hisar said that he has studied the Jewish Agency's memorandums, which have gone out to conference delegations, and praised the clarity of their wording and conclusions.

He made a good impression on us, but we know that he does not determine his delegation's policy.

I had a long talk with Hayim Greenberg,[61] who stopped in San Francisco on his way back to New York from Los Angeles, where he was lecturing. I met him on his visits to Palestine, but I had also known of him in my youth. He was one of the outstanding Zionist leaders in Russia. Greenberg

[61]Hayim Greenberg (1889–1953); born in Russia, emigrated to the U.S. (1924); a leader of the Labor Zionist movement and editor of its American journal, *Jewish Frontier.*

was well known both as a brilliant public speaker and lecturer and as a critic and translator: his translations of Ahad Ha'am from Hebrew into Russian earned him a high reputation in educated Jewish circles in old Russia, where many people who were interested could not read Ahad Ha'am in the original.

On his frequent visits to Palestine we often discussed the Arab question, which disturbs him from the moral angle as much as from the political point of view. Greenberg judges our relations with our neighbors against the background of our future with Asian peoples as a whole. In historical terms he sees our national rebirth and the Zionist movement as part of the broader reawakening of Asia and its yearning for national independence for its peoples. He rejects the binational solution to the Arab problem and also has reservations about proposed solutions that do not go far enough in considering the ethical objectives of the Zionist ideal.

Greenberg talked to me about the condition of American Jewry and the Zionist movement in all its parts, divisions, and institutions in this country. American Jewry, he said, has arrived at its moment of destiny: the Holocaust in Europe has left it the largest and richest Jewish community in the Diaspora, and it now has to carry out its historic responsibilities toward the remnants of European Jewry and to the Yishuv as well. The United States is now the most powerful country in the world and will have the strongest voice in the solution of many international problems. Jews hold a respected position in American public life and have many ways of influencing the government, if only they can learn how to unite and organize their forces, and marshal them wisely and effectively. However, there are many deep-seated causes for the existing divisions in American Jewry, and no one has yet found a way to bring the disunity to an end. Here is the challenge American Zionism faces: to win the Jewish public to its banner, attract and organize their support for our struggle in Palestine, and, most important of all, work for the right of the survivors of the Holocaust to enter Palestine. Greenberg sees good prospects for success in circles that in the past have opposed Zionism or have been apathetic to every public Jewish initiative. The tragedy in Europe has shocked many Jews who previously took no interest in Jewish affairs. Our struggle in Palestine has drawn left-wing Jewish groups, who until now identified us with British imperialism, closer to us. Sympathy for Zionism has also increased in non-Jewish circles, including those on the left, and there are influential people among them who may be of assistance to our cause here and abroad.

Greenberg went on to express his concern over our efforts in Washington. The Middle East policy of Roosevelt is a legacy that hardly seems promising, either for our immediate needs or for the longer-term objectives. So far the new president, Truman, has apparently not taken a position on a number of issues in American foreign policy, but there is reason to fear that since he has had few dealings with foreign policy he will turn for guidance to the State Department, which has never been friendly to Zionism. President Truman has not yet completed his appointments to his own staff of assistants and political advisers, but it can be assumed that he will replace Roosevelt's men with his own. They too may not be friends of ours.

Greenberg therefore thinks we have to be alert to and watchful of the changing situation in Washington, especially in the White House and the State Department. The American Zionist Emergency Council is doing a good job with Congress—its work is ongoing and important. Similar arrangements will have to be made with regard to the new resident in the White House. He wound up by saying that we have to remember we are not working in a vacuum; our efforts will be more than matched by the activities of the pro-Arab forces, who command large financial resources and powerful contacts within the administration, especially in the State Department and in military circles.

I spent the evening with the Shulman family. Herman Shulman spoke of the meeting called by the American delegation, which he had attended as a representative of the American Jewish Conference in order to hear questions and opinions from delegation advisers representing various American institutions and organizations. Every imaginable subject was touched on in a single session attended by the multitude of public bodies represented. As advisers to the United States delegation, the American Jewish Conference has a semiofficial status and enjoys the privilege of contact with other delegations to the United Nations conference. Shulman considers this kind of opportunity far more important for us than attendance at the advisers' gatherings, where talk, not action, dominates the scene.

Friday, May 18 (Shavuot)

We received the reply of the conference's secretary-general to Goldmann's letter of May 15. In his letter, Hiss defends the distribution of the Pact of the League of Arab States as an official conference document by saying that the pact is an official treaty among the seven signatory states. Its distribution to conference delegations was officially decided upon "inasmuch as it constitutes a background reference document relevant to the agenda of the conference." He then goes on to say that with regard to the question of giving document status to the Jewish Agency's letter, the Steering Committee has directed that distribution of this kind of material be made "only in instances in which, at the discretion of the general secretary, the material is relevant to the subject matter of the conference deliberations." The purpose of the conference is to draft a charter for an international organization. This being the case, Hiss concludes his letter, he does not feel in a position, "under the various circumstances referred to," to distribute the Jewish Agency's letter "at this time."

Naturally Hiss's reply disappointed and angered us. The Arab League pact is allowed to circulate as "background material," while our letter reflecting on the Annex Regarding Palestine in the pact is rejected; this despite the fact that on the subject of the Palestine Mandate the Jewish Agency has official standing, while the Arabs do not.

I met with Fadhil al-Jamali and Nasrat al-Farsy at lunch. The latter is a former Iraqi minister of foreign affairs as well as a member of his country's conference delegation. Al-Farsy is a brother-in-law of my close friend Daoud Pasha al-Haidari, a minister in several Iraqi governments, and formerly the ambassador to Teheran; during the last war he served as the Iraqi ambassador to the Court of St. James's. Al-Haidari's father was the last Sheikh al-Islam in the days of the Ottoman Empire, before Kemal Atatürk abolished that post.

Both al-Haidari and al-Farsy are Kurds and have close ties with the Jewish community of Baghdad. In difficult times Jews used to appeal for their help and were never disappointed. My wife and I visited al-Haidari when he was the ambassador in Teheran, and we were the guests of honor at a meal to which prominent Iraqi Jews who had settled in Iran were invited. In his after-dinner speech al-Haidari praised our work in Palestine and criticized his wealthy Jewish guests who did not contribute toward the upbuilding of the Jewish national home in Palestine!

From hints dropped by al-Jamali I could see how jealous the Iraqis are of the Saudis' having received a great deal of press and radio publicity, especially Crown Prince Feisal, the chairman of the Saudi Arabian delegation. When I asked al-Jamali why he does not put on a picturesque kaffiyeh to attract journalists and photographers, like the Saudis, he smiled and said that there are more important things than dress that may have helped the Saudis gain publicity. He did not say so outright, but he obviously meant the assistance rendered to the Saudis by American oil companies. In addition, al-Jamali, who is a Shi'ite, probably feels little sympathy with the Wahhabi kingdom of Abdul-Aziz ibn-Saud.

Al-Farsy said he wonders how ibn-Saud will use the vast American oil royalties he is receiving and whether he will seek the help of Arab or American experts in developing his country. He doubts, however, that the bedouins will ever master proper and effective farming or industry. The bedouins in Arabia are so deeply rooted in the nomadic life and in the traditions of the desert that a complete revolution in their way of life and cultural pattern is inconceivable, in al-Farsy's opinion.

Al-Jamali, who himself comes from bedouin stock in southern Iraq, disagrees sharply with al-Farsy's view. He asserts that most desert inhabitants have greater natural abilities than city dwellers, or fellaheen. If there are suitable conditions for the bedouin to be educated and to learn a skill or trade, then their latent talents will find an outlet. Iraq's own experience has shown this convincingly, and in al-Jamali's opinion there is no reason why, in time, bedouin life should not develop along similar lines in Saudi Arabia—on condition, of course, that the fanatical Wahhabi rule does not obstruct the process of change and progress.

---

125 *San Francisco   April 30–May 25*

I had a long talk with Gabriel Gonzalez-Videla,[62] the Chilean senator and conference delegate, a man of wide knowledge in world problems with progressive social and political views. He expressed at once his admiration for and support of Zionism. During our conversation he severely criticized British policy in Palestine, warning against the illusion that we can change the white paper by parliamentary methods and by negotiations with the British. He commented that the British have never given up any of their imperial possessions except after military defeat. Whitehall, in his opinion, considers the Muslim world more important for Britain than the Jews, especially because of the Muslims in India. The current situation in India strengthens the British need to exploit the Muslim factor in the fight against Indian nationalism; it is the powerful traditional weapon of "divide and rule." He thinks that we should do all we can to reach a settlement with the Arabs and not rely on British largesse. Even if it is possible to get more out of the British than we have managed so far, we will increase thereby our dependence on London and widen the gap between ourselves and our Arab neighbors. In the long run this will be foolish; we will still have Arabs on every side of us and will need an accommodation with them.

Gonzalez-Videla expressed his support for the Biltmore Program, but doubts if we can succeed in translating it into reality under present conditions. He agreed that at San Francisco we have to see that our rights under the Palestine Mandate are not injured and promised the full support of his delegation to this end.

[62]Gabriel Gonzalez-Videla (1898–   ); president of Chile (1946–52); formerly Chilean minister in France and ambassador in Brazil; has written books on political subjects.

Saturday, May 19 (Shavuot)

I met with Feridun Cemal Erkin, first assistant secretary-general of the Turkish Ministry for Foreign Affairs, a conference delegate. I first got to know him in Ankara, during the war, as a rather unfriendly kind of person. Every time I asked for his help for Jewish refugees from Nazi-occupied Europe on their way to Palestine, he let me down on some pretext or other. Erkin is one of the confidants of Nauman Menemencioglu, the powerful secretary-general of the Turkish Ministry for Foreign Affairs, and has responsibility for Middle East affairs. In his official position in the ministry he will undoubtedly exercise considerable influence on Turkey's stance on the Palestine question. I learned from Yalçin that he has a good chance of being appointed ambassador to Washington, replacing the aged Huseyin Ragip Baydur. The pro-Arab Erkin in Washington will certainly do us no good.

At the outset I explained to Erkin the legal status of the Jewish Agency as defined in the Mandate and our national rights embodied in it. He knew that our memorandums, and "many other Jewish memorandums," have been received by his delegation, but he has not yet studied them. I asked him if he does not think the establishment of the Arab League may pose certain problems for Turkey: it could, for example, raise stronger irredentist hopes among the Arab public, leading perhaps to a demand for the return of Hatay (Alexandretta) to Syria. He replied that the Hatay matter is closed and that neither the Arab League nor Syria have any right whatever to reopen it.

He would not be drawn into further discussion of the Arab League, however, and began to question me about the Palestine situation and our plans for a possible solution. I told him about the Biltmore Program. He answered that the Arabs will never accept it, nor will Britain, who helped set up the Arab League—especially after being successful in organizing a wider grouping of Arab states than it was able to after World War I. He added that Turkey's policy on Palestine has been one of neutrality and that their policy will be guided, as in the past, by Turkey's own interests and its international obligations to contribute to the preservation of peace and stability in the world.

I later met a well-known Turkish journalist who is acting in an advisory capacity to his country's delegation and apparently is a member of the inner circle within the delegation that decides tactics at the conference. In World War I he was a staff officer in Jamal Pasha's military headquarters in Syria and Palestine and spent some time in Jerusalem. When I first met him in Ankara I was struck by his undisguised hostility toward Arabs and by the fact that he still recalled their treachery toward Turkey during the 1914–18 war. Every time the Arabs were mentioned in today's conversation he warned us not to depend on any agreement made with them —even one "signed by all the kings, the emirs, and the pashas in the Arab world." According to him, since the dawn of history Arab tribes have fought among themselves and then broken every treaty they ever put their signatures to, because every peace settlement in their eyes is no more than a truce. This attitude of mind, he said, is as true now as it ever was, and time has changed nothing of substance in the mentality of their leaders.

He impressed me by his penetrating understanding of our needs and problems. I told him about my talks with members of his delegation, emphasizing the importance of Turkey's stand, as the most influential and advanced country in our part of the world, on the short- and long-term aspects of the Palestine problem. I went on to refer to both the immediate need for us to guard and preserve the integrity of the Palestine Mandate until a permanent solution of the problem materializes, and the need to gain support for Jewish statehood in Palestine along the lines of the Biltmore Program. He replied that to his knowledge, his government has not yet adopted a clear political line on the matter and will be in no hurry to do so until the Great Powers—particularly Great Britain and the United States—show their hand. It will be very hard for Turkey to quarrel with the British if they stand their ground firmly on the Palestine issue and ask for Turkey's support. According to my friend, Turkey attaches much more importance to the British factor in the matter than to the Arab one.

He doubts whether we stand much chance of changing the pro-Arab policy of the British government, because Anthony Eden regards the setting up of the Arab League as one of his greatest personal achievements and frequently praises its role in contributing an important share to the strengthening of Pax Britannica in the Middle East. The French have no influence on British policy in the Middle East; the Americans will look after their own interests—mainly oil—and leave the British to take care of the Soviet threat, since at present Britain alone has the military bases to protect against that threat. Equally, the Americans will let the British make such internal arrangements in the Middle East as they see fit for the preservation of peace and stability in the area.

I lunched with Emanuel Abraham Tamrat, a Falasha holding the post of director general of the Ministry of Education in Addis Ababa, who is a member of the Ethiopian delegation to the conference. He is a friend of Dr. Jacob Feitlovitch's and has been one of his pupils and active supporters in raising the educational standards of the Falashas in Ethiopia.

He told me about Emperor Haile Selassie's sympathetic attitude toward Zionism and our work in Palestine, with which the emperor has been familiar since his exile in Jerusalem, and about his understanding for our national aspirations. Ethiopia too, he said, is an island in a Muslim sea. The emperor also knows about Orde Wingate's[63] dedicated support of Zionism and about the great service rendered to the Yishuv by this friend of our two peoples. Under the Italian occupation, Tamrat said, the Falashas did not suffer more than any other Ethiopians and were not discriminated against because of their Judaism. However, their material conditions have deteriorated with the falling off of the flow of donations they used to receive, mainly from the United States. Tamrat will be meeting Dr. Wise, whom he mentioned as one of the group of American friends of the Falashas, to ask for the renewal of assistance.

According to Tamrat, although the chairman of the Ethiopian conference delegation is the prime minister, not even he can decide any matter of importance without prior reference to the emperor. The delegation keeps close ties with that of the United States, the go-between being John Spencer, the American adviser to the Ethiopian minister for foreign affairs, who has come to San Francisco from Addis Ababa for

[63]Orde Charles Wingate (1903–44); ordered to Palestine (1936) as an intelligence officer to study the political and security situation; trained special night squads, composed of Jewish volunteers, to help the British army beat back Arab terrorists; strong partisan of the Zionist cause; ordered to leave Palestine (1939) because of his criticism of British pro-Arab policy; served in Ethiopia (1940–41) as head of guerrilla forces fighting for Ethiopian liberation; killed in a plane crash in the Far East; Wingate Institute (a center for physical culture) in Israel is named for him.

the purpose. The Ethiopian delegation's attitude to any question on the conference's agenda will be greatly influenced by that of the United States.

Reuven Zaslani and Gershon Agronsky returned to New York today. I am now the only Palestinian left in San Francisco "minding the store" and maintaining contact with the people Reuven and Agronsky were in touch with while they were here.

Sunday, May 20

Dr. Goldmann and I went to see Mostafa Adle, chairman of the Iranian delegation and a former minister of justice. Goldmann explained what we are asking of his delegation and then broadened the discussion to raise the matter of the Arab League's "decisions" on Palestine. Adle agreed that the Arab League's congress in Cairo had no legal right whatever to change the international status of Palestine. The Palestine Mandate and its future, he stated, are the responsibility of the United Nations as the legal heirs to the League of Nations, possessing the sole right to alter its terms.

When Goldmann attempted to bring the discussion to a more practical level and clarify the position Iran will adopt at the conference on the subject of mandates, Adle replied that he and his delegation have many reservations concerning the Arab League, its character, and its objectives. However, behind the league stands Great Britain, and Iran has to take this into account. His people are proud of the historic event of the Jewish people's return from Babylonian captivity to Zion by permission of their king, Cyrus, and know about our recent achievements in the country where we are trying to restore national life again. The tombs of Esther and Mordecai in Hamadan, he went on to say, are regarded as historic monuments and are protected by the state; he trusts, therefore, that we will understand that his delegation is favorably inclined toward the Jewish people and the Yishuv. However, in view of the political circumstances he described and the present tension along Iran's borders with the Soviet Union, his country will take a neutral stand on Palestine and avoid becoming involved in the controversies among all the parties concerned.

Before we parted, Adle asked that the fact of our having met with him "remain confidential": the same old "Unter den Linden" story by Heine!

I spent several hours with Alexander Ul, a correspondent of the New York newspaper *PM,* sympathetic to our cause. I supplied him with material on Arab collaboration with Nazis and Fascists both before and during the war. Ul said he will try to have it published in his paper.

He told me he has recently been investigating the extent, and economic and political significance, of the activity by the big American oil companies in the Middle East. In the course of his search he has discovered how strong the influence of companies with interests in that part of the world has been on United States policy in the Middle East. He stressed the point that it would be wrong to think that the only beneficiaries of the oil concessions in the area are the companies who hold them: the United States armed services and the Department of the Interior, which is responsible for energy matters in the country, are also keenly interested in the exploitation of Arab oil. The United States fleet in the Indian Ocean needs oil from sources as closely situated as possible, and the same is true of the American army of occupation in Europe. The Department of the Interior is eager to bring the home stock of oil (which was allowed to fall sharply during the war) up to a level sufficient for normal home consumption and for possible security emergencies.

The oil wells in the United States itself cannot produce enough for the purpose, but the Arab countries have reserves that are among the largest in the world and can help a great deal. According to confidential information that has come into his hands, Ul said, the estimated reserves of oil in the Persian Gulf (Iran, Iraq, Qatar, Kuwait, Saudi Arabia, and Bahrein) come to between two hundred and three hundred billion barrels, while those in the United States hardly reach fifty billion. Eighty percent of the oil reserves in the Middle East are found in Arab territory, especially in Saudi Arabia and Bahrein. Anyone, Ul said, can see how these figures are bound to affect the thinking and decisions of those responsible for the oil, as well as for the military and foreign affairs of the United States.

What he was driving at, he explained, is that the United States government itself has at least as much interest in the area as the oil companies; as a matter of fact, the federal government helped them obtain their concessions and is concerned that operations in the Arab countries proceed smoothly and without interference from any quarter, local or foreign.

Ul also told me that official representatives and agents of American oil companies have been doling out vast sums of money throughout the Persian Gulf—particularly in Saudi Arabia and Kuwait—to prevent non-American oil companies from securing new concessions in countries where the Americans have already established themselves. As far back as 1942 the American government became actively interested in expanding oil production in Saudi Arabia and in guaranteeing its easy availability for the Allied war effort, both in the Indian Ocean and in Europe (the latter through the laying of a pipeline from Saudi Arabia to the Mediterranean). Although nothing practical came of the original idea of government financial participation in the pipeline project, the oil companies were helped in different ways by the federal authorities to carry it out. An important step in that direction took place in January 1944, when an agreement was signed by the United States government and Aramco, which by then had formally secured the oil concessions in Saudi Arabia, providing that the government, while having no financial stake in the project, will build the pipeline, remain its owner, and be responsible for its maintenance.

The State Department has supported the arrangement from start to finish and has striven to assure for itself the right to fix the policy of the oil companies in the countries in which they operate. However, when the agreement was published there was an outcry throughout the United States, including the two houses of Congress. Leading the opposition to the agreement were those oil companies that do not participate in Aramco. In addition, the British government objected to the agreement, for the American companies had obtained "unfair advantages," in their view, over British concerns—and this despite the fact that the proposed pipeline will end at Alexandria or at Haifa, ports that are both within the British sphere of influence. The United States Senate set up a committee to inquire into the matter, headed by Senator Joseph O'Mahoney from Wyoming; the committee has not yet reported, but all the signs are that the Congress will reject financial participation of the federal government in the pipeline project, and it will be for the oil companies themselves to decide whether to lay the pipeline at their own expense.

Ul is going to publish the results of his research and draw

attention to the continued danger of American Middle East policy being dependent on the oil companies, a dependence that will certainly influence policy trends and methods and limit the freedom of action and maneuverability of the United States in the area.

To illustrate the dangers he foresees for the future of our work in Palestine posed by an American policy that is based on Arab oil, Ul mentioned President Roosevelt's much-publicized talk with King ibn-Saud and the political implication of what Roosevelt said later referring to that talk. The principal danger, Ul thinks, lies in the State Department and the army; in the Department of the Interior, however, the influence of the independent oil companies is growing stronger, and Aramco's pressures are resisted by the increasing opposition of local producers of oil. They oppose building the oil pipeline in the Middle East and are active in congressional circles, trying to limit Aramco's say in American government policy on oil matters generally. Secretary of the Interior Harold Ickes has recently moved much closer to the view of the "independents," but since it was Ickes who signed the agreement with Aramco on behalf of the government he cannot easily retreat from his previous position in the matter.

The hour I spent in Ul's company was a very useful and informative one.

I later told Goldmann the substance of my talk with Ul, and he mentioned his discussions on the subject with American government officials in Washington and with members of Congress. Dr. Abba Hillel Silver, said Goldman, is also active in the matter, warning his influential friends in government circles in Washington of the risk of Zionism's being sacrificed for the sake of the oil companies. Goldmann thinks the subject deserves our closest attention because of the oil companies' growing power and influence on political decisions of the American government.

When I went to the conference press bureau to collect its daily bulletin, I came across an Arab journalist from Lebanon whom I had known in Beirut from the time when I worked as a Reuter's correspondent in Lebanon and Syria and as a correspondent for the newspapers *Davar* and *Palestine Post.* A reporter for the Beirut newspaper *L'Orient,* he told me about the growing tension between the Syrian and Lebanese governments. The Maronite members of the Lebanese government want a reasonable settlement and an improvement in their relations with France, which for generations has protected the Maronite community against the excessive aspirations of their Muslim and Druze neighbors. The Syrians, on the other hand, are strongly opposed to any understanding with France. The chairman of their conference delegation is Faris al-Khouri, a Protestant born of a Greek Orthodox family, and this latter community has often bred more extreme Arab nationalists than their Muslim neighbors. It is easy to recognize in his description the fundamental differences in political outlook represented by the reaction of the two delegations to current events in their home countries.

My journalist friend also told me that the Lebanese minister in Washington, Charles Malik, is receptive to British and American influence, but that his rather weak personal character cannot stand up to the pressure of Abdallah Yafi, the former prime minister and Muslim member of the Lebanese delegation, who renders his wholehearted support to the Syrian nationalists' demands. The influence of the French on the Lebanese delegation's decisions is nil in these circumstances.

The Maronite Church, he mentioned, is deeply concerned about Lebanon's having joined the Arab League and looks upon Zionism and the Jewish national home in Palestine as their natural ally against Muslim expansionist designs in the area.

Not surprisingly, the *L'Orient* reporter is himself a Maronite and is close to the Maronite patriarch, Antoine Arida, and his court. When I accompanied Dr. Weizmann to his meeting with the patriarch in Paris in 1937, this reporter was a member of the patriarch's entourage and was aware of our meeting. On that occasion the patriarch voiced his support (though in carefully chosen words) for the establishment of a Jewish state in Palestine and expressed the hope that it would have a common frontier with Lebanon. Bishop Abdallah Khouri, who was serving as the patriarch's "foreign minister" on this visit to Europe, insisted that nothing be published regarding what the patriarch said to Dr. Weizmann, or even the fact of their having met. After the bitter attack on the patriarch by the press because of his pro-Zionist speech at a reception given in his honor by the Jewish community of Beirut, the bishop was afraid of further attacks if the patriarch's meeting with Dr. Weizmann were made public. My friend and I exchanged memories of that occasion and expressed our hope for future cooperation between our two communities.

I had dinner this evening with Russell Porter, the *New York Times* reporter covering the Trusteeship Committee's proceedings. He thinks that the discussions on the future of the trusteeship system may reach a crisis in the coming week because of differences among the Great Powers on a number of important points and the growing ferment among small states, most of whom consider that the time for mandates has passed and think the whole system should be brought to an end. The Arab delegations at the conference, he told me, are debating whether to seek recognition of the Arab League as a regional organization similar to the Pan American Union, founded in 1890, and to cooperate with the union in defining the function of the "regional arrangements" included in the Dumbarton Oaks proposals.

Porter also told me that the Egyptian delegation is directing the activities of the Arab states in the deliberations of the Trusteeship Committee. Other members of the committee regard the close coordination of policy and tactics among Arab delegates as proof that the Arab League is an accomplished fact in world affairs and that this bloc of five members in the United Nations is a factor to be reckoned with.

Britain, in Porter's view, is doing all it can to influence the part played by Arab states on the committee, and indeed at the conference in general. But he is sure that this cannot continue much longer and that the league will sooner or later become a liability to Britain, both in the Middle East and on the international scene. Some Arab delegates have already been saying things to him that assure him his judgment is correct. I explained our general view on the future of the mandates system and stressed the Arabs' aim at the conference: to undermine our rights as embodied in the Palestine Mandate. He promised to use some of my arguments in one of his articles on the subject.

Monday, May 21

At this morning's regular meeting of the Jewish organizations, Goldmann, Monsky, and Shulman reported on their contacts with conference delegates about the support for our claims as listed in the memorandums of the Jewish Agency and the American Jewish Conference. Robinson analyzed the "Working Paper for a Chapter of the Charter on Dependent Territories and Arrangements for International Trusteeship" and stressed the vital importance to us of paragraph 5, contained under Section B in the paper, which reads:

Except as may be agreed upon in individual trusteeship arrangements placing each territory under the trusteeship system, nothing in this chapter shall be construed in and of itself to alter in any manner the rights of any state, or any peoples in any territory.

Although the "Working Paper" was circulated in behalf of all five Great Powers, including the Soviet Union, the wording of paragraph 5, initiated and insisted upon by Britain with the support of the United States, serves to ensure that there will be no arbitrary change in the position of existing mandates without the consent of the Mandatory Power. The reference to the rights of peoples and not to a *single* people in the territory under a mandate of the League of Nations is meant to protect the rights of the Jewish people in Palestine, as defined by the terms of the Palestine Mandate. According to reliable information, the Egyptian delegate on the Trusteeship Committee has already launched a bitter attack against this clause to our disadvantage; although he does not refer explicitly to the Palestine Mandate, this is his clear intention. He has proposed that paragraph 5 speak of "the people of any territory" instead of the plural form, "peoples," so as to make certain that only the rights of current inhabitants of the territories will be protected; the rights of the Jewish people in Palestine recognized by the Balfour Declaration and incorporated in the Mandate would thus be eliminated altogether.

All the signs are that the Arab objective at the conference will also be to secure a decision that will make the transition from mandate to trusteeship automatic and not subject to any further agreements. If accepted, that will pave the way for the cancellation of the special character of the Palestine Mandate and will put the future of the Yishuv at the mercy of the Arab majority in the country.

The Egyptian effort has so far failed to achieve results, for the amendment was rejected by the committee. However, as long as deliberations in the committee continue we have to expect repeated Arab attempts to delete from paragraph 5 anything that will assure the continuing integrity of the Palestine Mandate ensuring the rights of the Jewish people.

Assessments made after Robinson's survey show, on the whole, that the Arabs have no chance of success in their efforts; there is no risk of the Trusteeship Committee's going against the wishes of the United States, Great Britain, and Australia on the basic questions of the status of mandates and the method of transferring them to the trusteeship of the United Nations.

Herman Shulman reported that Harold Stassen has told him that Arab intentions are perfectly clear to him and says he will scotch any proposal that would endanger our interests. Fraser, he said, has been carefully watching the work of the committee, and there is complete understanding between them on what is at stake as far as the Palestine Mandate is concerned. Shulman explained that in opposing Arab amendments to paragraph 5, Stassen is also thinking of America's own problems in the Pacific and wants his government released from any restrictions on its freedom of action with respect to territories in that area of strategic importance to America. Despite these optimistic forecasts, the importance of continuing our work among delegates and journalists was underlined by all the speakers.

I received a letter from Mahmoud Fawzi,[64] a counselor at the Egyptian legation in Washington, saying that there is no chance of his coming to San Francisco and suggesting that we meet in New York or Washington.

When Fawzi was Egypt's consul general in Jerusalem (1941–44), he and I and our two families became friends. He is an intelligent and cultured person who knew how to gain influence among both Jews and Arabs in Jerusalem, and he became one of the most popular members of the consular corps in the country. In our many talks Fawzi often sharply criticized the policies of Haj Amin el-Husseini, the former mufti of Jerusalem, and his followers, who, in his opinion, did more harm to the Arab cause than to anyone else. During his term of office in Jerusalem he contributed to closer cultural and economic relations between his country and the Yishuv, initiating a number of mutually beneficial activities in these fields. After serving in Jerusalem, Fawzi was transferred to the ministry of foreign affairs in Cairo and, a few months before the conference in San Francisco, was appointed counselor in the Egyptian legation in Washington. When I arrived in the United States I got in touch with him, and we arranged to meet in San Francisco. Fawzi suggested that he introduce me to some of his colleagues on the Egyptian delegation to the conference, including the chairman of the delegation, Abdel Hamid Pasha Badawi, and to Mahmoud Pasha Hassan, the Egyptian minister in Washington. I therefore had made no efforts to meet the Egyptians, preferring to wait until Fawzi came, and also had not asked my

[64]Mahmoud Fawzi (1900–   ); born in Cairo and studied law in Rome and the U.S.; filled important diplomatic posts and was Egypt's permanent representative at the United Nations (1947); minister for foreign affairs (1966); deputy prime minister and political adviser to President Gamal Abdel Nasser; prime minister (1970) and vice-president (1972).

friend Senator Mahmoud Abul Fath to arrange a meeting for me with some of his colleagues. I shall now have to initiate something on my own regarding the Egyptians, who are playing an active and leading role among the Arab delegations.

I talked with Faris al-Khouri, the Syrian prime minister, who is chairman of his country's delegation to the conference. I first met him when I was the Reuter's correspondent in Syria and Lebanon and have kept in touch with him on my frequent visits to Damascus on Jewish Agency business —especially when, in 1936–37, we conducted a dialogue with the Syrian National Bloc on an Arab-Jewish understanding leading to a peaceful settlement of the Palestine problem. Faris and his brother Faiz al-Khouri were among the leaders of the National Bloc, and Faris, particularly, had considerable personal say in and influence on the policy and tactics of the bloc in its struggle for Syrian independence. Faiz, the younger of the two, was rather more understanding of our objectives; Faris's hostility to Zionism, on the other hand, sometimes went further than that of the most extreme Muslims in the bloc's leadership.

It was Dr. Farid Zeineddine who arranged my meeting with Faris al-Khouri. I did not expect it to be very productive, but I wanted to hear the views of the leader of the Syrian delegation on certain general questions and especially on those that are causing us concern.

He received me in his suite at the Mark Hopkins Hotel, and before I even finished the customary cup of coffee he declared in a rather pompous way that the establishment of the Arab League has in effect annulled the Balfour Declaration, together with the special privileges the Mandate accorded to Jews in Palestine. Henceforth only the Jews who now live in Palestine will enjoy the rights, and they will have to fulfill the same obligations as other inhabitants of Palestine, Muslim or Christian, and shall be equal in all respects to their coreligionists who live in other Arab countries. He denied that the British inspired the establishment of the Arab League: it was, he said, the result of natural and historic developments in the Arab world. He stressed, however, how significant it is, from the Arab point of view, that Britain has not objected to an Arab representative from Palestine taking part in the Arab League's work, as agreed upon by the Arab states at their congress in Cairo. He said that it hardly looks as if London will support any plan to partition Palestine or to create a Jewish state, as suggested by the Peel Royal Commission. Zionists will be well advised, he said, to hasten to normalize their relations with their Arab neighbors in Palestine; the Arab League, of course, will be prepared to help to this end. He knows, he said, that we will certainly try to engage for our cause the support of the influential American Jewish community, but the Arabs, too, now have considerable influence on U.S. policy in the Middle East, and we ought to reflect on this before attempting to weaken the prestige of the Arab League by challenging its right as the spokesman for the Arabs in Palestine. He added that we had better put aside for our own good any idea of cooperation with France against the Arab League in an effort to compel Syria and Lebanon to recognize a special position for France in their countries. It is now apparent that no major power in the world will back up the French claim in that respect, and he added that the French seem to have forgotten that Syria and Lebanon are independent states, free to act as they please.

Al-Khouri invited me to attend the press conference that he (on behalf of the Syrian delegation) and his Lebanese colleagues are holding tomorrow to explain their governments' policies regarding the problems of the Levant.

We met for about half an hour. I tried to explain our attitude to a possible understanding between our two peoples based on the Biltmore Program, but al-Khouri grew increasingly restive and would hardly let me talk. I deliberately refrained from raising the subject of the Trusteeship Committee's deliberations on the mandates issue, and he too said nothing about the matter.

I spent the evening in the company of Spanish Republican refugees who are lobbying among the friendly delegations to prevent the entry of Francisco Franco, the Spanish dictator, into the United Nations. Most of the group have come to San Francisco from Mexico, where they found a hospitable refuge after fleeing Spain. The majority of them are pessimistic as to the chances of restoring the Spanish Republican regime. Not a single one trusts the Soviet Union to help them. In the course of the civil war, most of them alleged, Stalin fought his own war with the Republicans, who, although sympathetic to the Soviet Union, were not prepared to accept orders from Moscow with which they disagreed. The Spaniards, they feel, have suffered like the Jewish people from betrayal by democratic countries claiming to defend freedom and human rights. The indifference of those countries before and during World War II has cost the lives of millions of innocent Spaniards and Jews. The foreign policies of the Great Powers —including Soviet Russia—will continue to be conducted in their own selfish interests and not according to the solemn declarations made by their leaders in wartime, which were intended mainly for propaganda purposes of the moment. We sat drinking dry California wine; the gloomy mood of my Spanish companions increased during the course of the evening—they despair about the future of humanity and the United Nations itself. We are apparently not the only people in San Francisco who have come with the expectation of finding understanding for their claims and looking for just solutions. Will we, at the end of our struggle here, have become as gloomy in our mood as the Spaniards with whom I spent the evening?

Tuesday, May 22

We were not aware of the fact that in the official document containing the Pact of the League of Arab States, distributed by the secretariat among the conference delegations, the Annex Regarding Palestine in Appendix B to the pact was omitted. We have found out that the Egyptian delegation, which asked Hiss to deal with the matter, presented him with a copy of the pact from which the annexes have been deleted. It is clearly a deliberate act on the part of the Arabs, who hope thereby to mislead the conference when the mandates issue is dealt with by the Trusteeship Committee, while avoiding the accusation of tampering with the present international status of Palestine prior to any UN decision on the matter. When he learned what happened, Robinson started at once to prepare another letter to be sent from Goldmann to Hiss; we shall issue it for publication and send it to the delegations at the earliest possible date.

Judge Proskauer and I had breakfast together. He told me about the conversations he has had with members of the British delegation. Proskauer said the British were impressed by his reference to the fact that American public opinion is united in its opposition to the white paper of 1939 and the limitations on Jewish immigration to Palestine. A British delegate asked him why the United States does not open its own doors to the survivors of the Holocaust, at least to those in camps in the American-occupied zone in liberated Europe.

Proskauer replied that he is concerned about that as well; but whether the United States government can do that or not, the British authorities—because of the international obligations they assumed in the Palestine Mandate—have the responsibility of facilitating the entry of Jews into Palestine. Proskauer (in his lawyer capacity) then explained to the delegate the contradiction between the policy of the white paper and the obligations of the Mandatory Power toward the Jewish national home, especially concerning immigration and agricultural settlement.

I thanked Proskauer for his valuable help and promised to let our people in Jerusalem and London know the substance of what he told me. I reported on our conversation to Goldmann, who has done much to bring about the current good relations with Proskauer.

At our morning meeting we heard a report on further concentrated Arab attacks at the Trusteeship Committee's deliberations on a number of provisions included in the "Working Paper for a Chapter of the Charter on Dependent Territories and Arrangements for International Trusteeship," now before the committee, which have a direct bearing on the Palestine Mandate. In the latest deliberations in the committee the Egyptian delegate, again leading the attack on clauses vital to the preservation of the special character of the Palestine Mandate, proposed to make a deletion from Section B, paragraph 1 of the "Working Paper," which provides that the trusteeship system to be established by the United Nations should set up suitable machinery for the administration and supervision of "such territories as may be placed thereunder by subsequent individual agreements." The last three words in the paragraph, "subsequent individual agreements," were Egypt's target. The amendment was defeated. If accepted, it would have made the transition from mandate to trusteeship system automatic and not subject to any further agreement. The British and American delegates, supported by the delegates of a number of other states, argued that since the existing mandates are a result of *individual agreements* under the mandates system, they can be placed under the new trusteeship system only by the same type of agreements. A similar attempt made in the committee by the Iraqi delegate to achieve the same purpose was also rejected.

Defeated on an essential point of fundamental importance, the Arabs then turned their attention to other clauses in the "Working Paper." This time it was again paragraph 5—now the clause in which Jewish rights in the Palestine Mandate are qualified as those of a people and not just as those of inhabitants of the country. As on the previous occasion it was the Egyptian delegate who opened the attack on the wording of paragraph 5, by proposing again that the plural form "peoples" in the paragraph be replaced by "people of any territory." In support of his amendment the Egyptian delegate argued that only the rights of the inhabitants of a mandatory territory should be protected as a "democratic matter of substance," especially since the wording of paragraph 5 does not indicate the peoples whose rights it intends to protect.

Harold Stassen, supported by a number of other delegates on the committee, opposed Egypt's amendment on the ground that if accepted it would "freeze existing situations in mandatory territories and prevent their further progress." Stassen added that paragraph 5 is intended to serve as a "safeguarding clause" not only for the protection of "any peoples in any territory," but also that "nothing in the Trusteeship Chapter should be construed in and of itself to alter in any manner . . . the terms of the Mandate," as stated in the clause.

Feeling that their chances of carrying the committee with them in changing the language of paragraph 5 are hardly promising, the Iraqi delegate, supported by his Egyptian colleague, suggested postponing further discussion on the paragraph in order to give the Egyptian delegate an opportunity to discuss the matter further with Stassen, to "harmonize their points of view."

Our people who saw Stassen were impressed by his firm stand in preventing any damage to our interests and by his determination not to give in to any pressure to reach a compromise with the Arabs at our expense.

It is clear, however, that the Arabs will make further attempts to advance their objectives. We must remain alert and active as long as the deliberations in the Trusteeship Committee continue.

I attended the press conference called by the Syrian and Lebanese delegations. Not many journalists were present, so the Arabs themselves tended to stand out; I recognized quite a few delegates and press officers from Arab countries. Alongside Faris al-Khouri sat the Syrian finance minister, Naim al-Antaki, and the Syrian minister in Washington, Nazem al-Koudsi. Next to Wadih Naim, the Lebanese minister of the interior and of public education, the delegation chairman, were seated Charles Malik and Joseph Salem, who is the Lebanese minister in Egypt.

Al-Khouri opened the conference by criticizing France for her "illegal interference" in the affairs of Syria and Lebanon and by protesting the French use of colonial troops against demonstrators in Damascus and Aleppo.

Answering journalists' questions, al-Khouri said that Syria and Lebanon have received assurances from the United States government that it will not consent to any special status for France in their countries. The position of Great Britain in the matter is less clear. A French journalist asked why the Syrian government is not opposed to the military bases that the British are now constructing on their territory. Al-Khouri replied that the question "has no bearing on the subject under discussion." He added that French troops will only be allowed to remain in Syria as part of the Ninth Allied Army, not as a separate force independent of the Allied army stationed in the country.

In answer to another question, al-Khouri declared that Syria made "an important contribution" to the war effort of the democratic powers and is therefore entitled to share in the fruits of the victory over "the common Nazi enemy." At the close al-Khouri explained the significance of the Arab League as a new factor in international affairs. Any armed attack on one member will oblige the rest to come to its aid militarily; this was explicitly agreed on, al-Khouri emphasized, at the Cairo congress that founded the Arab League.

A Lebanese journalist of long acquaintance commented as we were leaving that I should note, of course, that the Lebanese delegates were passive throughout: al-Khouri had dealt with all the questions and the Lebanese "had not opened their mouths." He told me that before the press conference there had been a heated argument between the two delegations as to the form any criticism of the French by al-Khouri should take. Malik had taken the Syrian side and agreed to read out the joint announcement in the name of the two delegations so as to demonstrate their identical views.

At lunch, Henry Monsky told me about the great efforts the American Jewish Conference is putting into its work in San Francisco. The AJConference was founded in New York in August 1943, with the participation of 123 representatives of sixty-four Jewish organizations, as well as 379 delegates from local communities all over the United States, giving a total affiliated membership of two and a quarter million Jews. He and his colleagues in B'nai B'rith put a great deal of work into organizing the AJConference, and they have managed to bring under its wing Jewish bodies who in the past have either not cooperated with each other or have worked together haphazardly. It is, said Monsky proudly, one of the few instances in the history of American Jewry where elections of AJConference representatives have been taken by secret ballot, and this gives added weight and authority to the AJConference discussions and decisions.

Monsky regards the San Francisco conference as a historic event in the life of our people, since it has brought about the creation of a common front of Jewish communities in the free world for the defense of Jewish rights. This is bound to be especially important with regard to decisions to be reached and practical arrangements to be made by the new international organization of the United Nations, as they affect Jewish life in the Diaspora and the future of Palestine. He said that the American Jewish Conference initiated the invitation to San Francisco of representatives of Jewish organizations in Great Britain and Canada. He believes that the walkout of the American Jewish Committee from the American Jewish Conference was not attributable to matters of principle, but to the antidemocratic character of the AJCommittee, which would not give up the oligarchic tradition it has maintained since the days of Jacob Schiff and Louis Marshall. Monsky said that Proskauer found it difficult to breathe the popular atmosphere of the American Jewish Conference, which is so entirely foreign to that of the organization he heads.

Monsky asked if the Yishuv understands the importance of the American Jewish Conference to its struggle. To win support of American public opinion and the United States government, he said, it is not enough for American Zionists to rally behind us; we must have the whole Jewish community of America on our side. B'nai B'rith alone has more members than all the Zionist organizations put together. It is

B'nai B'rith and sixty-three other American Jewish organizations, rallied by the American Jewish Conference for common Jewish causes, that give Monsky the right, as chairman of the AJConference, to ask Secretary of State Edward Stettinius to be sure that every proposal the United States puts before the United Nations conference on the future of mandated territories assures the rights of the Jewish people in Palestine and the future of the Jewish national home, as laid down in the Balfour Declaration and incorporated in the Palestine Mandate. It has been made clear to the United States government that the overwhelming majority of Jewish organizations in the country, by supporting the Biltmore Program, have identified themselves with the struggle for a Jewish commonwealth in Palestine. In Monsky's view the intervention in our behalf by the American Jewish Conference will bring fruitful results, both at this juncture and in the future.

Monsky went on to say that because of its material strength, which has continued to grow rapidly despite the tremendous cost of the war—its direct cost and the vast assistance to U. S. allies—the United States is now not only militarily but also economically the most powerful country in the world. Undoubtedly, the views of the United States must carry great weight in political decisions in every part of the world. It is therefore most important that we direct our efforts toward acting in an organized and systematic way, in order to strengthen our position in this country, and toward using public opinion in all its expressions for the support of our needs and demands—with the intention of having the United States government determine its Middle East policy with us fully in mind. The American Jewish Conference can, in his opinion, play an important role to this end.

We agreed to continue our conversation in the near future.

Maurice Cohen arranged a meeting for me with Dr. Wellington Koo,[65] the Chinese ambassador in London and China's representative on the War Crimes Commission. In the Chinese delegation to the conference Koo is second only to the foreign minister, T.V. Soong. Koo's important position in the delegation comes from his long experience in international affairs, dating from when he was, for many years, his country's permanent representative to League of Nations.

I found Dr. Koo to be acquainted with the problems of Palestine. He recalled meetings in Geneva with Dr. Chaim Weizmann and expressed his condolences on the disaster that has befallen our people in Europe, saying that the Chinese people, too, know the pain of persecution and discrimination based on race or nationality. As an Asiatic people, the Chinese are interested in the solution of the continent's problems by peaceful means and in solutions that are just, so that further crises and upheavals in the future may be avoided.

When I mentioned the Annex Regarding Palestine in the Pact of the League of Arab States, Koo denied the right of any country or institution other than the United Nations to change in a unilateral or arbitrary way the special character of any mandate operated under the authority of the League of Nations. The main issue, in his view, is not that of the British Mandate in Palestine; the danger he foresees is to the future of the United Nations if it goes the way of its predecessor, the League of Nations, and does not put down at its very inception any attempt at lawlessness in international affairs. He went on to say that the new international organization has to be pragmatic and firm in what it does and must

[65]V. K. Wellington Koo (1888–   ); Chinese minister of foreign affairs (1922–24); prime minister and minister for foreign affairs (1926–27); Chinese ambassador in Paris (1936–41), London (1941–46), and Washington (1946–56).

know how far it can go in imposing international discipline without clashing with the principle of national sovereignty. But the decisions of the United Nations taken at this conference have to be carried out in the right spirit and in accordance with the principles of its Charter. If not, the end of the organization will be no better than that of its predecessor; it has to be remembered that the League of Nations' shortcomings cleared the way for the disasters that have struck many peoples and countries.

I tried to turn the conversation more specifically to the Palestine question, but Koo would talk no further, presumably because of concern that his relations with the British government in his work as ambassador in London might be affected in some way if the substance of our talk were made public.

Si Kenen introduced me to correspondents from the New York Yiddish press who are covering the conference. I described for them the situation in Palestine and spoke on recent developments in the Arab world. Their questions were friendly, including those from Communist journalists. However, they know little about the subjects, apparently from the lack of a regular flow of news or normal communications between the United States and Palestine during the war and because of the strict censorship in Palestine.

Wednesday, May 23

In our second letter to the secretary-general of the United Nations Conference on International Organization, dispatched today, Goldmann charges that the Arab states have filed an "incomplete and misleading document" with the United Nations conference—an "unprecedented action in violation of all normal international procedures at an international assembly." The letter refers to the Pact of the League of Arab States, which was distributed by the secretariat as a conference document. It recalls that on May 15 the Jewish Agency protested against this distribution because the pact's Annex (1) in Appendix B seems to classify Palestine as an "Arab state" and even to designate "an Arab representative from Palestine to take part in its [the Arab League's] work." The letter goes on to say that it has now been disclosed that in filing the pact with the secretariat, the annexes, including the one on Palestine, were omitted:

The omission is serious, as it tends to give a false impression of the character and content of the pact. To our knowledge, indeed, the filing of such an incomplete and misleading document at an international assembly is unprecedented and is certainly in violation of all normal international procedures.

In view of the official distribution of the pact by the secretary-general of the conference on the ground that it constitutes a background reference document relevant to the agenda of the conference, it is obviously necessary that the delegates should not have before them a partial and misleading version. This is all the more pertinent in view of the fact that one of the annexes thus suppressed is in such clear conflict with the international status of Palestine and with the well-established international obligations contained in the Palestine Mandate.

In conclusion, Goldmann renewed his request to Hiss that the Jewish Agency's May 15 letter to him, together with this letter, be distributed as a conference document like the Pact of the League of Arab States.

We attached to the letter the annexes to the pact.

At our morning meeting Wise, Monsky, and Goldmann gave more information on the deliberations in the Trusteeship Committee. The Arab delegates are working in total coordination: the proposal of any Arab delegate is immediately supported by one or more of his Arab colleagues. Egypt's delegate is leading the game, and naturally it is he who introduces most of the amendments and decides the tactics. Despite the obvious fact that the Arabs' aim in the committee is related exclusively to one objective, the abolition of any reference to Jewish rights in Palestine in the new UN trusteeship system, the name "Palestine" is never mentioned by a single Arab delegate—or indeed by any other delegate on the committee!

Dr. Wise was told by Stassen that Fraser has decided to bring the discussion on points relating to Palestine to an end within the coming few days, and all the signs are that paragraph 5 will be confirmed without substantial change. The Trusteeship Committee's decisions on the trusteeship system, which will form a chapter of the United Nations Charter, will go to Commission II of the General Assembly for confirmation and from there to the plenary session of the conference for final approval. Wise and Goldmann have been advised that there is no reason to think that the plenary session will make any basic changes in the committee's decisions confirmed by Commission II, since both the Trusteeship Committee and Commission II reflect the balance of forces in the General Assembly of the conference. The president of Commission II is Field Marshal Smuts, on whose support we can count fully.

Wise, who knows Stassen well, told me about his military and public career. He is a young man who reached the rank of commander in the U.S. Navy during the war and returned only a short time ago from the Pacific. He entered political life with enormous energy, and great things are expected of him in the public life of the United States. His attitude to

Jewish problems has been very warm, and he has already shown his friendship in many concrete ways at the Trusteeship Committee meetings.

Later, during lunch, Shulman told me that our position on the Trusteeship Committee would have been much more difficult if instead of Stassen the United States delegate had been Senator Tom Connally or Congressman Sol Bloom or Virginia Gildersleeve. Personal contact with any of them would have been a great deal harder than it is with Harold Stassen, who is ready to see our people and listen to their suggestions at any time.

Victor Riesel, a *New York Post* writer on labor questions, interviewed me about the Histadrut's activities and its contribution to the raising of the living standard of Arab workers in Palestine. I learned from him about the structural organization of American trade unions and the way they operate. Riesel described the important role the trade unions play in American public life and the influence some of their leaders have on White House decisions in many fields, including foreign policy. He mentioned that in both the AFL and CIO Jews hold many leading positions; together, these two rival organizations represent the large majority of American workers. As long as we need American help, Riesel thinks we will do well to broaden and tighten our ties with trade union leaders. Far better, too, if we do not rely on only one of the two movements—the AFL or CIO—but try to establish close relations with both of them and use the help of either, depending on the needs of the time and the problems before us.

I have sent a note on this conversation to Israel Mereminsky, who is still in New York.

I had a long talk with Foy Kohler about the Arab League. He mentioned that the Soviet press published an article a few days ago entitled "British Toy," sharply attacking the league. It should be remembered, he said, that Russian policy, which supported the pan-Slavic movement in the Balkans and helped to advance its objectives in that part of Europe, was opposed in czarist days as it is now to the pan-Islamic and pan-Turanian movements. The Russians regard them as a threat to the integrity of the Russian empire and consider the ideological concepts of the two movements to be undermining the loyalty of Muslim and Turkish-speaking citizens living under Russian rule. It is not surprising, therefore, that the Russians see the Arab League as a British move mainly directed at themselves—part of the age-old struggle between the two powers for hegemony in Asia, based at present on a pan-Arab nationalism that represents a more advanced concept of unity than the old religious pan-Islamic or racial pan-Turanian movements.

I asked Kohler what the American attitude is toward the Arab League. He replied that he personally sees no harm in it. At the Dumbarton Oaks talks the United States delegation supported the idea of regional groupings of states, as the United States itself is a member of the Pan American Union; there is therefore no objection to the Arab states setting up a similar body of their own in the Middle East. From the political angle, he thinks it is too early for his government to take an official stand on the matter: the league has still to prove itself a positive, constructive factor in the development of the Middle East. The fact that the British helped set it up does not mean it has no value. Their desire to draw the Arabs closer together may contribute to the peace and stability of the entire area. Kohler added that it is a good thing that, instead of their traditional policy of "divide and rule," the British are now taking a more positive approach to the regional problems of the Middle East, an effort he thinks deserves support and encouragement. The independence of Syria and Lebanon opens up new opportunities for the British in the Middle East, which they did not enjoy after World War I because of the Sykes-Picot agreement on the division of zones of influence between Britain and France. This put many obstacles in the way of a single unified policy by either of the two governments and contributed, because of British-French rivalry, to many troubles in the area.

I asked Kohler if the Arab League, which is a British creation serving British interests, may not prove an obstacle to America's objectives in the region. He replied that United States interests in the Middle East are principally economic and cultural. As for the oil to be found in Arab countries, British and American oil companies are trying to reach a mutual understanding and have already made important progress toward this end. In Saudi Arabia only American companies will hold concessions; in Kuwait a formula has been reached that is acceptable to both British and American companies on the question of oil exploration in the territory under British protection. In Iraq an agreement among four Western oil companies has been working smoothly since before the war. Kohler sees no reason to fear serious disagreements among the international oil corporations themselves or a crisis in Anglo-American relations because of oil. The British military presence in the Middle East and its treaty obligations to the Arab states there for protection against aggression from outside oblige the United States, in Kohler's view, to act with great caution and not make things difficult for the British, who are carrying both political and military burdens for the stability and defense of the Middle East, an area of vital strategic importance for the Western powers.

In the course of our conversation I described to Kohler the

fragile nature of Arab unity under the British umbrella and mentioned the deep divisions in Arab society, which can hardly be wiped out by mere political arrangements. I sketched the historical background and the traditional relations in the Arab world of enmity and suspicion between Muslims and Christians, Sunnites and Shi'ites, Maronites and Druzes, Arabs and Kurds, Saudis and Hashemites, and between Egypt and the other Arab states. I suggested that the Arab League is bound to become in substance a Muslim bloc that will not only threaten the Jewish national home in Palestine, but will undermine the position of non-Muslims in the pluralistic Arab-speaking society. Arab nationalism should not be cast in the European mold. Arab nationalism is at bottom a predominantly Muslim-inspired and politically guided "nationalism." The Lebanese nationalism of the Maronites is a "Christian Arab nationalism," and the inhabitants of Jebel Druze have a "Druze nationalism," and so on. I concluded by saying that the Arab League under British guidance will be directed against factors interfering with British interests in exchange for a policy of appeasement at the expense of others in areas where British and Arab interests meet.

Of course it is hard to know what the future holds for the Arab world as a whole, I said, but there is the danger that, instead of contributing to the social and economic progress of its members, the Arab League will reinforce the tendencies toward aggressiveness and fanaticism in the Arab countries and will make understanding and cooperation more difficult, both within Arab societies with heterogeneous populations and between the different peoples of the area.

We had a long and an interesting talk and capped the evening by dining together at one of San Francisco's many Chinese restaurants.

Thursday, May 24

I have learned from American journalists of the intense effort being made by Arab delegations to have the Arab League officially recognized by the United Nations as a regional organization in the Middle East and to have incorporated in the United Nations Charter a clause giving such organizations the right to a permanent seat on the Security Council. Much of the Arab activity is directed at Latin American countries who (so I am told) support the idea. Actually, the campaign has only propaganda value, because the San Francisco conference has no power to decide the matter. No doubt the Arabs know this and wish to pave the way for a future attempt, meanwhile gaining some publicity for the league's existence and objectives.

Ray Brook told me that when Sumner Welles was deputy secretary of state he favored granting a permanent seat on the Security Council to regional organizations of states. Welles dealt with Latin American affairs in the State Department and believes that if the Organization of American States is accorded the right to a seat, the position of the United Nations will be considerably enhanced.

However, the efforts of the Arabs and the Latin Americans will probably encounter objections of a more than formal nature. The Soviet Union has no desire to see the United States gain further advantages at the United Nations, especially in the Security Council. Nor is it likely that the USSR will agree to a seat for the Arab League, which it sees as a British plaything. Even the British are likely to reflect carefully on whether it is in their interest for the Arab League to have a privileged position rather than remaining a pawn in their hands, dependent on their favors.

Yesterday the conference secretariat published a proposal by Arab delegations that there be included in the United Nations Charter the following definition of a grouping of regional states:

There shall be considered as regional arrangements organizations of a permanent nature grouping in a given geographical area several countries which, by reason of their proximity, community of interests, or cultural, linguistic, historical, or spiritual affinities, make themselves jointly responsible for the peaceful settlement of any disputes which may arise between them for the maintenance of peace and security in their region, as well as for the safeguarding of their interests and the development of economic and cultural relations [Document 553 II/4/A/9].

I came across no reaction to or assessment of this document in the morning papers.

At our morning meeting Wise, Goldmann, Shulman, and Monsky reported on their talks with members of the American and other delegations. Practically everybody they met said that there is no reason to fear the outcome of the Trusteeship Committee's discussion on clauses of importance to us, which are to be concluded in a day or two. Fraser and Joseph Bech, Luxembourg's minister for foreign affairs and the committee's rapporteur, are agreed on the need to pass on to other clauses in the "Working Paper" so that the committee may remain within the timetable allowed to it in the conference's schedule. There is, our people have been told, an increasingly tense atmosphere in the committee, and complaints have been made by a number of its members that the Arabs are going over their arguments again and again, despite the fact that they have failed to win the support of other members for their amendments.

I ate lunch with Harold Beeley, who confirmed that discussions on paragraph 5 will probably end very soon. Time is pressing, because the Trusteeship Committee and Commission II of the General Assembly still have to deal with other important clauses before finishing their work. In fact, Beeley said, it could have finished its discussions on paragraph 5 earlier, but when the committee rejected the Iraqi proposal to put off discussion of the subject without making a decision, Fraser, to appease the Arab members, allowed them to reiterate their arguments against paragraph 5. The Arabs talked on and on until a delegate of a small country, who was utterly sick of the repetitions and did not understand why the Arabs were doing what they did, asked the chairman what the point was of the committee's wasting so much time on "this word or that" instead of getting on with its work. Beeley thinks that many members shared the delegate's ignorance of why the paragraph under consideration has been causing so much trouble, particularly as the word "Palestine" has not been breathed by any of the Arab speakers—who instead claim that their arguments are based solely "on principle." Beeley said it was only after the British delegate explained privately to others on the committee the real reason for the Arab attack on the clause—a clause the British support—that many delegations realized what was going on. This applied especially to the Latin Americans, who were the main focus of the Arabs' attempt to win support. The Arabs had deliberately held up a decision on paragraph 5 so that they could continue their propaganda among the delegations outside the committee's deliberations and keep up their pressure on individual delegates on the committee.

Listening to Beeley, I could not help suspecting that the firm stand by the British delegation on paragraph 5 was probably not so much the result of a sudden pro-Zionist mood as the fear of opening a Pandora's box: once a precedent of change in the Palestine Mandate is created, who can prevent the Arabs or anybody else from demanding further changes in the Mandate, this time affecting direct British interests? Beeley explained that every decision of the Trusteeship Committee has to be approved by Commission II of the General Assembly before going to the plenary session for final confirmation. This, he added, is only a formality, and commission decisions are in practice final unless challenged at the plenary session.

When the conversation turned to general matters at the conference, Beeley mentioned that in the next few days Abdul-Illah, the regent of Iraq, and Nuri Pasha al-Said, the Iraqi prime minister, will arrive in San Francisco. Beeley did not conceal his sympathy for the Iraqi leaders, saying that they deserve credit for their courageous stand on the side of the democracies during the most difficult hour of the war in the Middle East.

I asked Beeley if he thinks that Arab delegates are less concerned with hitting at the Jewish national home than with outdoing one another in getting coverage in Arab newspapers in their own countries for their support of the Arabs of Palestine and with furthering their own political careers. He answered that although there is a certain rivalry in the Trusteeship Committee among Arab delegates, nonetheless the cooperation and coordination between them on important questions are much greater than their differences. The Palestine issue is an outstanding example of the understanding that now exists in the Arab camp. Beeley thinks we would be making a mistake if we regard this as merely an outcome of the Arab League's decisions at Cairo. What was agreed on at Cairo is the culmination of continuing developments in the Arab world, not the beginning of a new process. He went on to say that of course it would be easy for us to hold the British responsible for the changing picture in Arab states with the foundation of the Arab League, but said this would bring us no nearer to a true assessment of the situation or a just and lasting settlement with our neighbors. Even before the war the Palestine issue had become a general Arab question, not simply a conflict between us and the Arabs in Palestine.

Beeley then expressed a thought that seemed to me of special significance for gaining a better understanding of British policy in the Middle East and the entire Muslim world. In wartime, he said, Britain could put off attending to pressing problems in the British Empire and in countries where it has influence. Now Great Britain is, as a matter of fact, the dominating factor in the entire Middle East because France has lost the position it once enjoyed and the United States has no interests in the area of as vital importance as has Britain, outside of oil interests. The presence of a militarily and politically strong Britain is essential to the stability of the entire region and to its capacity to withstand Russian threats and probes, already evident in Turkey and Iran. In order to achieve that objective Britain has had to reach a firm understanding with the Arab states and put an end to any conflicts and disagreements that bar mutual cooperation. The difficult situation in India is an additional reason to avoid friction with the large Muslim community there, for without its cooperation it will be hard to find a lasting solution to the Indian problem.

Beeley thinks that it will be right and important for Britain and the United States to draw closer in their policies in the Middle East. It is easy to see that what he really means is that American policy in the region, and particularly regarding

Palestine, should follow the lines laid down by the Arab experts in the British Foreign Office. Incidentally, I could hear in Beeley's words an echo of what I detected in my conversations with Kohler and his colleagues, and the views they expressed on Britain's role in the Middle East were pretty close to those of Beeley.

I passed along the substance of my talk with Beeley to Goldmann and also to the Jewish Agency offices in London and Jerusalem.

In the last few days I have been collecting material on public bodies and organizations in the United States with ties and interests in the Middle East, to try to assess the opposition we have faced in the past and most probably will continue to face, openly and behind the scenes, both in our attempts to win American public opinion over to our side and in our contacts with official circles in Washington. So far I have been able to collect data on the following bodies:

(1) The Near East College Association, a leading cultural channel between the United States and the Middle East with headquarters in New York, is connected with eight educational institutions in Lebanon, Syria, Iraq, Turkey, Egypt, and Greece. These institutions were founded by American Presbyterians. By 1943 their total enrollment was more than five thousand students, the majority having Arabic as their mother tongue. The American University of Beirut is the largest and most important institution sponsored by the association. As for the contribution that the university has already made in raising the educational and professional standards of Arab countries in the area, the proof lies in the presence at the San Francisco conference of twenty-nine former students of the American University in senior posts in Arab delegations. Many Americans on the staff of the university served in the United States armed forces during the

war, as well as in the diplomatic missions and intelligence services operating in the Middle East. Some of them are now advisers on Middle Eastern affairs in different government departments in Washington, influential in the framing of United States policy in the region and in its implementation.

The association's public relations in America are looked after by Lowell Thomas, a writer and well-known radio commentator, who had much to do with the publication, after World War I, of the exploits of T. E. Lawrence in Arabia. The association and those connected with it have been conducting continuous propaganda activity on every Arab subject and have been helping to broaden the contacts with influential circles in Washington for Arab envoys.

(2) The Near East Foundation is another body rendering public and political assistance to the Arabs. It was established after World War I to assist social and economic development in the Middle East. Charles Crane, the founder of the organization, opposed the Balfour Declaration, and the hostility to Zionism of the commission of which he was a member (the King-Crane Commission) is history. For some years between the wars the foundation was represented in Palestine by George Antonius, a close adviser and confidant of Haj Amin el-Husseini's. Charles Crane was one of the first Americans to establish personal relations with King Abdul-Aziz ibn-Saud and the Imam Yahya of Yemen and to initiate a number of enterprises by Americans in Saudi Arabia.

(3) The Council for Near Eastern Affairs was set up in New York in 1942 for the purpose of studying the problems of the region. From its establishment it adopted a pro-Arab attitude on the Palestine question. Worth noting is the fact that one of its founders is a former member of the staff of the Zionist Organization of America, Hans Kohn, at present a professor at Smith College. The council distributes material supporting the Arab points of view on topical subjects and, when the Arab League was founded, published articles explaining its

importance as a regional organization advancing the cause of Arab nationalism.

(4) The Institute of Oriental Studies of the University of Chicago is directed by Professor John Wilson, who is perfectly open about his opposition to Zionism and does his utmost to strengthen Arab influence in academic circles in America.

Another important academic center in the same field is Princeton University. Professor Philip Hitti, Lebanese by origin and a historian of Arab countries, is active in marshaling support in academic circles for Arab causes and the fight against Zionism. The State Department often turns to him for advice and guidance on matters connected with Syria and Lebanon.

(5) The Foreign Service Education Foundation was founded in 1944 for the general training of United States diplomats, but it is in fact concerned mainly with the Middle East. Most of those attending its courses join its institute prior to taking positions abroad. The director of the institute is Dr. Halford Hoskins. Much of the foundation's work is financed by American oil companies with concessions in Arab countries. Hoskins and his colleagues are extreme anti-Zionists, and it is easy to imagine the guidance students receive on the Palestine question. There are close ties between the foundation and Aramco, which sends staff bound for senior positions with the company in Saudi Arabia to the foundation's institute before they assume their posts.

(6) The Arab-American Mining Company Institute is another American link with Saudi Arabia. In 1943 Karl Twitchell, a geologist-engineer and the institute's founder, led a team of agricultural experts sent by the State Department to Saudi Arabia more for political reasons than to study the agricultural problems of the country. While in Saudi Arabia he busied himself with investigating the ancient gold mines and sources of other precious metals in the Hejaz. He later

became one of the trusted contacts between the State Department and the court of King ibn-Saud. In February 1944 he showed his hostility to Zionism before the Foreign Affairs Committee of the House of Representatives when he defended the Arab case in the Palestine controversy.

(7) Regarding the American Arab population in general, their number in 1943 was little more than 100,000 (the census listed 107,420 persons whose mother tongue is Arabic as residents of the United States in 1940). Anne O'Hare McCormick told me that despite their numerical inferiority ("especially as compared with the five million Jews") and despite religious and sectarian divisions, the majority of the Arab Americans and their press—there are nine periodicals in the U.S. published in Arabic, three of them daily newspapers—support the Arab claims in Palestine. One of the first Arab organizations in the country, founded in 1943 in Flint, Michigan, for the special purpose of fighting Zionism, was the League of American-Arabs Committee for Democracy. It has the support of Senator Josiah Bailey of North Carolina and of W. E. Hocking, author of the anti-Zionist book *Arab Nationalism and Political Zionism*.

(8) The Institute of Arab-American Affairs, founded in 1944 in New York, has broadened its activities by establishing branches in Washington, Boston, Chicago, Detroit, San Francisco, and Los Angeles, and although it describes itself as a "purely educational body" it carries on active anti-Zionist propaganda. Its publication, the *Bulletin of Arab-American Affairs*, publishes articles aimed at underlining the importance to the United States of Arab friendship. The *Bulletin* is distributed among congressmen, journalists, clergymen, and various political organizations in the country. The president of the institute, Faris Malouf, is assisted by Ismail Khalidi, from Jerusalem, who directs the institute's activities. He is to be replaced soon by Dr. Khalil Totah, an old acquaintance of mine. A graduate of Columbia University, Totah served for

several years as principal of the Quakers' School in Ramallah. While in Palestine he became interested in our educational system and sought to cultivate friendly professional contacts with Jewish teachers, for which he drew fire from the country's Arab newspapers. Politically, however, Totah has always been an outspoken anti-Zionist, and I was not surprised to hear that he is becoming director of the institute. He should be a serious opponent because of his apparent "moderation" and his calm approach to controversial subjects.

Another organization, calling itself American Citizens of Arab Descent to Cement Arab-American Friendship, was founded in 1944. It publishes a quarterly, *Arab World*, engaging primarily in anti-Zionist propaganda, but the journal has a limited circulation and has not been appearing regularly.

———————

In my conversations in San Francisco I have been struck by the fragmentary knowledge our people display on the activities of the Arabs and their friends in this country, who seek to increase Arab influence in the public and political life of the United States and to weaken our position. There is no doubt that the new political and economic interests of the United States in the Middle East will make the task of our opponents easier and ours more difficult. I talked about it at length with Goldmann and Arthur Lourie.

———————

This evening I spoke about our problems to a gathering of members of all the Zionist parties and organizations in the city. The meeting was chaired by Leo Rabinowitz, president of the San Francisco Zionist organization. In addition to concern over the situation in Palestine and an understanding of the responsibility that rests on the official Jewish bodies in the Yishuv, the Jewish Agency and the Vaad Leumi, several people in the audience voiced support for the dissident acts taking place in Palestine and criticized the official policy of the Jewish Agency and Zionist organizations in the United States for not rising more actively to the needs of the hour in Palestine and the Jewish world. There is little doubt that dissident groups in the United States have apparently gained some hold on Jewish opinion (the dissidents are represented in San Francisco by Hillel Kook, alias Peter Bergson,[66] nephew of the late Chief Rabbi Kook). I have been told that Bergson and his associates have succeeded in attracting to their cause groups of people who have previously been indifferent to Zionism and non-Jews of high social and political position.

Friday, May 25

Yesterday was a great day for us. The Trusteeship Committee, after a long and stormy session, voted on paragraph 5 (as amended by the American delegation), and approved the following resolution:

[66]Peter Bergson (born Hillel Kook) (1915–); organizer and leader of the Hebrew Committee of National Liberation; joined Irgun Tzvai Leumi at its founding (1937); active in behalf of Irgun in Warsaw and London; came to U.S. (1940); cofounder and leader of the Committee for a Jewish Army of Stateless and Palestinian Jews, the Emergency Committee to Rescue the Jewish People of Europe, the American League for a Free Palestine, and the Hebrew Committee of National Liberation; member of first Knesset (1949– 51) as representative of Herut.

Except as may be agreed upon in individual trusteeship arrangements made under paragraph 4 and 6 placing each territory under the trusteeship system, nothing in the chapter should be construed in and of itself to alter in any manner the rights of any state or any peoples in any territory, or the terms of any mandate [Document 552, II/4/23, May 24, 1945].

The vote: twenty-nine delegates for, the five Arab delegates against, with no abstentions.

The private meeting between Harold Stassen and Abdel Hamid Pasha Badawi, minister of foreign affairs and chairman of Egypt's delegation, to reach a compromise on the wording of clauses in the "Working Paper" on which the views of the two delegations differ, produced no results. Stassen made it clear to the pasha that the disagreements between them are on points of substance and that his delegation would not retreat from the position it has taken and fully explained. Stassen insisted firmly on the need to protect all the rights of all the parties incorporated in the League of Nations mandates.

According to reliable information, the angry Badawi started shouting, and Stassen reproached him for his behavior. Later the incident became a topic of conversation in the corridors and reached the press. At the opening of the session Stassen, without referring to his talk with Badawi, made a formal statement regarding the fundamental importance of paragraph 5 as a "safeguarding clause intended to preserve and to protect all the existing rights, which will remain unchanged and will neither be increased or diminished in the Trusteeship Chapter in the United Nations Charter." At Fraser's suggestion, the statement was put on record.

The Arabs did not give up their intention to continue the fight, however, and the Iraqi delegate, sensing the general mood of the committee and its support for Stassen's statement, jumped up, as he had done on a previous occasion, to propose a postponement of further discussion on paragraph 5 on the ground that the paragraph involves questions of great importance to "certain delegations" and that more time would be required for further study of the paragraph. The Egyptian delegate seconded the proposal. The proposal was defeated.

Then the Arabs changed their tactics and chose to renew their attack, this time by the Syrian delegate, on the expression "any peoples"—now, however, not trying to change "peoples" to "people," but proposing that the rights be limited to "peoples of the territory concerned." The intention of this proposal was clear: to abolish the rights of the Jewish people in Palestine and to restrict them to the current Jewish inhabitants in the country alone. This proposal, too, was defeated.

On both occasions no one in the committee supported the Arab amendments, although there were some abstentions. The results of the votes were quite obvious to people concerned about the mood of the committee. And when the Egyptian delegate tried to prolong the discussion, Fraser, by then weary of the Arab tactics, turned to him and said: "Listen, you fellows, out in your part of the world you know good horses when you see them! Why look this one in the mouth?"

He then put paragraph 5 to a vote, which entirely isolated the Arabs from the rest of the committee in their position.

Before the meeting adjourned, Fraser said that the vote had been taken with the understanding that it would not preclude subsequent consideration of the paragraph. It is not clear whether he meant that the committee may consider the matter again or that it will be done in Commission II, where the committee's report will have to be confirmed before being passed to the plenary session of the General Assembly for a final decision.

We were told by Wise, Goldmann, Monsky, and others about what had occurred at the Trusteeship Committee meeting. Robinson analyzed the significance of paragraph 5 as it now reads: while our existing rights under the Mandate will remain unchanged, the way will not be closed for subsequent agreements regarding the future of Palestine, in which the Jewish Agency's recognized status under the Mandate will be of great international importance in the formal presentation of our demands and in our dealings with the Mandatory Power itself.

At our second meeting later in the day, additional information was given on what happened in the Trusteeship Committee. We know that when the Syrian delegate wanted the rights limited to "peoples of the territory concerned," he was supported by Soviet, Cuban, and Haitian members, but all of them abstained when the proposal was put to a vote. At the final vote on paragraph 5 the Soviet delegate as well as the delegates from Cuba and Haiti joined those who voted for the clause as proposed by Stassen. An amusing sequel was related by Monsky: after the vote the Egyptian delegate proposed "textual amendments and linguistic improvements" in the clause already approved, to allow the Arab delegates "to consider anew how they should cast their votes." Fraser rejected the proposal. But our people think that this last-minute intervention by the Egyptian and the Iraqi delegates may have induced Fraser's remark that the vote taken would not preclude subsequent consideration of the paragraph, thus giving the Arabs the satisfaction that the way is still open for possible second thoughts on the matter.

Robinson thinks that the Arabs will try to prevent the final insertion of paragraph 5 in its present form when it is put before the plenary session of the General Assembly, rather than in Commission II. They may do it, however, more for publicity reasons than in the expectation of being successful, after their defeat at the Trusteeship Committee meeting.

Kenen reported that the spokesman for the American delegation told the press that the paragraph the Arabs seek to amend is "a general safeguarding clause for everyone's rights everywhere" and said that amending it would prejudice a number of situations throughout the world. This, he said, includes American rights in the Pacific and various international treaties around the globe.

It is clear that in supporting our interest Stassen is actually acting in accord with America's own interests, as indeed the British position emphasizes even more.

Wise, Goldmann, Monsky, Israel Goldstein, Shulman, Robinson, and others spent the last few hours before the meeting of the Trusteeship Committee discussing the matter with members of different delegations. Referring to his meetings with a number of American delegates, Shulman mentioned the great importance of the Jewish Agency's memorandums, especially the supplementary memorandum, as sources of most valuable and instructive information on the Palestine problem and our demands. Many delegates learned about the subject for the first time in our well-explained and clearly presented case against the Mandatory government.

Robinson, calling our attention to the fact that there are still two stages for paragraph 5 to pass through before it is inserted in the Trusteeship Chapter of the Charter (Commission II and the plenary session of the General Assembly), said again that the Arabs can try to annul the decision of the Trusteeship Committee at either stage but are more likely to try it in the plenary session. He stressed the importance of not reducing our activities before the work is complete.

Summing up the situation, Goldmann reminded us of

Churchill's statement of February 27 in the House of Commons that the United Nations conference will not deal with solutions to the Palestine problem and that the matter will be dealt with only after the war. From the decisions taken at Dumbarton Oaks it transpires that in its discussions on the trusteeship system the conference will not consider the affairs and problems of any particular country under the mandates system of the League of Nations. This being the case, he said, our task is to concentrate on the protection of the legal status quo and make sure that the rights of the Jewish people and of the national home under the Palestine Mandate emerge intact. We also have to see that the new trusteeship system will be attuned to our needs. This, it seems, we may have already achieved. He went on to say that while our political aim will be to bring an end to the Mandate and establish a Jewish commonwealth in Palestine, before we reach that objective we must safeguard what we already have and resist further Arab attempts to change it to our disadvantage. Arab activity at the conference has already indicated clearly enough what we can expect. There is great moral and political significance in the fact that the Arabs have lost the first round in the postwar battle with Zionism on the international scene. But there are still more—and difficult—battles ahead of us.

In conclusion, Goldmann expressed his satisfaction with the general course of deliberations in the Trusteeship Committee and with the trend among most delegations to increase effective international supervision over territories that may eventually be placed under the trust of the UN.

Wise and Monsky praised the friendly understanding and help rendered to us by the American delegation, especially by Stassen, at every stage of the proceedings in the committee, where Stassen was the spokesman for his delegation, and on other matters on which we have sought their help. Goldstein gave an impressive review of the contacts we have made in numerous delegations. Kenen spoke about our press and public relations.

Wise spoke, too, about the understanding we have found especially among the delegations of small states, particularly those from Latin America. Both Wise and Goldmann stressed that the understanding between the American and British delegations on the need to protect the integrity of the existing mandates in every part and detail has contributed greatly to our success. The fact that the Soviet Union voted for paragraph 5 with the United States and Great Britain, and that France and China joined the other Great Powers as well, lends weight to the committee's decision and is also of international political significance.

I then summarized the lessons that we can draw from the Arab stand, emphasizing the common front put up by the Arab delegations on the Palestine issue in this, their first appearance at an international gathering as members of the Arab League. The Palestine question, I said, is a heaven-sent opportunity for them to demonstrate their unity and enhance the league's prestige. By raising the Palestine issue they could conceal the differences between Syria and Lebanon, Hashemite Iraq and Saudi Arabia, and the other Arab states and Egypt, which is seeking to lead the Arab League and use it to further Egypt's own objectives.

I observed that in the committee's discussion on paragraph 5, the Arabs only directed their fire at those parts of the Palestine Mandate that refer to the rights of the Jewish people and the national home, saying nothing whatever about Britain's position and rights as the Mandatory Power in Palestine. I suggested that there is either some sort of understanding on the matter between the Arab and the British delegations, or the Arabs themselves refrained from raising points that might cause friction with Great Britain, especially now that London is the principal supporter of Syria and Lebanon against France's remaining hold over them. Anthony Eden, as the chief patron of the Arab League, can well be satisfied with its debut at the conference.

I also commented that the Egyptian representative on the Trusteeship Committee apparently masterminded the attacks of his Syrian and Iraqi colleagues on paragraph 5, but that the Lebanese delegate took little part and the Saudi Arabian delegate took no part at all in the committee discussion, although both delegates voted with the rest of their Arab colleagues. The Saudis, I suggested, were probably swayed by the firm position of the United States delegation and wanted to avoid what might appear as a conflict. And the Maronite members of Lebanon's delegation were perhaps reflecting with hidden satisfaction on the rights of "peoples" rather than "one people" in a territory, as defined in paragraph 5, since they now face, after the withdrawal of the protection of France, the nightmarish fear of a Muslim "Greater Syria."

I ended by warning about the possibility of increasing danger in the future from the Arab League: the more the Arab camp is ridden with internal conflicts and divisions, the greater will be the efforts of the British and their Arab allies (despite their own differences) to strengthen the Arab League at our expense.

Ray Brook has learned from the Egyptians that they and other Arab delegations are giving serious consideration to raising the issue of paragraph 5 again later on. In order to soften their defeat, practically all the spokesmen for the Arab delegations have stated that they did not come to San Francisco with any thought of settling the Palestine problem. Moreover, the spokesmen assert that the Arab delegations have no specific country in mind when offering amendments and take the attitude that the United Nations Charter should "deal in generalities" only.

My friend Mahmoud Abul Fath, speaking to a number of journalists, said that the trusteeship question in relation to Palestine cannot be settled in San Francisco. As to the question itself, he continued, Arabs and Jews alike should be thought of as citizens of Palestine, just as in the United States there are no laws applicable specifically to American citizens of French or British origin. Nationals of other countries are protected here by international law as individuals. In Palestine it should not be a matter of Jewish or Arab rights but of the rights of citizens, concluded Abul Fath in his "explanation" of the Palestine question. He avoided further discussion with the journalists when asked about Arab-Nazi collaboration during the war and about King Farouk's sympathy for Hitler and Mussolini.

Another friend of mine, Fadhil al-Jamali, when asked by reporters for comments on the Trusteeship Committee's decision and its possible effect on the Palestine question, replied, according to Ray Brook, that "on a democratic basis, there is no reason or logic in granting special privileges to Jews living in Palestine." You can expect, said Brook ironically, not only the Egyptians and the Iraqis but the ex-mufti of Jerusalem himself to appear tomorrow as a defender of democracy if it serves his objectives. The ignorance of the great majority of people everywhere, and the selfish political interests of many who know but do not care about truth and justice except as it best serves them and their countries, leave plenty of latitude for maneuvering by the Arab leaders, including those who yesterday belonged to the pro-Nazi camp.

————————————

At our press conference, which was well attended by American and foreign correspondents, Goldmann explained that paragraph 5's importance for us and the preservation of our rights under the Mandate should not be interpreted as the ultimate goal we are working for: we will continue to fight for the basic aims of the Zionist movement, as outlined in the Biltmore Program.

Some American reporters at our press conference had already heard from the spokesman for the United States delegation about what took place at the meeting of the Trusteeship Committee. The spokesman, replying to questions, had explained the importance of paragraph 5 in protecting the rights of the Jewish people in Palestine and had described it as being a fundamental principle that must be upheld wherever there are problems of several different nationalities present in a single political unit. Some reporters had also spoken to the Arab representatives and heard their reactions to the committee's decision. They said the Arabs intend to renew their efforts later on and that they had told the committee chairman so after failing to achieve their aims at the present stage of deliberations. Goldmann referred the reporters to Fraser for comment.

The secretariat of the General Assembly has informed the press that the United States, Britain, France, and China approve the insertion of a new chapter in the Dumbarton Oaks security proposals dealing with colonial peoples and strategic areas. The Soviet delegation at the United Nations conference, while indicating approval, is awaiting final approval of this chapter from Moscow.

In addition to paragraph 5 there is also an important and direct bearing of the new Trusteeship Chapter's provisions on the Palestine Mandate, in paragraphs 3C and 4 of the chapter. Paragraph 3C says that "it would be a matter for subsequent agreement as to which territories would be brought under a trusteeship system and upon what terms"; and paragraph 4 says that "the trusteeship arrangement for each territory to be placed under trusteeship should be agreed upon by the states directly concerned, including the

Mandatory Powers. . . ." It follows from the text of these two paragraphs that Great Britain, as the Mandatory Power for Palestine, will remain a decisive factor in any possible change of the present status of Palestine.

I lunched with Jouve and Gorse and told them how much we appreciate their delegations' support in the Trusteeship Committee deliberations on matters of great importance to us. Gorse mentioned the deep disappointment among the Arabs at their failure, not so much because they failed but because not one delegation sided with them on the decisive vote. The Iraqis accuse the Saudis of not working hard enough on their American friends to prevent them from helping the Zionists. The Syrians now have further grounds on which to accuse France of ignoring Arab interests. Only the Egyptians, who have been less preoccupied than the Syrians or the Iraqis with the Palestine question, minimized the importance of the Arab defeat; they have warned their Arab colleagues not to present what happened in a way that will give added publicity to the Zionist victory, damage Arab prestige, and be detrimental in future battles they may have to fight at the conference.

Gorse has close personal ties with the Egyptian delegation.

I went to hear Dmitry Manuilsky at a press conference organized by the Ukrainian Soviet delegation. Accompanying Manuilsky, the delegation chairman, were Vladimir Bondarchuk, Pyotr Pogrebniak, and Nikolai Petrovsky, members of the delegation, and a large entourage of aides and bodyguards. The only speaker—he also answered questions—was Manuilsky himself, who repeated almost verbatim what Molotov said on a similar occasion a few days ago. A reporter asked how he explained the wartime collaboration of many

Ukrainians with the Nazi occupation army. Manuilsky denied that this had occurred and accused the questioner of spreading "slanderous lies." Another reporter asked a question in Ukrainian, to Manuilsky's acute embarrassment. Apparently he does not speak the language at all or at least could not understand the question well enough. He quickly received an explanation or translation from someone seated near him. Manuilsky spoke in Russian and French, and the two interpreters—a man and a woman—translated what he said into English.

Like Molotov, Manuilsky closed the proceedings quickly, despite the shower of questions put to him. His manner was less sharp and aggressive than Molotov's, and he seems to be a more congenial person who has a sense of humor, which is more than one can say for Molotov.

Emanuel Tamrat (the Falasha) introduced me to Ato Aklilou Abte-Wold, vice-minister for foreign affairs of Ethiopia, a delegate to the conference. At the outset, as in most meetings with Ethiopians, I listened to the tale of the friendship of King Solomon and the Queen of Sheba and heard of the close historic ties between our peoples, ties strengthened still further at the time of the Emperor Haile Selassie's exile in Jerusalem, and of our two peoples' relationship with Orde Wingate. Wingate, while devoting himself to his military duties in Ethiopia, had also applied his energies to helping the population as a whole. He and one or two Palestinian Jews who were with him did much for the cause of a free Ethiopia, which will always be remembered by them with gratitude.

I told Abte-Wold about the situation in Palestine and the problems we face. He took down part of what I said and told me he would report our conversation to the emperor himself and to the prime minister, who is also the delegation chairman. After our talk Tamrat mentioned the great influence Abte-Wold has at the imperial court and dwelt on the benefits that could flow from our developing closer ties with Ethiopia, where the founding of the Arab League has increased fears of the dominance of Islam, the traditional enemy of Ethiopia.

The long and busy day was capped by dinner with several of our team of workers at the conference.

Most of the Jewish representatives are due to leave San Francisco in the next few days, for it looks as though there is now no pressing reason for them to stay on. In the short time I have been here I have gotten to know several people better than the rest, and to form some opinion of their abilities in the special circumstances of our difficult task. I have already struck up friendly relations with some, forged in the battle we have been fighting together on many fronts. Although the San Francisco conference has brought many Jewish organizations under a single roof only temporarily, in the course of our work together we have developed a team of people with widened knowledge in international affairs and newly acquired experience in diplomatic procedures and techniques. Dr. Jacob Robinson stands out above everyone in his profound knowledge and penetrating approach, both legal and political, to our problems at the conference. Herman Shulman has shown great ability and sound political judgment. I am sure that there will be further opportunities to use his talents in the course of our struggles in America. Henry Monsky has played an important role as the representative of a broad American Jewish public outside the Zionist camp, thus widening the character and scope of American Jewry's support for our demands. I also think that Proskauer's joining us in the attack on the white-paper policy of the British government was an important asset to us. The strong anti-Zionist bias still prevailing among many of his colleagues in the American Jewish Committee and Proskauer's own opposition to our political aims, as defined in the Biltmore Program, do not diminish the great public importance of the AJCommittee's joining in the struggle for our immediate vital needs, restricted by the white paper.

Nahum Goldmann, who represented the Jewish Agency at Geneva before the war and knew his way around the maze of the League of Nations, also knows many of the delegates at this conference and has been using his contacts to great benefit. His strength lies in his versatility, his rapid acclimatization to the particular conditions of the moment, and his ability to make quick decisions. I have observed, however, that when these rapid decisions have to be followed by action, they are not always coordinated well enough with his colleagues'. It seems to me that of all the Jewish leaders I have met, Nahum Goldmann best represents the broad approach, both in knowledge and in practical experience, when explaining our case to delegates from different countries. I have also developed a friendly relationship with Louis Lipsky, a cultured person and a nonconformist in his opinions on many aspects of general American and Jewish life and problems in this country.

But it is Dr. Stephen Wise who has dominated the Jewish scene in San Francisco. His personal charm, brilliance in conversation, and great talent for public relations, in addition to his majestic appearance and nobility in dealing with people, princes and commoners alike, have made him one of the most popular and highly respected figures in the corridors of the conference. He knows everybody he wants to know and manages to have direct access to any leader of any delegation he desires to see and talk with. He has been a great asset to us and has contributed much to the success of the Jewish presence in San Francisco during the conference.

San Francisco, May 26–June 8, 1945

II *The "Unholy Alliance"— Russia and Arab League*

Saturday, May 26

This morning's press highlighted the adoption of paragraph 5 by the Trusteeship Committee, together with comments on the importance of this development for the protection of the rights of the Jewish people in Palestine. Most papers presented what our side had to say about the decision, as well as the Arab reaction. Several writers sympathetic to our cause stressed that the postwar Zionist political struggle has begun with an important achievement in the international forum but still faces a long, difficult road before achieving its ultimate aims.

The *New York Times,* reporting on the event, headlined its story on the action taken by the Trusteeship Committee ARAB BLOC'S FRUSTRATION and noted that Harold Stassen played a leading role in blocking an effort by the Arab bloc "to freeze the status of the Palestine Mandate." The *Times* went on to stress the fact that the Arabs' behavior at the Trusteeship Committee proceedings was only one of numerous manifestations at the conference of their keen awareness of the importance of regional groups within the United Nations. Most of the Arab tactics, the *Times* said, were designed to strengthen even further the Arab League's position at the conference.

Alger Hiss's reply to Goldmann's May 23 letter has been received by the Jewish Agency desk in the Butler Building. The secretary-general of the conference repeats what he said in his letter of May 18, stating that the Pact of the League of Arab States was distributed as "a background reference document relevant to the agenda of the conference because it is a charter for a regional organization of the type envisaged by the Dumbarton Oaks proposal." He goes on to say that "the international secretariat feels that it has discharged its responsibility in this matter. The secretariat is not in a position to insist that any delegation make arrangements for distribution of particular documents or materials such as the annexes which you sent me."

Further on in his letter Hiss says that "the annex text which you quoted in your letter of May 15, 1945, would actually fall specifically in the category of material that would not be eligible for distribution or consideration at this conference, as it refers to a specific territory, rather than to general principles of broad application." Adding that he regrets not seeing his way clear to acceding to Goldmann's requests to distribute our letters, because he feels "obligated to adhere to the firmly established policy of not suggesting to delegations that material not relevant to the drafting of the Charter be reproduced and distributed," Hiss concludes by informing Goldmann that he is forwarding copies of their correspondence to the chairman (Abdel Hamid Pasha Badawi) of the delegation "that requested us to reproduce the English text of the pact, as furnished by him."

Goldmann learned from a reliable source in the secretariat that John Ross, Hiss's deputy, is of the opinion that the Jewish Agency's letters should be included in the *Daily Bulletin of the United Nations Information Office,* but Hiss is opposed to that, too. We have decided to send copies of our correspondence with Hiss to all delegations, with the relevant material attached.

———————————

I went with Goldmann to see Jan Masaryk and Stojan Gavrilovic. As at the previous meeting with them, Goldmann again requested the Czechoslovak and Yugoslav delegations to issue statements confirming their readiness to participate in an international agreement that would transfer to the Jewish people all, or certainly most, of the property belonging to Jews murdered by the Nazis who left no heirs, to be used for the resettlement of Holocaust survivors in Palestine. Goldmann pointed out the public importance of such an announcement, as it would encourage other states where Jews suffered under the Nazi occupation to follow the lead of Czechoslovakia and Yugoslavia. Masaryk at once agreed to issue such a statement during the conference, and Gavrilovic promised to cable Belgrade seeking permission to do so. Masaryk was greatly moved throughout our talk and expressed his shock at the terrible fate that has overtaken European Jewry, including the Czech communities, with their ancient traditions and material and spiritual riches.

Most of our representatives—including Monsky, Shulman, and Arthur Lourie—left San Francisco yesterday, and others are planning to leave in the next few days, for we assume that their tasks have essentially been accomplished and that their presence at the conference is therefore no longer required. In consultation with Goldmann, who returned to New York today, we decided that I should stay on in San Francisco to be on guard should the Arabs try to raise the Palestine question in Commission II or at the plenary session of the conference. Despite the statement by an Arab spokesman that the Arabs "did not come to San Francisco with any thought of settling the Palestine question," there are indications in Arab quarters, as reported by some press correspondents today, that "consideration is being given [by the

Arabs] to the possibility of raising the issue [of the Mandate] again later on."

I also will have to maintain contact with the Czechoslovaks and Yugoslavs and to meet again with the chairman of the Greek delegation, to ask his government to issue a statement in a similar vein concerning Jewish property in Greece. A cable was sent to Moshe Shertok, in Jerusalem, informing him of the extension of my stay.

Louis Lipsky and I talked at lunch about the political tasks facing the American Zionist movement. Lipsky attaches great importance to our success with the Trusteeship Committee and thinks it came about largely because of the close cooperation of the Jewish public bodies belonging to the American Jewish Conference, which demonstrated the unity of American Jewish opinion and the solidarity of most American Jewish organizations with the Zionist struggle against British policy in Palestine. In his opinion it is essential to enhance the standing of the American Jewish Conference in order to prevent official circles in Washington and the American public from gaining the impression that Palestine is of concern only to Zionists. The AJConference also helps weaken the influence of Jewish bodies that vacillate on the Palestine question, especially the American Jewish Committee: there is no way of knowing what its position will be on matters vital to us at future stages of our political struggle.

Besides strengthening the pro-Zionist front in American Jewry, Lipsky thinks we should also broaden and intensify the political activities of the American Zionist Emergency Council. Lipsky mentioned that on his visit to America in August 1943, Dr. Weizmann had succeeded in persuading Abba Hillel Silver and Stephen Wise to serve as joint chairmen of the council. They then drew into the AZEC's work most of the leadership in American Zionism and were for a time successful in reducing the traditional rivalries among the Zionist organizations. However, Lipsky thinks that the harmonious working of the AZEC was affected from the start by the conflicting personalities of the chairmen. Silver, who is younger and more radical, does not find the older and more inflexible Wise a congenial person to work with; they also differ in basic concepts about policy and methods of execution. Arthur Lourie, the political secretary of the Jewish Agency's London office, spent the war years in the United States and was appointed director of the AZEC. His presence on the staff strengthened the AZEC because of his vast knowledge and experience in Zionist affairs, but most of the AZEC's activities remained in the hands of local officials who had Silver's approach to problems and were loyal to him personally. Silver lives in Cleveland, where he is rabbi of a prominent Reform congregation, but he devoted a good part of his time and energy to the AZEC's work. Wise, on the other hand, is busy with numerous public and academic affairs, and his personal contact with the AZEC and its staff was rather slight and irregular.

The continuous and increasing tension between the two chairmen finally reached a breaking point when, in addition to the complicated personal relations between the two men, the question of the AZEC's relations with the United States government arose. In October 1944, on the eve of the presidential elections, the two candidates, President Franklin D. Roosevelt and Governor Thomas E. Dewey, declared their general support for Zionism. At this juncture, it was thought, the AZEC could have prompted the chairman of the Senate Foreign Relations Committee to renew closed hearings on the Palestine question, which had been suspended earlier owing to a War Department warning that "further action on them [the hearings] at this time would be prejudicial to the successful prosecution of the war." It could now be assumed that with the president's formal approval, by including the

Biltmore Program in his platform, the work of the congressional committees would be successful.

On November 7 Franklin D. Roosevelt was reelected for a fourth term as president of the United States, and on December 11, 1944, Secretary of State Edward Stettinius argued before the Senate Foreign Relations Committee against taking any decision on Palestine, as passage of a resolution favorable to Zionism "at the present time would be unwise from the standpoint of the general international situation." Under White House pressure, and no longer acting from considerations of campaign needs, the committee decided against further deliberations on the Palestine question. Similar pressure by the administration on the Rules Committee of the House of Representatives held up the House Foreign Affairs Committee's favorable decision, passed on November 29, in support of a Jewish commonwealth in Palestine.

It was then, explained Lipsky, that a quarrel broke out in the Zionist leadership between Silver, who wanted strong pressure put on the White House, and Wise, who favored a more cautious approach, which would avoid the publicity on the subject that Silver demanded. Wise hoped to achieve more by his tactics than by allowing the Palestine question to become an issue of open confrontaion with the president. Lipsky mentioned the mutual suspicions—which resulted in additional tension in their relations—stemming from the political differences between the Republican, Silver, and the Democrat, Wise. Although there was active support for Silver's aggressive policy from a considerable segment of the Zionist Organization of America, Mizrachi, and even some leaders of the moderate Poalei Zion and Hadassah, Silver's intemperate behavior and ad hominem attacks on his adversary prevented their practical agreement about anything. When he lost the support of the AZEC's majority for the line he had proposed, Silver resigned (in December 1944). The split in the AZEC ranks, Lipsky said, has damaged the public image of the American Zionist movement and weakened the AZEC's influence in several fields of operations. Silver's departure from the AZEC also led to the resignation of a number of its members and officials, and this, too, has had its effect on the efficiency of the body.

Now gathering around Silver is a group of Zionists, primarily from the ZOA, who believe his approach to Zionist tactics vis-à-vis the administration to be the right one. Silver's followers carry on their activities inside Zionist organizations and are using the Yiddish press to gain support for their views. On the other hand, with Wise its sole chairman, the American Zionist Emergency Council is cooperating more closely with the Jewish Agency than in the past. This has come about largely through the friendly personal ties between Wise and Goldmann, ties that Goldmann does not enjoy with Silver. Silver's group, calling itself the American Zionist Political Committee, is no real threat to the AZEC's position and prestige, which are based, as in the past, on the Zionist political parties and organizations in this country represented on it, as well as on the full support of the Jewish Agency executive in London and Jerusalem. If the split in the ranks of American Zionism continues, however, Lipsky thinks it may interfere with the marshaling of Jewish energies to wage the difficult battles that the Zionist movement foresees in America, including those for gaining the support of the general public, the political parties, and people in administration circles in Washington.

Lipsky suggested that before I return home I should study the situation in the United States more closely and go to Washington to get the feel of it firsthand. He returns to New York tonight.

I was invited to a party this evening in honor of Vicente Lombardo Toledano, head of the Mexican Federation of Labor, which was held at the home of an official of the long-shoremen's union. The guest of honor told me about his sympathy and support for our aspirations, and declared his readiness to help us in any way he can. He advised us not to depend on promises of help from any quarter before we have ourselves prepared to fight in every way for what we consider vital to our cause. He said he is glad the British labor movement is with us and that American workers are on our side. He thinks we should broaden our information activities to include Latin America, whose influence in international affairs is growing stronger because of the number of votes it commands at the United Nations. Left-wing forces in Mexico, he said, have considerable influence on government policy, and we can rest assured of their help in gaining the support of his government in matters of vital concern.

I suggested to Toledano that he visit Palestine. He promised to do so on a future trip to Europe.

Sunday, May 27

I talked at length with Fadhil al-Jamali. Like other Arab delegates, al-Jamali discounts the significance of the Arab defeat in the Trusteeship Committee, arguing that the Palestine question is not on the conference agenda, and therefore no decision reached can have any effect on the outcome of the struggle between Jews and Arabs over the future of Palestine. I asked him why, if this is the case, the Arabs concentrated all their energies on the attack on the original draft of paragraph 5, especially after it became clear that they were completely alone in their attempt to make basic changes in it. Al-Jamali would not be drawn out and treated me to a long lecture on the right to self-determination of every people in the majority in a specific territory. As for the Arab fight in the Trusteeship Committee, it had been one of principle; and with regard to Palestine, the Arab League has already taken a perfectly clear stand on the question, he said.

After a short pause, as if considering his argument further, al-Jamali made the following significant statement: he would not be revealing any secret to me in saying that the British government had prior knowledge of the inclusion of the Annex Regarding Palestine in Appendix B of the Pact of the League of Arab States signed in Cairo on March 22, 1945, yet it had made no protest. And so from now on, al-Jamali stressed, every British government will be obliged to respect the stand adopted by the united bloc of Arab states with respect to Palestine. Al-Jamali considers this much more valuable than the Arabs' not having achieved their objectives in the Trusteeship Committee. After all, he said, Palestine is ruled by Great Britain, not by an international body; that is what matters, not resolutions.

I asked al-Jamali about relations between Iraq and Britain. He replied that they had never been better. The British government is most appreciative of the loyalty shown by the Hashemite dynasty in Iraq and Transjordan during the war, and this has strengthened the position and influence of the two countries in London. Anthony Eden regards Iraq as the focal point of British strategy for the entire region, more important than Egypt because of Iraq's proximity to the Soviet Union and because of its oil. With the American control of Saudi Arabian oil, Iraq's economic value to Britain cannot be exaggerated; as a result of Iraq's being included in the sterling area, Britain will be able to purchase oil for the rebuilding of its industry, so badly hit by the war, on easy terms and without recourse to dollars.

As to Arab-Jewish relations, al-Jamali declared flatly that

there can be no basis for any settlement or understanding between the two peoples as long as the Jews aspire to set up an independent political unit in an area where the majority of the inhabitants are Arabs. The British have at last realized their error in supporting the Peel Royal Commission's partition plan, and al-Jamali said he thinks there is no likelihood that the plan will be revived under the present circumstances. The only way open to the Jews of Palestine is to recognize their position as a permanent minority and agree to live side by side with the Arab majority, as Jews have done in Iraq. Iraqi Jews, al-Jamali concluded, have a "secure and respected position," especially in the economic life of the country, and there is no reason why the Jews in Palestine should not achieve the same.

Before we parted, al-Jamali mentioned that he is going on to New York to receive the Iraqi regent, Abdul-Illah, and his high-ranking entourage, which is to include my old friend Daoud Pasha al-Haidari, I learned. Al-Jamali also told me that among those accompanying the regent will be Archibald Roosevelt, assistant American military attaché in Baghdad, who during the war traveled through the Arab lands with his cousin, Kermit Roosevelt, in order to draw Arab leaders closer to the United States.

Archibald Roosevelt is the grandson of President Theodore Roosevelt and belongs to the Republican branch of the Roosevelt family. Although Archibald Roosevelt's attitude to Zionism has not been as hostile as his cousin Kermit's, it is safe to assume that when the regent comes to America, Archibald Roosevelt will utilize his many contacts in the State Department and the Pentagon to smooth the work of Abdul-Illah and his ministers, including undermining our claims in Palestine and gaining support for the Arab point of view.

I had a half-hour meeting with Huseyin Ragip Baydur, Turkey's ambassador in Washington. Yalçin, who arranged the meeting, also attended. He has been a friend of Baydur's from the time they worked together in the Union and Progress party of the Young Turks. Yalçin told me of Baydur's close personal ties with Turkish President İzmet İnönü and of the great respect Ankara has for his views on every question concerning American-Turkish relations.

Yalçin suggested that besides explaining to the ambassador our views on the Palestine question, I should describe the assistance we are receiving from American Jews who are supporting us in our political struggle for a just solution of the question. I did so and found that he knows scarcely anything about Jewish organizations in the United States, that all he does know of American Jews is that "the Jews have great influence and power" in all sectors of American life. Apparently he thinks Rockefeller is a Jew and that all America's railroads belong to Jews!

In the course of the conversation Baydur remarked that the American public and government are currently interested mainly in developments on the American continent and in the Pacific Ocean, and pay scant attention to events in other parts of the world. To illustrate his point he recounted a conversation he had had with a distinguished member of Congress. After a long talk, in the course of which Baydur had tried to describe his country's problems, the American politician asked him what part of Africa Ankara was located in! It did not occur to the ambassador, of course, that he himself had said an equally ignorant thing to me only a few minutes before about Rockefeller and America's railroad barons. A lesson to be learned from my talk with the Turkish ambassador is that it will be dangerous for us to take for granted that the Palestine question is familiar or well understood in the United States, not only by foreign envoys but by the American public—including large sections of the Jewish population.

---

197 *San Francisco   May 26–June 8*

I lunched with Saloum el-Mokarzel, the president of the National Lebanese Society of America and editor of its paper, *Al-Hudah,* the larger of the two Arabic-language dailies that are published in New York, (in Brooklyn to be specific).

I had met el-Mokarzel through a Lebanese friend who is a frequent contributor to the paper. *Al-Hudah,* which is read mainly by the Maronite community, has a circulation of about five thousand. The other daily, *Al-Samir,* is sold mainly among the Arab Greek Orthodox community, who also have another publication, *Marat al-Arabi,* which appears on an irregular basis; it too is published in Brooklyn, where immigrants from Arab countries are scattered among the almost solid Jewish population of the borough. The Druze community has its own paper, *El-Bayan,* which appears in Washington three times a week. Other Arabic-speaking communities in the United States have their own journals, but none of them come out on a regular basis.

All this was related to me by el-Mokarzel, who describes himself as a friend of Zionism because of the mutual interests of the Jews of Palestine and the people of Lebanon—the "national home" of Christian Arabs and their social and cultural center in the Middle East. He spoke about the illustrious past of his newspaper (which was founded by his late brother, Naim el-Mokarzel) and about its contribution to the preservation of the Arabic language among persons who have left Lebanon and other Arab countries for the United States. He boasted that its writers have won praise throughout the entire Arab world for their development of new forms of the Arabic essay and verse. Almost all, el-Mokarzel declared, are Maronites from Lebanon. He is proud of the fact that the first Arab immigrant to the United States was a Lebanese Maronite who came to America in 1854 and settled in Boston. In the Catholic cemetery in Brooklyn there is the tomb of Antonius el-Bishlani, a Maronite priest buried in 1856. Following the Maronites, Arabic-speaking immigrants came from other communities in Lebanon, each with their own spiritual and secular leadership. There is little social contact, he explained, between Arabic-speaking communities in America, particularly between Muslims and Christians. In the United States there are 150,000 to 200,000 people of Arab origin, according to him, although it would be difficult to identify many of them because of assimilation among the younger generation, who are changing their Arab names to American ones. The Arabic language, too, is gradually being forgotten and is largely preserved in the Muslim community, chiefly for religious reasons.

El-Mokarzel spoke about anxiety in the Maronite community in the United States over the recent events in Lebanon, which point to the intention of Lebanese and Syrian Muslims to erode the Christian character of the country and ultimately incorporate it into a "Greater Syria." From information reaching el-Mokarzel from reliable circles in Beirut, it is apparent that Christians there have no great faith in the assurance Lebanon obtained under the Alexandria Protocol of the Arab League, which emphasized the league's "respect for the independence and sovereignty of Lebanon in its present frontiers." El-Mokarzel apparently has intimate ties with the Maronite Church in Lebanon, and he also keeps up a correspondence with some of the Maronite youth leaders, who are protecting the community's interests and are ready to defend themselves against both internal and external subversion.

El-Mokarzel mentioned the prospect of a conference of all American Lebanese organizations, to be held soon to demonstrate solidarity with their brethren in the homeland. His society also intends to invite representatives of similar organizations in Latin America, in order to heighten the impact of the gathering.

El-Mokarzel went on to say that the Arab League is soon going to open an information office in Washington; arrangements have already been made by the Egyptian legation there. Although there are still differences of opinion among Arab envoys in the capital about the character of the office to be set up and who should run it, it will probably start functioning this summer. According to el-Mokarzel, one of its main tasks will be to rally friends of the Arab cause in America and build up their strength against the Arab League's prime target, Zionism.

Before we parted, el-Mokarzel mentioned that he has heard from our mutual friend, the Lebanese journalist who had brought us together, about my friendly ties with Lebanon's Maronite leaders, including the patriarch, Antoine Arida. He invited me, as an ally in a common cause, to visit his paper's editorial offices when I go to New York and be introduced to his colleagues in the National Lebanese Society and on the staff of the paper.

This evening I lectured to a group of Hadassah women on the situation in Palestine and our relations with the Arabs. From the questions I was asked after my talk, I learned about the wide scope of interest and the desire for information regarding the life and problems of the Yishuv. I was impressed by the quality of some of the questions and by the keen desire to help us in our coming struggles in different fields, social, economic, and political.

One of the participants in the discussion voiced support for the views of Dr. Judah Magnes on relations with our neighbors. She proudly called my attention to the fact that Dr. Magnes was born in Oakland, near San Francisco. This was a bit of new information to me about a man whom I greatly respect. Although disagreeing with some of his views on the Yishuv's relations with the Arabs, I admire his unshaken faith and his dedicated work for closer relations and better understanding between us and our neighbors. When I first went to Beirut to continue my studies, he encouraged me to get to know our neighbors directly, especially the Arab intelligentsia. It was principally with them, Magnes believed, that we would one day have to deal to reach a settlement and establish normal relations on the basis of just and lasting peace, cooperation, and mutual respect.

Monday, May 28

I learned from Beeley that Commission II of the General Assembly, whose president is Field Marshal Smuts, will discuss the decisions of the Trusteeship Committee only after the committee has completed its deliberations and resolved all the items on its agenda. Beeley says that the South African representative on the Trusteeship Committee has been active in the defense of our rights and has opposed Arab efforts to alter paragraph 5 in the "Working Paper," changes that would threaten the integrity of the Palestine Mandate. In Beeley's opinion, neither in Commission II nor in the plenary session of the General Assembly should we expect any real difficulty in having the decisions of the Trusteeship Committee confirmed, because representatives on the Trusteeship Committee have acted on their governments' instructions. These instructions also determine the stand of the representatives on Commission II and of the delegations in the plenary session, which will make the final decisions on any subject dealt with by the conference.

Jouve told me about the important contribution to the paragraph 5 discussions of the Trusteeship Committee made by France's representative, Ambassador Naggiar, who defended our rights cogently and fought every Arab attempt to jeopardize our interests. I later cabled Goldmann the substance of what Jouve said, suggesting that he send a message of our appreciation to Naggiar.

Jouve went on to say that we should be careful not to assume that British policy on Palestine has changed just because they did not support the Arabs in the Trusteeship Committee. The British behaved as they did on this occasion because it suited them to oppose the Arab demands, not because of any faithfulness to the Balfour Declaration. Jouve thinks that neither should we rely too much on the Americans, whose attitude toward Middle East problems will be chiefly determined by economic and political considerations relating to their oil interests, not by concern for the Yishuv's prosperity or Zionist aspirations in Palestine. Britain and the United States will unite in trying to oust France from its historic footholds in the area; but the Anglo-American relationship, despite their common interest in preventing Russian penetration, will sooner or later turn sour as their own rivalry intensifies over economic domination of the Middle East and its oil resources. Jouve claimed that France's presence in the Middle East is deep-rooted and has endured for centuries and said that the Anglo-Saxon allies will not easily oust France from the position it held in the area before the war.

We have learned from a reliable source that after Roosevelt met King ibn-Saud, the United States government made a series of basic and far-reaching decisions on financial and military assistance to Saudi Arabia. The men primarily responsible for this were Secretary of the Navy James Forrestal[67] and Secretary of War Henry Stimson.[68] Edward Stettinius, the secretary of state, had backed his colleagues' initiative, and the three presented Roosevelt with a memorandum that included the following items. (1) In the Middle East, where two great world powers, the United States and the Soviet Union, come into contact, Saudi Arabia will be able to maintain its territorial integrity and independence only if economically strong and politically stable. (2) The vast oil resources in Saudi Arabia under a concession held by American companies rely on the United States government to safeguard them and to assure their further development. (3) Saudi Arabian oil is important to the United States itself, as well as being a source of world supply. (4) The military authorities urgently desire certain facilities in Saudi Arabia for the prosecution of the war, such as the right to construct military airfields and flight privileges for military aircraft en route to the Pacific war theater.

The American government, it was suggested, should take the following steps to secure the agreement of King ibn-Saud to establish military bases in Saudi Arabia for the use of the United States air force. (1) Congress should be requested to appropriate funds for use in meeting the urgent financial requirements of Saudi Arabia, the size to be determined by the secretary of state. (2) The American Export-Import Bank should extend to Saudi Arabia development loans to finance

[67]James V. Forrestal (1892–1949); secretary of the navy (1944–47); secretary of defense in the Truman administration (1947–49); an extreme opponent of Zionism and Israel; following differences of opinion with the president he was dismissed from office in May 1949 and later committed suicide. A few days before his death he telephoned me from his hospital bed and told me of a change of heart toward Israel.

[68]Henry L. Stimson (1867–1950); secretary of state (1929–33); although a Republican, he was Roosevelt's secretary of war (1940–45); his attitude to Zionism was often influenced by his anti-Zionist advisers in the State and War departments.

long-range projects for economic and social improvements. (3) The military authority should give immediate consideration to projects such as the construction of airfields in areas of Saudi Arabia deemed to be of strategic importance.

According to our source, Roosevelt confirmed this program, and King ibn-Saud, too, gave it his full consent.

Although the initiative of the three secretaries was motivated primarily by military considerations, their memorandum to the president, as we have been informed, contains elements of long-range strategy—both military and political —in the Middle East. Here we find a clear indication of American interests in our part of the world transcending temporary military considerations. Oil is evidently one of the main factors, probably the most important one, in American policy decisions. Reference in the memorandum to the Soviet Union also suggests concern for the future of a region that lies so close to the USSR and is of growing strategic importance to the United States.

According to our source, different departments in the American government have already been engaged in implementing some of the suggestions contained in the memorandum, especially those connected with military requirements.

In light of the contents of the memorandum, American–Saudi Arabian relations cannot be viewed as simply economic in character or as affecting only those United States oil companies with concessions in the country. Though it may not yet be formal, there already exists a far-reaching arrangement between the United States and Saudi Arabian governments, which is bound sooner or later to have political consequences affecting our own interests. Roosevelt's remarks following his talk with ibn-Saud can now be better understood than they could before.

I passed the information on to London and Jerusalem.

Plenary session of the United Nations Conference on International Organization (UNCIO). Delegate from Saudi Arabia speaking

The Ethiopian delegation. Second from right, Ato Aklilou Abte-Wold

The Saudi Arabian delegation. Seated, Crown Prince Feisal, chairman

The United States delegation. Sitting (l. to r.): Rep. Sol Bloom, Sen. Tom Connally, Secretary of State Edward R. Stettinius, Jr., Sen. Arthur H. Vandenberg, Rep. Charles A. Eaton, Harold N. Stassen

Jan Masaryk,
chairman of the Czechoslovak delegation

Stojan Gavrilovic,
a member of the delegation from Yugoslavia

Andrei A. Gromyko, the Soviet
ambassador in Washington

V. M. Molotov, chairman of
the delegation from the USSR

Dmitry Manuilsky,
chairman of the
Ukrainian Soviet delegation

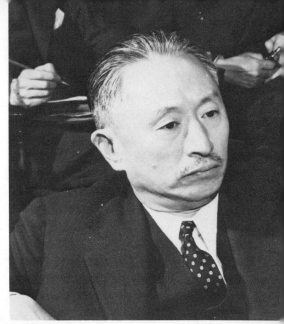

V. K. Wellington Koo,
a high-ranking member
of the Chinese delegation

Carlos Romulo,
chairman of the
Philippine delegation

Abdel Hamid Pasha Badawi,
chairman of the
Egyptian delegation

Faris al-Khouri,
chairman of the
Syrian delegation

*Anthony Eden, chairman of the
delegation from the United Kingdom*

*Peter Fraser of New Zealand,
chairman of the UNCIO Trusteeship Committee*

Sir Firoz Khan Noon,
a member of the
Indian delegation

Field Marshal Jan Christiaan Smuts,
chairman of the delegation
from the Union of South Africa

The San Francisco Opera House (left), site of the UNCIO meetings

The San Francisco City Hall with UN flags in the courtyard

A British journalist whom I came to know well when he visited Jerusalem before the war, who now serves on the staff of the British Office of Information and Publications in New York, told me about the office's activities against us. He says that one of the subjects that kept the office busy even in the most trying days of the war was the anti-Zionist propaganda campaign, intended to win the support of American public opinion for the Palestine white-paper policy and neutralize Zionist influence on the American press. The well-known pro-Arab writer Freya Stark was attached to the office for a time in 1943. She was sent from London for the special purpose of furthering anti-Zionist activities among Americans concerned with the Middle East. The Foreign Office judged that Freya Stark's name and her reputation as a writer on Middle East affairs would help her succeed in her mission. She was assisted in the United States by Anne O'Hare McCormick and Clare Boothe Luce, the wife of Henry Luce, publisher of *Time* and *Life* (both magazines, which are worldwide in circulation, have anti-Zionist leanings), who is herself a writer and anti-Zionist publicist. With Anne McCormick's help, Freya Stark made her way to the *New York Times* and met the publisher, Arthur Hays Sulzberger, also an outspoken anti-Zionist. Henry Luce opened his magazines to Freya Stark, to which she contributed blatantly pro-Arab and anti-Zionist copy.

It was harder, however, for Freya Stark to gain the assistance of Dorothy Thompson,[69] who although pro-British does not share Freya Stark's views on Zionism and Palestine. When she tried to gain entry into Dorothy Thompson's pa-

[69]Dorothy Thompson (1894–1961); a prominent American journalist and widely read columnist, for many years a sympathetic advocate of the Zionist cause; she later changed her views, becoming a vehement opponent of the Jewish national home and the state of Israel.

per, the *New York Herald Tribune,* she encountered opposition from Helen Reid, the paper's publisher, who is a convinced pro-Zionist.

In Washington, Freya Stark relied on the personal backing of the British ambassador, Lord Halifax, and the assistance of Michael Wright, the embassy's Middle East expert, who put her in touch with officials in the Office of Near Eastern and African Affairs of the State Department. It did not require much time or effort for her to reach a complete understanding with the anti-Zionists in the State Department who deal with Arab affairs and Palestine. From some of them she received generous assistance for her activities.

My friend told me about the regular exchange of views between the British embassy in Washington and the State Department on the Palestine question, and about the understanding that exists between them on the anti-Zionist policies of the white paper. The State Department holds that the United States government should support these policies because of the fundamental common interests of the two powers in the Middle East. Wallace Murray, chief of the Division of Near Eastern Affairs, has often expressed to his British colleagues barely disguised anti-Semitic views about the "Jewish cabal" that makes his work difficult.

He also warned me not to underestimate the abilities of the British Office of Information and Publications in New York and its influence on highly placed people in the United States. We should also realize, and prepare ourselves for the fact, that as our work here increases so too will the activities of the opposing British propaganda.

I learned a great deal today from Foy Kohler. I met him by chance in the conference building, and we chatted over a cup of coffee in the cafeteria. I asked him about the qualifications of men accepted into U.S. foreign service. He described to me the serious staff crisis the State Department is facing at present, because of the lack of qualified personnel in most geographical sections of its work and the dearth of candidates with specialized knowledge of regions of the world where American involvement had been trivial in the past. The shortage is especially marked in the Russian section. They are now paying the price, Kohler said, for their failure to set up schools of Russian studies in institutions of higher learning; before the war there were only two such schools in American universities. In large measure this state of affairs is due to the fact that the United States recognized Soviet Russia as late as 1933, and the absence of normal relations between the two countries was no encouragement to a young man looking to a career in diplomacy and seeking to equip himself in a discipline where he could make progress and put it to good use. As a result, there are very few people in the State Department who know Russian, and fewer still who know enough about the new Russia and the Soviet regime. The problem has become urgent and most important in the light of an increasing volume of work resulting from the wartime cooperation between the two countries.

This, however, is not the situation in the Office of Near Eastern and African Affairs, Kohler said. Many young Americans who have spent years in the area, and know its languages and problems, could easily be engaged for diplomatic duties, except that a large number of them lack the necessary academic qualifications. He thinks that, as they do in the case of Soviet Russia, the department will in the future have to train men in this field. Kohler mentioned that manpower is at present one of the most urgent problems in the State Department, which needs more people capable of carrying out the policies decided upon by the different branches of the American government dealing with foreign affairs.

I spent the evening at the home of Mr. and Mrs. Leo Rabinowitz. From what he had to say about the composition of the Jewish community in San Francisco and its social divisions, I can tell that he does not belong to (and doubts whether he could be accepted by) the Jewish establishment of the city, which is dominated by rich Jews of German origin—and this despite the respected public position of my host, a well-known attorney and president of the local Zionist organization. There is apparently still a wide gulf between families of East European origin and those whose parents came to the United States from Western Europe. Rabinowitz's parents arrived in America from Minsk in the 1880s, and he was born in the United States. However, he told me that throughout his years of study and legal practice in this city, to which he came as a child, he made more friends among the Christians of all sects than among German Jews. I wonder where a Palestinian Jew, born, like Rabinowitz, in Russia, is placed on the scale of tribal classification by the president of the American Jewish Committee and his colleagues?

Tuesday, May 29

An agitated Si Kenen telephoned me this morning. He said that at last night's session of the Trusteeship Committee the Iraqi delegate again raised the question of paragraph 5, claiming that in earlier discussions on the paragraph he had reserved the right to reopen the issue—despite the fact that the committee has already made its decision on the matter. The Soviet delegate supported his Iraqi colleague, and, after an exchange of views between delegates, the chairman apparently had no choice but to agree to the Iraqi delegate's request. The Soviet delegate, while supporting his Iraqi colleague, asked for a general discussion on mandates and trusteeship systems, as well as on the matter of paragraph 5 of the "Working Paper," as desired by the Arabs. Kenen and I decided to find out more about what happened and then to contact New York for instructions on how we should react.

I telephoned Beeley, who confirmed what Kenen told me. Beeley said it would appear that the Soviet delegation received instructions from Moscow to use the proceedings at the Trusteeship Committee meeting to make a well-publicized protest against the colonial policies of the Western powers by opposing paragraph 5, which probably seems to them a cover for the perpetuation of mandatory regimes. The Soviet delegate tried at yesterday's committee meeting to show that article 22, paragraph 4, of the League of Nations Covenant, which states in part that "certain communities formerly belonging to the Turkish Empire have reached a stage of development where their existence as independent nations can be provisionally recognized," contradicts paragraph 5.

Although I doubt that the Soviet move has as its deliberate or primary intention the undermining of our mandated rights, now that Syria and Lebanon are independent, Palestine is the only possible target for an attempt to invoke this paragraph of the League of Nations Covenant in connection with paragraph 5. However, it is hard to believe that the Soviet government, on whose instructions their representative on the committee acts, does not realize the significance of its proposals for the future of the Jewish national home. I reminded Beeley of the fact that every Arab attempt in the past to turn article 22, paragraph 4, to their advantage has been rejected by the British government and by eminent international lawyers (including Sir William Finlay and others), on the ground that article 22 does not apply to Palestine because of the sui-generis character of the Palestine Mandate, which includes explicit provisions for the establishment in Palestine of a national home for the Jewish people.[70]

According to Beeley, the Arab delegations have jumped at the opportunity that has unexpectedly come their way—unexpected, because at the earlier sessions the Soviet delegate supported the committee's resolution on paragraph 5. Bolstered by the apparent change in the Soviet position, the Arabs have broadened their demand—a demand, no less!—now wanting the complete deletion from the "Working Paper" of paragraph 5, which they say is "lacking in utility and logic." The Russians are again backing the Arabs and demanding the deletion of the clause in its entirety, arguing that its retention would freeze the status of peoples dependent on mandatory rule, and impede their progress.

Once again, however, Stassen stoutly defended the clause's importance as a shield for the existing rights of cer-

[70]This view was clearly expressed and explained in a letter from Winston Churchill, the colonial secretary, to the Palestine Arab delegation on March 1, 1922: "With regard to article 22 of the Covenant of the League of Nations, I am to observe that this article, insofar as it applies to territories severed from the Ottoman Empire, has been interpreted by the principal Allied powers in articles 94 to 97 of the Treaty of Sèvres. Syria and Iraq are explicitly referred to in article 94 of that treaty as having been provisionally recognized as independent states, in accordance with the fourth paragraph of article 22 of the Covenant of the League of Nations. Article 95, on the other hand, makes no such reference to Palestine. The reason for this is that, as stated in that article, the Mandatory is to be responsible for putting into effect the declaration originally made on the 2nd of November, 1917, by the British government, and adopted by the other Allied powers, in favor of the establishment in Palestine of a national home for the Jewish people" (Correspondence with the Palestine Arab Delegation and the Zionist Organization, Great Britain, *Parliamentary Papers,* 1922, Cmd. 1700).

tain peoples under a mandatory regime, and asked that there be no alteration in the decision already made on the matter. Lord Cranbourne, the British delegate, strongly opposed the Soviet proposals, saying that if accepted it will bring civil war in Palestine between Arabs and Jews, for each is bound to interpret its right to self-determination in the spirit and manner it chooses. He added that there will also be grave problems elsewhere, especially in Africa, involving the danger of conflict between different segments of the population, which often include tribes with opposing interests.

The French, Chinese, Australian, New Zealand, South African, and several South American delegates supported the American and British position. The discussion was tense, particularly after one of the Arab delegates declared, on behalf of his Arab colleagues, that their continued participation in the committee—and in the whole United Nations conference—depends on the adoption of the Soviet proposals. The discussion was adjourned late last night and will be resumed in two days.

Following my talk with Beeley, I telephoned Goldmann in New York on the latest developments. He asked me to see Fraser as soon as possible and to stress our grave concern over what has happened in the committee. He suggested that when I meet Fraser I should emphasize the following points. (1) Paragraph 5 fully protects the rights of every state as well as of every people living in any specific mandated territory; what is provided in paragraph 4 of article 22 of the League of Nations Covenant is included in the adopted paragraph 5, and therefore there is no need for any further mention of the subject in the United Nations Charter. (2) The Soviet proposals in practice affect only one territory, Palestine; if they are adopted, the rights of the Jewish people in Palestine will be undermined, rights that are now recognized by the Palestine Mandate and in the future are to be protected by paragraph 5. (3) If, nevertheless, it is decided to take up the subject of the rights of communities referred to in article 22, paragraph 4, then the rights of the Jewish people must be explicitly cited as being incorporated in the terms of the Palestine Mandate.

Goldmann suggested that I list these points and after my talk with Fraser leave a written record of our position with him. If the situation worsens Goldmann and Lipsky will return to San Francisco. Monsky has been in touch with Stassen, and at Monsky's instructions Kenen will meet Benjamin Gerig, the deputy secretary-general of the United States delegation, and provide him with the same material I will be giving to Fraser.

Fraser's secretary understood the urgency of the matter and arranged for me to see him during the morning, when he usually rests in his room and does not receive visitors.

Fraser received me in his pajamas in his modest room in the Sir Francis Drake Hotel and listened carefully to what I told him in Goldmann's name. He referred to the Soviet-Arab partnership as an "unholy alliance" and said he thinks we should not view the Russian proposal as directed at the Jewish national home. He and his colleagues regard it as a tactical device for propaganda purposes. The Russians know very well that their proposals do not have the slightest chance of adoption since even the Chinese, who among the Great Powers are the closest to the Soviet point of view on colonial matters, will not support them against the United States, Great Britain, and France. What matters to the Soviet Union is for the Arab League to notice that when the British opposed the league's members in something of vital concern to them, the USSR was the only Great Power to stand by them. It is probable, Fraser surmises, that Stalin himself decided on the maneuver after hearing a report on the line taken by the Soviet representatives to the Trusteeship Committee, who voted with the majority in favor of paragraph 5 of the "Working Paper." For reasons of prestige, no official in Moscow would dare alter the position taken and voted for by a delegate at an international conference without a personal confirmation by the boss in the Kremlin.

As for the Arabs, said Fraser, their joy will be short-lived, for he has decided to finish the matter off at the next session of the committee, which is fixed for Thursday. He is quite certain that paragraph 5, which the committee had already passed by a decisive majority, will go to Commission II of the General Assembly in the form already adopted. Fraser is relying on Smuts, president of Commission II, to know how to handle any attempt by the Arabs or Russians, or both, to question the decision and to attempt to torpedo its confirmation by the commission.

Before we parted I left Fraser with a written copy of the points I had raised.

Mr. Peter Fraser, Chairman   May 29, 1945
Trusteeship Committee
Sir Francis Drake Hotel
San Francisco, California

Dear Mr. Prime Minister:

It has been reported to us that a new attempt is being made to amend the Trusteeship Chapter by the incorporation of a reference to article 22, paragraph 4, of the Covenant of the League of Nations. We have not yet seen a copy of this amendment and it is therefore difficult to comment on it. We believe, however, that it would be improper to incorporate reference to this provision of the League Covenant for the following reasons:

1. Paragraph 5 of the Trusteeship Chapter provides for safeguarding the existing rights of any state or any peoples in any territory. If any rights exist in consequence of article 22, paragraph 4, of the Covenant, those rights are, therefore, fully protected by paragraph 5 of the Trusteeship Chapter.

This inclusion of an additional provision specifically safeguarding rights under article 22, paragraph 4, is, therefore, unnecessary and irrelevant.

2. Moreover, this is an effort to incorporate reference to a specific territory, Palestine, which is the only one of the "communities formerly belonging to the Turkish Empire" still under mandate, and not yet independent. The Trusteeship Chapter has been carefully drafted to avoid reference to any particular area or to the particular rights of a people in any area.

3. The incorporation of a clause of the Covenant of the League which has been the subject of controversy in the past in relation to Palestine might be regarded as intending to prejudice rights, the very thing that the committee is seeking to avoid, and would be contrary to the procedure which it has followed throughout its deliberations.

4. If specific reference is to be made to rights of these specific communities then specific reference must also be made to Jewish rights and the terms of the Palestine Mandate. Presumably this is precisely what the committee would wish to avoid, particularly since the existing paragraph 5 protects the rights of all peoples.

We will appreciate your favorable consideration of the contents of this letter. Should you desire any additional comment from us, we would appreciate the opportunity of a meeting with you at your convenience. Your secretary may reach me at Douglas 7717.

Sincerely yours,
Jewish Agency for Palestine
(by Eliahu Epstein)

I arranged for Fraser's secretary to keep me informed of developments.

I spoke to Goldmann by telephone about my talk with Fraser. We agreed that before Thursday's session I should try to see the French and Chinese delegates to the Trusteeship

Committee and if possible a Russian delegate, in order to explain our position to them as I have to Fraser.

Goldmann mentioned that there is no need for us to worry about Stassen's position: it is as clear and firm as ever. Goldmann has heard from the editor of a New York newspaper that the British are even more concerned than the Americans about the Soviet proposal, and that Georges Bidault and Stettinius, like Eden in London, regard it as directed especially at Britain. The Russians, according to this assessment and also Fraser's evaluation, intend their proposals to damage Britain's prestige and reliability in the eyes of the Arab League. It is also designed to demonstrate the two-faced nature of British policy in the Middle East, which supports first one and then the other party to the Palestine conflict in accordance with British interests of the moment.

Frenchmen I met at the conference building are incensed at the battles being fought between the French army and Arabs in Damascus and elsewhere in Syria. They all accuse General Spears of devoting his whole stay in Beirut, as head of the British mission in Syria and Lebanon, to weakening French influence and French standing in these countries. The Syrians, they claim, would never have dared act against France as they have without encouragement from Britain and its agents. One Frenchman told me that not since Fashoda[71] have Anglo-French relations been so bad and that Frenchmen, whatever their political views, will always remember Britain's treachery. France has time-honored influence in the Levant, with an unbroken history in the region from the time

[71]A town in southeast Sudan; its seizure by a French force created a serious international crisis in 1898, almost causing war between Great Britain and France.

of Louis XIV. At the end of World War I, France and Britain reached an agreement on the division of zones of influence in the area (the Sykes-Picot agreement); now the British are violating this understanding repeatedly and viciously.

Russell Porter, the *New York Times* reporter, confirmed all that Beeley told me this morning about last night's events at the Trusteeship Committee meeting. The Iraqi delegate who revived the issue of paragraph 5 at yesterday's session introduced himself this morning to press reporters he met in the corridors as the man who would go down in Arab history as the "savior of Palestine from the Jews." The Egyptians are more cautious in their assessment of the situation and seem to realize that the Russian maneuver was motivated by quite different considerations from the Arab League's concern for the future of the Arabs in Palestine. It was the Syrian Faris al-Khouri, not the Egyptian delegate, as reported in some newspapers, who suggested that the Arab delegations walk out of the conference if their proposals are not accepted. But no one, not even the Arabs themselves, take the threat seriously, although the Arab delegates Porter spoke to expressed their solidarity with al-Khouri's suggestion.

Porter has sent his newspaper a detailed report on last night's session at the Trusteeship Committee and included a lengthy explanation of the significance of the Soviet and Arab proposals on the future of the Jewish national home in Palestine.

This evening Kenen and I reviewed the day's events, which have taught us—among other things—how dangerous it is to assume that our matter is sewn up as long as the proceedings of the Trusteeship Committee continue, and as long as the Arabs are prepared to use any tactics to achieve their aim and deprive us of our rights. After the committee's approval of paragraph 5, which was unanimous except for the Arab delegates, we certainly had no reason to think that there was the slightest cause for anxiety or that things would not go smoothly. Suddenly, however, the Russians proposed something no one expected, something wholly contrary to their position at the time of the discussions and the subsequent vote, and at one stroke the whole matter has been turned upside down! After their total failure with the Trusteeship Committee, the Arabs themselves certainly did not expect that the resumption of discussions on the subject would produce different results. They have jumped at the chance the Russian move has given them. Although their ultimate objectives are completely different, we think it is safe to assume that prior to last night's session of the Trusteeship Committee there was contact between the Arabs and the Russians so as to coordinate their members' actions at the session. Kenen and I agree that we have to be ready for possible new surprises and to be watchful until Commission II and the plenary session of the General Assembly itself have finally confirmed what was decided by the Trusteeship Committee.

Wednesday, May 30

This morning I received a copy of a telegram Goldmann sent to heads of conference delegations, drawing their attention to Porter's report in the *New York Times* explaining the threat to the rights of the Jewish people in Palestine if paragraph 5 is abrogated. Goldmann asked for their support of the paragraph and its inclusion in the Trusteeship Chapter of the United Nations Charter. Among those who received the telegram were the delegations of the five Great Powers.

As part of our efforts in case discussion on the Arab-Russian proposals is resumed in the Trusteeship Committee tomorrow, I met during the morning first with Liu Chieh, minister at China's embassy in Washington and deputy secretary-general of his country's delegation at the conference, and later with Ambassador Naggiar.

Liu Chieh occupies a senior position in the embassy. He studied at Columbia University and has many Jewish friends in the United States. He has done a good deal of reading on Zionism and has a clear idea of our problems. He explained that, on the question of trusteeship, the view of the Chinese delegation differs from that of the British and French, for these powers' intentions are merely to continue colonial rule under a more respectable name. He said that China remembers very well what the Mandatory Powers did under the cloak of the League of Nations mandates. In his view it is vital, at whatever cost, to prevent the United Nations from being used to give renewed life to this deplorable chapter in history. On this point, he stated, the Chinese position is closer to that of Soviet Russia than to the position of the Western powers. However, as long as the future of the British Mandate in Palestine remains undecided, he feels that there is no moral or legal justification for changing its terms to the detriment of any party whose rights are presently protected. He ended by saying that he has no doubt that the Chinese representative on the Trusteeship Committee will be guided by this consideration and that we have no reason to fear on China's account. I left with him a copy of the document I had given Fraser, and Liu Chieh promised to pass it on to the chairman of his delegation.

There was no need for a lengthy meeting with Naggiar. He thanked me for Goldmann's telegram, which expressed our appreciation for his support on the Trusteeship Committee, and assured me there is no cause for concern about Russian and Arab efforts to have the committee's decision overruled. He told me that among the supporters of the Arabs at the committee's session last night was General Carlos Romulo, chairman of the Philippine delegation, who on this occasion was sitting in for the regular representative of his country on the committee. Naggiar suspects collusion between him and the Arabs, with Romulo probably hoping to gain some kind of advantage at the conference, not necessarily for his country but rather for himself, with Arab assistance. Naggiar regards Romulo as an unprincipled go-getter, ready to do anything to advance his personal ambitions.

Before I left Naggiar he asked me if the present tense situation in Syria may not encourage the Arabs in Palestine to renew their aggressive acts against us, this time with British connivance. He thinks that the Syrians would not have dared call for the removal of French troops from their country without Britain's agreeing to the move. France's departure from Syria will make it simpler for Great Britain to dominate the entire region, except perhaps for Saudi Arabia, where the United States stands in its way. Then only the Jewish national home in Palestine would disturb the harmonious Anglo-Arab relations that London has dreamed of for so long. Naggiar doubts that we can reach any understanding with Britain that might foster progress toward our political independence in Palestine. No matter what political party is in power, the British government will not be able to resist the temptation to simplify the contents of the dual Sykes-Picot agreement to a singular "Sykes agreement," Ambassador Naggiar said with a smile. With each passing day it seems clearer to him that France and the Jews will have to pay the price for the system that Eden and his advisers on Arab affairs have formulated for the Middle East. This is the main lesson to be learned from the founding of the Arab League and the current events in Syria and Lebanon. Thus the world-weary French diplomat concluded his aperçu of events in our part of the globe.

Besides all my pressing duties, a new task suddenly fell on my shoulders. I had to spend time explaining at length to an employee of one of the American Zionist organizations, supposedly an expert in public relations, that the establishment of the Arab League cannot possibly be to our advantage and that its existence will in fact make the struggle for our rights in Palestine more difficult. I also doubt that the league will make a contribution to the peaceful coexistence of those peoples living in the area who are not ready to accept Arab domination. The woman, who is a journalist, was impressed by her talks with several Arab delegates at the conference and had written an article for Pearl Buck's monthly, *Asia*, that constituted a hymn of praise for the Arab League as "a factor for social and political progress in the Middle East." It was with the greatest difficulty that I persuaded her to ask for the return of her article and extracted her promise not to publish it elsewhere—in its present form, anyway.

After this talk I was very disturbed by the realization that there is hardly anyone among the Zionist organizations represented at the conference who has the necessary knowledge and authority to explain capably the Arab problem in all its guises and with all its implications for our own aspirations in Palestine.

Goldmann and Lipsky arrived from New York this afternoon. I brought them up to date on what Kenen and I have done since hearing of the unexpected turn of events on the Trusteeship Committee. We decided that Lipsky should attend to the American side of things and Goldmann should deal with leaders of friendly delegations.

Goldmann invited me to dine with him and his guest, Geneviève Tabouis,[72] the well-known French journalist.

Madame Tabouis was famous in prewar days as an expert on international affairs. I could see at a glance, however, that the legendary Tabouis of the League of Nations days is no more. Her whole world—*her* France—has been pulled from under her. Her personal relations with de Gaulle and his aides, to the extent that they exist at all, are tense. After managing to escape from occupied France to the United States, she began to write for local newspapers. At first she made a good living, but as time went on her influence declined, and now there is hardly a newspaper in this country interested in her opinions on international questions. But she has apparently not given up her desire to be considered a source of "exclusive news." She is trying to get information from the few remaining statesmen she used to know in Geneva who are at the conference, which information she is ready to share with others.

She spoke about what is happening behind the scenes at the conference, about the growing distrust among the five Great Powers, each preoccupied with selfish interests and caring nothing for the challenge facing them to create a better, more stable world than the one that has passed away. She thinks all the indications are that the United Nations will be no more effective than the League of Nations in international

---

[72]Geneviève R. Tabouis (1892–   ); niece of French diplomat Jules Cambon; diplomatic correspondent for many French, British, and American newspapers; in the interwar years she covered many international conferences, including the assemblies of the League of Nations; published a French weekly, *Pour la Victoire,* in New York (1939–45); returned to France in 1946, where she continued her journalistic activity.

affairs, and says that there may be even more dangerous consequences for world peace in the future because Hitler has destroyed the political and moral foundations of conduct between nations.

Madame Tabouis's main interests at the San Francisco conference—and apparently the focus of her activity here—have a certain prewar flavor, peculiar to Europeans of her class and kind. What is Otto Hapsburg doing in San Francisco? What are the representatives of Mihailovitch, who are hanging around in the lobbies of the conference, up to? Why have the Polish anti-Communists come from London? She is also occupied in trying to help diplomats of the former countries of Estonia, Lithuania, and Latvia, who are busy pushing their claims against the Soviet Union. The problems of real interest to her belong to an order that has passed. She is a person who apparently cannot come to terms with the new postwar world and the American way of doing things; the rapid changes in fortune so characteristic of the country's general way of life and its violent contrasts are often beyond the understanding of an outsider, especially one, like Madame Tabouis, with such deep roots in conservative pre-1939 European society.

After we made our farewells to Madame Tabouis, Goldmann and I continued to talk for a long time, touching upon different subjects connected with our problems in Palestine and at the conference itself. In the course of our conversation Goldmann suggested that I delay returning to Palestine when the conference is over and stay in America for at least six months, possibly longer, to assist in the political work of the Jewish Agency in the United States. He stressed the growing importance of the United States in world affairs and the dangers we face from increased Arab efforts to gain U.S. support. My knowledge of the Middle East, he thinks, will be of great value in the agency's contacts in Washington with the State Department and different political groups in the capital, as well as with the American press. He suggested that I think over his proposal and added that he will be very glad to work with me.

I said that I will consider the offer and that I will consult Eliezer Kaplan about it when I see him in New York. I told Goldmann I will have to ask Moshe Shertok and David Ben-Gurion for their opinions. Ben-Gurion is due to arrive in New York in the next few days.

Thursday, May 31

Yesterday I telephoned the office of the Soviet delegation and requested a meeting with an official dealing with trustee-ship matters. After a rigorous cross-examination—about what institution I represent, in what capacity, and so on—I got an appointment with K. V. Novikov, the secretary-general of the delegation. Today when I was shown into Novikov's room, in the delegation's offices in the Sir Francis Drake Hotel, I noticed the memorandum of the Jewish Agency and those of other Jewish institutions lying on his desk. Incidentally, we had had the Jewish Agency memorandum printed in Russian and sent it on May 11 to the Russian, Ukrainian, and Byelorussian delegations. The Russian text included the history of the Palestine Mandate, information on the national home and its achievements, and a description of the course of British policy in Palestine and the breach of the terms of the Palestine Mandate. The memorandum in Russian summarized our claims to the United Nations conference in the same form as the one submitted in English to other delegations.

I told Novikov that I had come to see him to express our concern about the position his delegation adopted at the last meeting of the Trusteeship Committee. I explained that what their representative on the committee suggested has brought into question the legal foundations on which Jewish rights in Palestine are based. I stressed that the existing Mandatory regime is not at all what we were working for: our objective is political independence and freedom from any form of foreign domination. But as long as this remains beyond our reach, I went on, we have to protect the rights granted to us under the Mandate. Palestine, I said, does not appear on the UNCIO agenda, but any change in its present internationally recognized status would hurt us and impede us in our struggle for Jewish statehood.

I told Novikov about the Biltmore Program and emphasized that behind the Arabs who are attacking our rights stands the Arab League. And behind the league stands Great Britain, whose policies perpetuate the feudal and backward status quo in the area, aided by reactionary Arab elements opposed to the economic and social progress that the Jewish national home is bringing to the Middle East. I cited the example of the former mufti of Jerusalem and his associates, tools of Hitler and Mussolini, and said that these collaborators with the Nazi and Fascist regimes were no different in their outlook and behavior from a good number of other Arab leaders who now represent their countries at international gatherings—including the San Francisco conference. I finished by asking Novikov if he realizes the harm the Soviet proposal can do to our rights under the Mandate as long as Palestine's political future remains undecided.

Novikov replied that he will bear all this in mind and transmit the substance of my remarks to "the proper quarter." He went on to ask me about the situation in Palestine, mentioning that he has heard of the "Jewish Red Cross delegation" the Yishuv dispatched during the war to Russian troops serving in Iran. Referring to the amicable character of that delegation, I told Novikov about my meeting in 1942 with Sergei Vinogradov,[73] then Soviet ambassador in Ankara, about rescuing Jews from Nazi-occupied countries and taking them to Palestine. I explained that my call on the ambassador was connected with our request that the Soviet navy not cause difficulties for the boats carrying Jewish refugees to Palestine from Romanian ports on the Black Sea. Novikov, without commenting on my remarks, asked about the absorptive capacity of Palestine and about what countries we hope to bring immigrants from if we overcome the political difficulties now standing in our way. He also inquired about the attitude of American Jewry to the idea of a Jewish state in Palestine.

Our conversation, which was in Russian, lasted about forty minutes. Although I left without any response or even a hint of a reaction to this presentation, it seems to me that our talk was worthwhile, since it gave me the chance to explain not only our case before the Trusteeship Committee but also our plans and intentions for the future of Palestine. I came away from my talk with Novikov with the feeling that we should pay more attention to our contacts with the Russians.

I called again on the Greek minister for foreign affairs, John Sofianopoulos, and told him about Goldmann's latest talks with Masaryk and Gavrilovic regarding property in German-occupied Europe that belonged to murdered Jews who left no

[73]Soviet ambassador in Egypt until his death in September 1970.

heirs. I handed him the American Jewish Conference memorandum on the subject and put particular emphasis on the fact that it expresses the attitude of the majority of American Jews—and indeed of Jews the world over. I said that according to information we have received from Jerusalem, about 90 percent of the Jews of Greece were murdered during the German occupation, and the value of their property is certainly not less than 22 million Palestine pounds (equivalent to the same amount in pounds sterling). Sofianopoulos stated that his government has not yet completed gathering information on the war losses suffered by Greek nationals and said he could not comment about the injury done to Jews in his country. I explained that we are willing to accept any among the remnant of Greek Jewry who have relatives in Palestine and drew his attention to our right to assistance in absorbing them. At the close of our conversation I mentioned our desire to strengthen our ties with his country, including economic cooperation, and pointed to the assistance we may expect to receive from the Greek and Jewish communities in the United States, both of whom carry considerable economic weight. I told him that Eliezer Kaplan is presently in America and will certainly be glad to investigate the possibilities in this regard.

Sofianopoulos was less reserved than at our earlier meeting. He showed sympathy for, and interest in, the proposal to use the property of heirless Greek Jews who died in the Holocaust to help rehabilitate Greek Jews who have survived and wish to join their relatives in Palestine. He promised to cable his prime minister about our talk and to suggest that a special investigation be made as soon as possible into the value of the property of Jews who had perished under the Nazis. He said that the program we have proposed to his Czech and Yugoslav colleagues and now to him would have to be handled by a suitable international body. The body must be able, and would be entitled, to obtain the consent of the United Kingdom (as the Mandatory authority) in securing the facilities necessary to carry out its program successfully. Expressing interest in what I said about our economic relations with Greece, he suggested that when I get to New York I should contact the Greek consul general to arrange a meeting between Kaplan and the Greek commercial counselor in Washington.

Before I left I raised the question of the recent developments in the Trusteeship Committee and conveyed our concern over the latest turn of events. I handed him a copy of the document I submitted to Fraser. Sofianopoulos promised to speak to his representative on the committee, but said nothing of substance on the matter.

I had heard that in the newsreel being shown in the Butler Building's cinema, some of our soldiers serving with the Palestinian Brigade in the Italian theater of war appear in sequences shot on the front, and I asked Jouve to join me in seeing it.

When we were seated, Jouve told me the following poignant story. Joseph Paul-Boncour, a former premier of France (1932–33) who is now a delegate to the conference, came to San Francisco almost directly from the jail in which he was confined by the Germans throughout the war, where he was in complete isolation from what was happening in the world. After being freed he had apparently had no time before leaving for San Francisco to catch up with all that happened during his imprisonment. When he arrived in the United States he tried to contact some old friends, among them Wendell Willkie, and first heard of Willkie's death by telephoning his home and asking to speak to him! What is even more saddening to him is that so many conference delegates have been asking: "Who is this man Paul-Boncour?" *Sic transit gloria mundi.*

I was sorry to hear from Jouve that he is leaving San Francisco and returning to Paris. He suggested that I keep in touch with Gorse and Naggiar and mentioned, too, the name of Henri Bonnet, the French ambassador in Washington. In Jouve's opinion he is a man of outstanding abilities who is well able to grasp our problems. Jouve is sure that Bonnet will help us as best he can: he has considerable influence in Paris, and his judgment on political affairs is highly respected. Jouve promised before leaving San Francisco to speak to Bonnet and recommend that he see me.

I invited two Palestinian sailors to lunch, students from the Haifa Maritime School, who during the war served as members of the crews of American merchant ships now anchored at San Francisco. Fine, tough fellows, they recounted to me their adventures in war service in the Pacific carrying supplies to the American troops. After the war they intend to return to Palestine and use their experience in the development of our merchant fleet.

I met with several American reporters and explained to them the meaning of the Soviet proposals in the Trusteeship Committee and the consequent threat these represent to our interests. A correspondent from *PM,* the New York leftist daily, which has good contacts with the Soviet delegation, said that the Russians do not intend their move to hurt us or help the Arabs. What counts with them is establishing the principle that they desire to cultivate the friendship of peoples still under colonial rule. He added that the Russians are expert in this sort of propaganda exercise and in this case, by receiving the desired publicity, have actually achieved their objective. Besides, the journalist considers that right now the problem of Europe is uppermost in Soviet thoughts and thinks they only raise colonial questions as a lever against Britain if it opposes Russia on the European issues. The USSR wants as much ammunition as possible to strengthen its bargaining position in negotiations with the Western powers.

Ray Brook was there and told me about his talks ("not for publication") with the Iraqi regent, Abdul-Illah, and prime minister, Nuri Pasha al-Said. Brook knows both of them well from his visits to Iraq.

Abdul-Illah repeatedly emphasized that during the war he and his uncle, Emir Abdullah, were the only Arab rulers to risk their lives by remaining loyal to the democratic powers. Others—including King Farouk—were ready to renounce their obligations to their British ally and had even tried to do so. Ibn-Saud kept lines open to both sides and sheltered traitors of every description, among them Rashid Ali al-Keilani, who, once he was in Saudi Arabia, continued plotting against Arab regimes loyal to the democracies and contributing to their war effort. The regent complained that there is little appreciation of the Hashemites' loyalty and the dangers to which they were exposed during the war by the American government, which now pays so much attention to King ibn-Saud and helps him both politically and economically. Nuri Pasha met Brook privately, and he too complained that the Americans favor Prince Feisal and the Saudi Arabian delegation over the other Arab delegations; he spoke contemptuously of "the bedouins who have become statesmen overnight." Nuri Pasha hinted at a lack of sufficient initiative and activity on the part of his country's delegation on a number of matters, and said he regretted not having come to San Francisco at the opening of the conference to direct the Iraqi delegation more effectively.

According to Brook, Nuri Pasha, prodded by his friends in the British delegation, has been busy since his arrival persuading Arab delegates to intensify their attacks on France, and thus demonstrate Arab unity with regard to the fate of Syria and Lebanon. Brook thinks the propaganda campaign has borne fruit: practically every Arab delegate is now using the opportunity to proclaim solidarity with his Syrian and Lebanese brethren fighting the "French aggressors." It is evident, however, that the Lebanese are less opposed than their fellow Arabs to the events in their country and have been confining themselves to only passive identification with the anti-French propaganda that the Syrians are pouring in the ears of anyone who will listen.

This evening Goldmann, Lipsky, Kenen, and I had dinner together.

From Goldmann's and Lipsky's contacts with numerous delegates a picture has emerged, a picture, they feel, that should not cause us undue worry as to the outcome of the Trusteeship Committee's deliberations. There is no sign that the Soviet Union is actively seeking the support of other delegations for its proposal. This strengthens our assumption that the Russians are not in fact prepared to press the matter further, either because they realize they have no chance of success or because they calculate that their maneuver has already brought the desired publicity and therefore achieved its aim. It is not even certain that the Russians will renew their proposals at the committee's next session.

Goldmann believes that Fraser wants to push ahead with the committee's work and quickly polish off the remaining subjects on its agenda. He has been under pressure from the presidents of the conference[74] and will do all he can to dis-

---

[74]As agreed on at Dumbarton Oaks, the conference had four presidents, one each from four of the five Great Powers: Edward R. Stettinius, T.V. Soong, V.M. Molotov, and Anthony Eden. The

courage long-drawn-out discussions on any subject still on the agenda. Even if the Russians insist on pressing for further discussion on their proposals, Fraser has indicated there will be no danger—either then or later on—that Commission II or the plenary session of the General Assembly will change the text of paragraph 5 as adopted by the Trusteeship Committee. Lipsky reported that Harold Stassen and other American delegates hold a similar view. Other heads of delegations Goldmann consulted are also optimistic about the outcome of our campaign to keep the paragraph as it stands. Despite this, we agreed that this time neither Goldmann nor Lipsky will leave San Francisco until there is not the slightest doubt that we will emerge successfully from the struggle.

Friday, June 1

Jouve telephoned to say he had arranged a meeting for me with Ambassador Henri Bonnet. I met him at his hotel. Bonnet told me that when he was a member of de Gaulle's Committee of Free France he worried about the position of the Jews of North Africa. He knows the problems we face now and voiced his support for Zionism. He thinks that a

---

French, who did not attend the Dumbarton Oaks talks, interpreted the omission of Georges Bidault, the French minister for foreign affairs and chairman of his country's delegation, as an act of deliberate discrimination, accusing especially the Americans and the British of an anti-French attitude and of offending France's international standing and prestige.

Jewish state ought to be a refuge both for the remnant of European Jewry and for Jews who suffer discrimination in their countries of residence. Its basic function, however, should be to serve as a framework for the creation of an independent spiritual and social life, in which the Jewish genius can express itself fully and freely for the benefit of the Jewish people and mankind. The Nazis have insinuated their anti-Semitic poison into the minds of millions of people throughout the world, and he said it would not surprise him if anti-Semitism continues to manifest itself in European countries that have been under Nazi occupation, even though Hitler and his Third Reich have been obliterated. Bonnet feels that the establishment of a Jewish state would raise Jewish self-esteem and oblige the world to treat the Jews like any other member of the family of nations.

He told me about the Arab League's preparations to open an information office in Washington. The Egyptians, according to his information, are doing most of the work, and Abdul Rahman Azzam Pasha, the secretary-general of the Arab League, is soon due in the United States to complete the arrangements. The office will probably concentrate on propaganda directed against France and Zionism, the two matters on which the Arabs are united at the moment. Bonnet has heard that the Lebanese are not too pleased at the development because the propaganda line that the Arab office will peddle will probably be that of pan-Arabism, distorting the true character of Lebanon in American eyes. But Lebanon's say in the Arab League is minimal, and divisions among its Christian communities detract from its ability to stand up to Muslim pressures, both in Lebanon and throughout the Arab world.

Bonnet invited me to visit him in Washington if I go there after the conference ends.

I reported on my talk with Bonnet to Goldmann, who said that the news of the Arab League's opening a Washington office underscores the need to broaden our own activities in the American capital, to combat the anti-Zionist propaganda campaign the league will mount.

I talked with Stane Krasovec, of the Yugoslav delegation, whom I met at the suggestion of Gavrilovic. Krasovec is interested in developing economic ties between the Yishuv and his country: he has visited Palestine and is impressed by our industrial capabilities. Our goods can help Yugoslavia a good deal—it was ravaged during the war and has suffered terribly. I thought Krasovec should talk with Eliezer Kaplan in New York.

The headlines in the morning newspapers were filled with the events in Syria and Lebanon. The *New York Times* reported the danger of an outbreak of fighting between the British and French, a danger prevented only at the last moment by de Gaulle's giving in to Churchill's ultimatum that French troops cease firing against the Syrians and withdraw to their barracks. This had the effect of forestalling possible clashes between the British and French troops in Damascus and other Syrian towns, and reducing the danger of further political complications in the already-tense relations existing between the two governments. Truman has sided with London in the affair.

I met Raoul Aglion in the Butler Building. He spoke of the indignation he and his colleagues in the French delegation feel about the developments in Syria and about the way Britain and America are sapping France's prestige and challenging de Gaulle's authority in the eyes of the world. He complained about France's isolation and said that when the

French delegates meet their British counterparts they hardly greet them or exchange courtesies.

I inquired if he knows how the French intend to handle Haj Amin el-Husseini, who according to press reports has been captured by the French army in southern Germany and is now in French hands. He promised to look into the matter.

I spent a large part of the evening with Dr. Henry Atkinson, who has returned to San Francisco as an adviser to the American delegation. He gave me a detailed picture of the American Christian Palestine Committee he heads. It was founded at the end of 1942 and is made up of Christians of all denominations. It has a membership of more than two thousand. One of the committee's first moves was to declare its support for the Biltmore Program. Atkinson expressed his satisfaction at the fact that among the founders of his committee are some of the most eminent Christian theologians: Reinhold Niebuhr,[75] John Haynes Holmes, Paul Tillich, and Ralph Sockman. Most members are Protestant, but there are also Catholics, some of whom are well known, such as Msgr. John A. Ryan. Dr. Daniel Poling, editor of the *Christian Herald,* one of the important and widely circulated Protestant periodicals, is an active member of the committee. Atkinson is a regular contributor to the magazine and also edits the Protestant *Church,* which is sold mainly to Baptists in the United States and Canada (Atkinson's country of birth).

Reinhold Niebuhr, Atkinson said, is one of the first

[75]Reinhold Niebuhr (1892–1971); professor of Christian ethics and the philosophy of religion at Union Theological Seminary in New York; editor of the quarterly *Christianity and Society;* testifying in 1946 before the Anglo-American Committee of Inquiry (on the Palestine question), he called for the establishment of a Jewish state in Palestine.

American spiritual leaders and people with great moral influence in public life to endorse the Biltmore Program and to support the Jewish right to statehood in Palestine. He reflects, in his views on the subject, the finest values of the American traditions of universality and liberalism, and he has exerted a tremendous influence in explaining to the general American public that the Jewish problem is something that concerns the whole Christian world as much as it does the Jews. Between the two wars he strenuously fought against isolationism and played an important role in swinging the country's public opinion behind the democracies and against Fascism and Nazism. Tillich and Sockman, who, like Niebuhr, are on the faculty of Union Theological Seminary, have done much to guide their students toward a penetrating understanding of the Jewish problem and Zionism. As a result, our friends and sympathizers among the Protestant clergy throughout the country have multiplied in number.

Atkinson maintains close touch with Senator Robert Wagner, chairman of the American Committee for Palestine, which has more than five thousand members, including cabinet members, former presidential nominees, more than sixty senators, two hundred members of the House of Representatives, twenty-five governors, and many prominent men and women in public life in every part of the United States, among them such well-known figures as Dr. Daniel Marsh, Professor William Albright, Professor Carl Friedrich, AFL leader William Green, CIO leader Philip Murray, Dr. Walter Lowdermilk, Secretary of the Interior Harold Ickes, and many other people dedicated to the Zionist cause. Wagner's organization has more than seventy active branches in the country's big cities. Both the American Christian Palestine Committee and the American Committee for Palestine receive constant assistance from the American Zionist Emergency Council, which was in fact instrumental in setting up this body. Atkinson thinks the two committees should merge: there is too much duplication in activities directed toward a single goal.

Atkinson urged me not to leave the United States without meeting Niebuhr: he, Karl Barth, and Paul Tillich, said Atkinson, are the most important Protestant theologians to emerge since the Reformation, and Niebuhr's support for Zionism is a milestone in the development of Christian thought that can help to promote better Christian-Jewish understanding in America and in the world as a whole. Atkinson thinks that liberal Catholic theologians such as Jacques Maritain and John Courtenay Murray could find inspiration in Niebuhr's perception of Zionism, especially as Niebuhr is held in such high esteem by liberal Catholics both in America and abroad. There is still a wide gulf between Protestant and Catholic attitudes toward a Jewish Palestine, and it is important, said Atkinson, to work for improvement in this field.

Atkinson warned me, however, not to assume that all American Protestants are sympathetically disposed toward Jews and Zionism. There are Protestant groups in this country—especially the Presbyterians—who sympathize with the Arabs and are opposed to Jewish national aspirations in Palestine. Some Protestant journals in the United States, including the Methodist *Christian Advocate* and the Episcopalian *Living Church,* opposed the founding of the American Christian Palestine Committee and continue to criticize its objectives. There are close personal and institutional ties between many leading Presbyterians in America and in Arab countries. The American universities in Beirut and Cairo and a number of other educational and benevolent institutions in Arab countries were founded by American Presbyterians and are still receiving their help. Atkinson showed keen interest in my studies at the American University of Beirut and in my impressions of the years I spent there.

I promised Atkinson that before I return home I will address his committee on the situation in Palestine and our relations with the Arabs.

Saturday, June 2

I received a cable from the Palcor news agency in Jerusalem, asking about the situation in the Trusteeship Committee and requesting an explanation of the Palestine press reports about the crisis facing the committee on our issue. The cable was based on a report in *Haboker* on June 1, which had relayed information from the Palestine Telegraphic Agency that "Zionists were so confident about the outcome of the Trusteeship Committee's deliberations on the matter of concern to the Jewish national home that there was nothing to worry about and they all returned to New York. Meanwhile," the item went on, "when the Russians came out with their proposals the only Zionist representative in San Francisco was Eliahu Epstein." I arranged with the Palcor reporter, Zev Brenner, for a reply to be sent to Jerusalem describing what had taken place on the Trusteeship Committee in the last few days, adding that Goldmann and Lipsky are back in San Francisco.

Fraser told Goldmann this morning that Arab tactics on the Trusteeship Committee have taken a new course: the Arabs will not ask for the renewal of discussion on paragraph 5 until they have mustered sufficient support among other delegations for their position. The Arabs know very well that, despite Soviet support, they will again be defeated if they move to amend the committee's decision on paragraph 5 without obtaining sufficient additional votes from other members of the body. It is also evident that the Russians, no doubt for their own reasons, are showing no inclination to raise the issue again. However, said Fraser, it would not be wrong to assume that there is some kind of liaison between the Arabs and the Russians, and perhaps some surprises are still in store for the committee.

Lipsky has heard that the Americans expect the Russians to choose a suitable moment for attempting to use their proposals in the Trusteeship Committee as a gambit for bargaining with the Western powers, trading the proposals against concessions from the West on subjects that really concern them. It seems to the Americans that Soviet-Arab cooperation on the committee is an ad-hoc arrangement, although it is too early to conclude that similar cooperation will not take place in the future on other matters as well. Both Goldmann and Lipsky think that we should remain alert and follow developments in close consultation with Fraser and the friendly delegations.

I had lunch with a leading Maronite Lebanese delegate to the conference. He is quite disturbed about the situation in his country. Although Lebanon is relatively quiet and the general strike that has broken out in several cities has not been accompanied by serious incidents of the sort taking place in Syria, where there are still clashes between French and Syrian troops, he fears that the shooting will spread to Lebanon if the Syrian situation is not quickly brought under control. The worse matters become in Syria, the more difficult it will be, in his opinion, to prevent the crisis from affecting everyday life in Lebanon, a country needing harmony among its various religious communities in order to survive as a state. My friend believes that the Lebanese Muslims, rather than the Christians, are more likely to react violently to events in Syria and stir up intercommunal trouble. The danger is that such a development could bring on the intervention of the Western powers, whom most Muslims now regard as enemies of Islam.

However, according to my luncheon companion, the Christian leaders also are responsible for the constant tension in Lebanon; they have done little to help find solutions acceptable to the different segments of the population. Maronite leaders, such as Émile Eddé, he continued, with their repeated and exaggerated stress on the Christian character of Lebanon, have caused unnecessary provocation to the Muslim leadership and have disturbed the internal balance of the country's pluralistic society. A farsighted policy would be for all the Christians in Lebanon to recognize the fact that though they now constitute more than half the population, because of the higher birthrate among the Muslims and Druzes, Lebanon will become a Muslim country in the near future. It would be better, therefore, for the Christian communities to work together in defense of their legitimate interests through a reasonable understanding with their Muslim countrymen than to expose themselves unprepared to the increasing danger of a minority status.

I asked him what effect he thinks the Arab League will have on intercommunal relations in Lebanon. He answered that as long as pan-Arabism does not become pan-Islamism and the league remains an organization of governments without interference in its member's internal affairs, it can make an important contribution to the progress of the Arab states. The league's future will therefore depend on the aims it sets for itself and the people who direct its activities.

Since it appeared that he knows Émile Eddé, I asked him about the former Lebanese president, a man who openly sought ties of friendship between his country and the Yishuv and favored the idea of an independent Jewish state allied to

Christian Lebanon. I told him about the meeting in Paris on June 22, 1937, between President Eddé, who was then visiting the French capital, and Dr. Chaim Weizmann, who came from London especially for the occasion.

The meeting took place in the Hotel Lutetia, where Eddé and his entourage were staying. Participating in the meeting were President Eddé, Dr. Weizmann, Eddé's private secretary, and myself. After the customary exchange of courtesies—the conversation was conducted in French—Dr. Weizmann took out his watch and said that in about half an hour's time the Peel Commission's report would be signed: it would include a provision for the partition of Palestine and the establishment of a Jewish state in parts of the Mandate territory. Eddé did not seem to react to Dr. Weizmann's remark and asked instead about the country's development, the absorption of German refugees, and Dr. Weizmann's scientific work. After a short while Eddé glanced at his watch, suddenly broke off the conversation, left his chair, and declared to Dr. Weizmann: "Now that the Peel Commission's report is an official document, it is my privilege to salute the first president of the coming Jewish state." Eddé went on to say that since he was the first to congratulate Dr. Weizmann on the historic decision for which the Zionist movement had fought so hard, he requested of the Jewish state's future president that its first international friendship treaty be with its good neighbor, Lebanon!

Both Eddé and Weizmann seemed moved by the occasion, which they marked by raising their glasses to the future happy relations between the two states. Eddé's secretary and I toasted the health of both presidents. The leaders parted with warm expressions of friendship, and every time I spoke to Eddé on my later visits to Beirut he referred, with obvious emotion, to that memorable meeting in Paris.

My friend listened intently but did not comment on Eddé's

remark regarding relations between Lebanon and the future Jewish state. He said only that Eddé, by accepting the nomination from the impotent French authorities in 1943 as the Lebanese "head of state," has been discredited in the sight of the Lebanese people and forced to leave the country's public life. His chances of making a comeback are slight—no better, my friend added sarcastically, than "the chance of a Jewish state being established in Palestine."[76]

This evening I addressed a local B'nai B'rith chapter about our problems and was impressed by the warmth of the reception. Most of those present were middle-aged people, at least a few of them still readers of the Yiddish press. The general feeling in the room was that neither America nor any other country will open its doors to the remnant of European Jewry, and that every Jew who cannot—or does not want to —remain in the place where his relatives were slaughtered should be able to go to Palestine. We in Palestine, I told the audience, will go on struggling for the right of free entry into the country for every Jew, refugee or otherwise; but for us to succeed in our task we must have the moral and material support of our brethren in the Diaspora, above all the great Jewish community of the United States.

[76]Émile Eddé died in 1949. His sons, Raymond and Pierre, lawyers like their father, are active in Lebanese political life.

Monday, June 4

I had a long talk with the *PM* journalist I. F. Stone. He and his colleague Alexander Ul have done us an important service by properly explaining our case before the Trusteeship Committee and supporting it in the press. They have also published much of the material we have given them.

We talked about the reactionary character of the Arab League, about the British intention to use the league against Zionism, and about what we are accomplishing socially and economically in Palestine. I explained to Stone the dangers we foresee from the pan-Arab movement for national minorities in the Middle East, and emphasized the connection between Arab nationalism and the political aspect of Islam, which poses a threat to Jewish aspirations in Palestine as well as to the Christians of Lebanon. I suggested the use that Britain can be expected to make of the existing religious and other divisions in our area, applying its traditional method of "divide and rule." The history of British rule in Palestine provides ample evidence of that. Stone promised to use the material I gave him on the subject in his articles for *PM* and the *Nation*.

Dr. N. B. called on me. He is a medical doctor of Kurdish extraction living in Philadelphia, a friend of the brothers Emirs Jaladat and Dr. Kamuran Ali Bedr Khan. Jaladat, the elder brother, lives in Damascus, where he edits a Kurdish-language periodical. He had written to his friend in Philadelphia, mentioned my being in San Francisco, and suggested that he meet me to bring regards and to hear of the brothers' work in behalf of the spiritual and political revival of the Kurdish people.

The Bedr Khan brothers belong to one of the oldest and most prominent Kurdish families of the old Ottoman Empire. They were among the founders of the Hoyboun party, which was set up after World War I to work for the political independence of the Kurds, as promised in the 1920 Treaty of Sèvres (between the Allies and Turkey). The treaty's provisions for Kurdish autonomy and the creation of a Kurdish state were later annulled in the wake of the political changes in the Middle East, particularly the victory of Kemal Atatürk. (I am reminded of the story about Clemenceau who, when hearing about the disintegration of the Treaty of Sèvres, remarked that it was only natural that any product of Sèvres, a city famous for its china, should be fragile and easily broken!)

The Bedr Khan family, which lived in the Turkish part of Kurdistan, was compelled to flee the country. They found refuge with the French authorities in Syria, making their residence in Damascus. Despite their broad European education and fluency in several languages, the two brothers continued to work for the cause of their people, chiefly by publishing material, in Kurdish, of a literary and political nature. Dr. Kamuran Ali, the younger brother, later went to Beirut, where he continued his activities. On my frequent trips to Syria and Lebanon I used to meet them and hear about Kurdish events and problems. Maurice Fisher[77] kept in close

[77]Maurice Fisher (1903–65); Israeli ambassador to France, Turkey, and Italy.

touch with them. He was an enthusiastic advocate of Kurdish independence and did all he could to help the cause when he was an officer in Lebanon with the Free French forces.

Dr. N. B. told me that in the course of the last twenty-five years at least two thousand Kurds from the former Ottoman Empire and Iran have settled in the United States; but to most Americans the Kurds are simply Turks, Syrians, or Persians who happen to speak Kurdish. Before coming to America most had worked in commerce, and they have continued to do the same in America. A number of young Kurds attended American universities, and the Kurdish community now includes doctors, engineers, and lawyers. It is hard to claim that there is an organized Kurdish community in the United States, since the relatively few Kurds are scattered throughout the country—unlike the Lebanese, who are better organized than any Arab community in North or South America. Kurds who are associated with any "landsmanschaft" are for the most part members of Islamic organizations, and a few Kurds have become leaders of these groups. Only recently, after an appeal from the Bedr Khan brothers, has Dr. N. B. managed to form a society of young Kurds living in the New York vicinity who send material assistance for the brothers' work in Damascus and Beirut. Since Dr. N. B. has relatives in Turkey, he has been careful not to publicize the existence of the group.

Acting on instructions from Dr. Kamuran Ali, Dr. N. B. had a memorandum sent to every head of a delegation at the United Nations conference, asking that the Kurdish problem be placed on the agenda and that an international commission be set up to investigate the Kurdish problem and propose a solution to the coming peace conference. However, not a single delegation—including those professing sympathy with the Kurdish cause—is prepared to become involved in a matter that might cause undesirable repercussions in its relations with the Turkish, Iranian, Iraqi, Syrian, and Soviet delegations (all five of these countries have Kurdish minorities). The efforts of Dr. N. B. and his associates have been to no avail.

Although he has lived in the United States for many years, Dr. N. B. has not ceased, he told me, to love his homeland or care about the sufferings of his people. He stated proudly that the Kurds will go on fighting for their freedom and national existence. Like their forefathers, they will not lay down arms against neighbors who have denied them their national rights. What value, he asked, do words like "justice" and "international morality" have, when all that concerns the forum of the world's peoples are the selfish interests of each state? What could I say in reply?

Dr. N. B. told me that there are a number of officials in the State Department who are sympathetic to the Kurdish case. However, in an off-the-record talk one such official told him that the Kurds should not expect American help, for by supporting Kurdish aspirations, the U.S. would complicate its relations with Turkey, Iraq, and Syria. These countries are all sensitive to "minority questions," especially Turkey, which does not even recognize the existence of the Kurds as a minority people, referring to them as "mountain Turks."

Dr. N. B. invited me to visit Philadelphia and meet his group so that I can relay my impressions to the Bedr Khan brothers when I return home.

I came across Mikulas Mara, Jan Masaryk's private secretary, in the Butler Building, and told him about our anxiety over the latest turn of events on the Trusteeship Committee, owing to the change in the Russian position.

Mara stressed the sincere and profound friendship Masaryk feels toward us and his willingness to help us in any way he can. As for the Russians, Mara said, they are not an easy people, and it is hard to shift them from any stand they take.

He expressed the hope that "despite this, things will sort themselves out." The Czechs are incurable optimists or, even more, confirmed fatalists.

Word reached me from London about Professor Harold Laski's sharp words of criticism of the British government for appeasing the Arabs at the expense of the vital interests of the Jews of Palestine. The British government, he asserted, helped the Arab countries gain representation at the San Francisco conference and is directing their policies there, but is preventing the spokesmen of the Jewish people from being accorded similar representation. Laski directed his attack against Churchill and Eden in particular. The Overseas News Agency relayed Laski's remarks, and a précis was carried by a local paper. I.F. Stone used this for an article in *PM*.

Laski had impressed me by his brilliance and by his moral courage when I met him in London before the war. I was introduced to him by Professor Roger H. Soltau, once his assistant at the London School of Economics and later my teacher at the American University of Beirut.

Before Jouve left he arranged for me to meet several French journalists. One asked me why we do not set up a federal state with Lebanon and gather Jews and Christians into a single political unit, which could stand up to the neighboring Muslim countries with greater strength and confidence. The Jews and the Christian Lebanese, the questioner claimed, are the most talented and progressive peoples of the region and in time can become the leading economic and cultural forces in the Middle East. I inquired whether any Lebanese leader had put the proposal to him and if he sees any chance of the Christians in Lebanon accepting it. He countered that it is his own idea, but nonetheless worth investigating and working for. I doubt whether even Eddé would support such a plan, suspecting a dominant Jewish role in such a federation. Cooperation yes, federation no! This would probably be the reply of our own leaders to such a proposal.

I telephoned Eliezer Kaplan, who is now in New York after touring the United States to raise funds for our urgent needs in Palestine and our work in liberated Europe. So far he has received more promises than hard cash, but hopes the situation will improve before he leaves for home.

His basic concern is to set up a central organization for raising funds in a proper, comprehensive manner. Of necessity it will be situated in New York. This organization will have to be capable of meeting the greatest need of the time: dealing with the dire situation of the Holocaust survivors, for whose settlement in Palestine prompt action and funds are demanded, of a kind never before required in our people's history. Although Kaplan has not yet completed his discussions with different Jewish agencies, including the Joint Distribution Committee, he finds on the whole both sympathetic understanding and willingness on everyone's part to meet at least a substantial proportion of our needs. Ben-Gurion will soon come to New York, and there will then be a thorough discussion of all the tasks facing the American Zionist movement at this testing-hour in Jewish history.

I reported to Kaplan on events in San Francisco, saying I regret that he cannot be here himself to see our scene of operations firsthand and to evaluate the gravity of the problems that beset us. These problems, I believe, can only grow more acute with the increase in Arab political strength, aggravated by the British policy of building up the Arab League. I also regret Moshe Shertok's absence: he could have seen the situation at close quarters and come to know personally some of the statesmen taking part in deliberations of interest to us and effecting decisions of international importance. As things have developed here, in the future we will have to keep in touch with a number of delegates and seek their support for our political struggles, whenever and wherever they are carried on internationally in defense of our interests.

Kaplan intimated that he knows about Goldmann's suggestion that I stay on for a while in the United States to join the Jewish Agency's Political Office in Washington, which will have to be properly organized to combat Arab influence in the capital effectively. Kaplan favors the idea.

I spent the whole evening writing. Rose Halprin, a Hadassah leader, had asked me to prepare material on the Arab question for publication and distribution among the leading members of her organization. Officially Hadassah has accepted the Biltmore Program, but there are members who support, in greater or lesser measure, the B'rit Shalom group in Palestine, who favor a solution along the lines suggested by Dr. Magnes and his associates. This could lead, in Mrs. Halprin's opinion, to a division in her own organization just when all efforts should be directed toward maintaining the unity of the Zionist camp in America and rallying all the influence it possesses in favor of Jewish statehood. A comprehensive analysis of the Arab question has therefore become an urgent necessity, she explained to me. It is also important, Mrs. Halprin stressed, for reliable information on the subject to reach all parties and organizations in the Zionist movement itself and the wider public of the United States, Jewish and non-Jewish.

Tuesday, June 5

Beeley informed me that the Trusteeship Committee over the past few days has not discussed the Russian and Arab proposals. Although the subject has not been stricken from the agenda, no one has asked that it be considered. The Iraqi delegate on the committee, who requested the postponement on the ground that "more time is needed for further study," has not indicated since then that the study has been completed.

Beeley stressed that we should certainly not look on this as a Russian retreat, still less as an Arab retreat; both remain committed to the renewal of a full-scale discussion of the matter in the Trusteeship Committee itself and beyond. They may well judge that conditions are ripe for reopening the struggle either at Commission II or at the plenary session of the General Assembly. Since the conference will probably go on until the end of the month, it is possible that a number of committees, including the Trusteeship Committee, will take an additional couple of weeks to complete their work. Until then the initiative to renew the discussion or not will be in the hands of the Russians and the Arabs. However, the request to renew it, from whatever quarter it comes, will be met by the firm opposition of the committee's chairman. His position will be supported by the majority of the committee, who do not question the decision already made with only Arab opposition. Assuming that, the Arabs may choose to carry their struggle to Commission II rather than face another defeat in the committee.

Beeley again voiced his confidence that neither paragraph 5 nor its wording is in any danger. The position of the British, American, French, and Chinese delegations is absolutely clear to the Russians. They can expect nothing tangible from their move, even if for propaganda reasons they stick to their proposals.

I met Senator Richard H. Nash, an Australian delegate, who is a leading member of the Labour party in his country. He mentioned that he has heard a great deal from his many countrymen serving in the Middle East about Zionist achievements and the contribution the labor movement in Palestine has made to the social and economic progress of the region. He noted in particular that all the Australians who have visited our agricultural settlements have returned home as devoted friends of our cause, especially those who have seen the social backwardness and the exploitation of labor in the neighboring countries. The Australian command in the Middle East, he said, has had many words of praise for the military efforts of the Yishuv, an island of devotion and loyalty to the democracies' war effort in a sea of espionage, subversion, and deceit.

I spoke to Nash about our problems and the grave crisis we have reached in our relations with the Mandatory government since the publication of the white paper of 1939. He believes that if the Labour party wins the coming elections in the United Kingdom there may be a complete change in the white-paper policies, which were the result of the totally discredited appeasement philosophy of Neville Chamberlain. Nash said that among the leaders of the labor movement in Britain there is an understanding of and appreciation for Zionist endeavors. What we have done, he thinks, is seen to be of benefit not only to Jews but to Arabs as well, for we are an example and challenge to them to overcome the obstacles standing in the way of their social and economic progress, obstacles that are unsettling to the stability of the region as a whole. Nash hopes to visit Palestine soon and see our work for himself.

Maurice Cohen, the "Chinese General," invited me to meet Hu Lin, editor of the popular Chinese newspaper *Ta Kung Pao*, who is a member of the People's Political Council. Cohen described him as one of the key men in the Chinese delegation and a personal friend of Generalissimo Chiang Kai-shek's.

Hu Lin's scrupulous politeness and his formal yet kindly way of speaking reveal his Mandarin origins. In English that is fluent (although hard to follow because of his accent) Hu Lin said that he has read extensively about Palestine and knows, too, of how the Jews have suffered since Hitler rose to power in Germany. The Chinese, he said, have good reason to understand Jewish suffering because of his own people's experience under the Japanese occupation. The Japanese were no better, he said, than the Nazis: the culture of both Germany and Japan rested on an unrestricted, selfish conception of their national destiny in the world rather than on established principles of morality, humanity, and justice with regard to relations with other peoples. Both the weakness and strength of China have expressed themselves throughout history in the unceasing search to reconcile the matter and spirit in the life of the individual and society. "We have not achieved the goal and perhaps never will," Hu Lin said, adding that the very pursuit of that objective has been important in the life of his people, preserving their spirit and shielding them from the many internal and external dangers that have beset China throughout generations. He knows, too, that the Jewish people bases its existence on deeply rooted faith and adherence to the values of righteousness and justice. He has nothing but respect for the capacity we have shown to overcome the many sufferings and obstacles in our path, particularly in renewing our national life in the land of our forefathers. He went on to ask me a series of questions about the cultural life of the Jewish community in Palestine, our educational institutions, and the press. He promised to print an article on Zionism in his paper and to visit Palestine himself if he is ever in the vicinity.

I lunched with Yalçin and found him disappointed at what he has seen at the conference. He feels all the signs show that, as in the past, the new United Nations will act as a thin cover for the Great Powers' policy of selfishness and naked force. Each of the powers will continue to follow its usual two-faced course in traditional power-politics fashion—one face for the "closed club" of the Great Powers and the other for international forums, which will remain, as in the days of the League of Nations, limited and of little significance for reaching binding decisions in matters of importance.

There is a danger, said Yalçin, that the USSR, which has enjoyed an elevated status since the war as a power of force and influence, may sabotage arrangements based on mutual trust in international relations. This would be a tragedy for mankind. After the horrors of the Hitler tyranny, the new world organization ought to be able to order international affairs in a comprehensive framework so as to guarantee a stable and lasting peace among peoples, but there is uncertainty over the intentions of Stalin and his entire regime. Yalçin has no confidence in a settlement in which one major power is subverting others and in which Russia is seeking territorial expansion rather than peace. He thinks that the Soviet ruler will try to utilize his military power in both Europe and Asia to extend his frontiers whenever he thinks he can get away with it.

I had never before seen Yalçin so tense and pessimistic. He feels that the Yishuv should not set its hopes too high as far as the United Nations is concerned. He believes that French behavior in Syria has shown a lack of political sense, for it will lead not only to the questioning of France's prestige by Muslims and Arabs elsewhere, especially in French North Africa, but also to further tension in France's relations with Great Britain and the United States as a result of the present crisis in the Levant. As for the Arab League, Yalçin thinks its establishment will strengthen overall Arab aspirations and demands. Britain, in his opinion, will find no joy in the Arab League. Sooner or later there is bound to be conflict between the league's sponsor and the Arab states, who before long will seek to develop closer relations with another Great Power, probably the United States, in order to balance their position and exploit whenever possible the conflicting interests of both Britain and the U.S. in the Middle East. The Turks have had many generations of experience in dealing with the Arabs and have come to learn how much the Arabs lack stability and endurance. Arab emotions are often far stronger than their reasoning and prevent continuity in their actions and behavior. Yalçin said that the famous medieval Arab historian, ibn-Khaldun, one of the greatest of all Islamic scholars, recognized this weakness in the Arab character and described it in his works. Time, said Yalçin, has brought no change in the situation: the Arabs by and large are still as they were in ibn-Khaldun's day.

This was one of my longest and most absorbing talks with Yalçin, a wise and cultured man. We parted in the hope that we will see each other again when I next visit Turkey.

Wednesday, June 6

Foy Kohler confirmed that the Arab League is preparing to open a Washington office. I gather from what he said that the State Department is concerned over the situation in Syria and fears the spread of fighting to Lebanon. I sensed from his remarks that the United States is not indifferent to the events in these countries; but apparently it is still too early to judge the situation thoroughly and in sufficient depth to determine a long-term policy and not simply respond to events as they take place. Kohler believes that with the end of the war a completely new chapter has opened in the Middle East. America's responsibilities in international affairs will be much greater than before, and this new situation, Kohler thinks, necessitates more comprehensive knowledge and radically different methods from those America employed in its isolationist period. He mentioned the setting up of special teams in most of the State Department's geographical sections to look into the problems of each area, assist in devising policy, and suggest how it can be realized. In our area American interests used to be confined mainly to trade and culture, and the political activities of the United States in the Middle East hardly went beyond such concern. Now it is necessary to repair this omission.

I was glad to hear Kohler say that a good friend of mine, Joseph Satterthwait, is coming to Washington from service at the American embassy in Ankara to join a team working on the Middle East.

My conversation with Kohler underscored the importance

of our work in Washington with the State Department and with other branches of the United States government involved in studying the different aspects of the Middle East situation. Undoubtedly, the results of this research will influence in one way or another the overall policy that the United States will adopt in our region. I reported on my talk to Goldmann and also took care to see that the information reached Jerusalem and London.

My Lebanese friend Charles Corm has sent me a letter of recommendation to Jamil Baroody,[78] his brother-in-law, and to Yacub Rafaël, editor of the Arabic newspaper *Al-Akhlaq,* which appears irregularly in New York.

Corm, a distinguished poet, is a popular figure in the social and cultural life of Beirut. He has for many years devoted himself to the cause of restoring the Lebanese to their "Phoenician origins" and freeing themselves from their ties to Arabism. He and Albert Naqqash—scion of one of the best-known Maronite families in Lebanon and former minister of public works—have set up the Society of Young Phoenicians, whose objectives are to revive and spread knowledge of Phoenician culture among the Lebanese. The archaeological discoveries at Tel Ras-Shamra near Latakia (in Syria) and the rich literary material in Ugaritic that came to light there inspired the group. Corm and his friends often cite the example set by the Zionist revival of the ancient Hebrew culture as a challenge to the "Phoenicians" in neighboring Lebanon. In one of his publications Corm portrayed the Society of Young Phoenicians as "Lebanese Zionism," advocating the establishment of close ties between his organization and the Zionist movement.

[78]Later the Saudi Arabian delegate to the United Nations.

When the late Dr. Victor Jacobson[79] visited Beirut in 1932 as an emissary of the Jewish Agency, he lectured to the Society of Young Phoenicians. Its members enthusiastically endorsed his hope for the renewal of neighborly relations— between the Jews of Palestine and the Lebanese—as in the days of Kings Solomon and Hiram! The biblical example took a practical turn when, at the end of the 1930s, a group led by Charles Corm and Albert Naqqash was founded in Beirut, with the object of drawing the Yishuv and Lebanon closer together and promoting joint social and cultural activities. The idea of a Lebanese-Jewish association was welcomed by us, and Moshe Shertok took it upon himself to prepare a set of guidelines.

Albert Naqqash, an engineer, had also proposed the establishment of a Jewish-Lebanese company to exploit the waters of the Litani River for irrigation and electric power to be used for development purposes in both Lebanon and Palestine. The Palestine Economic Corporation (of the U.S.) was interested in the project and sent its Palestine representative, Julius Simon, and the corporation's engineer, Isaac Wilentchuk, to investigate the idea in situ with Albert Naqqash. The project had a reasonable chance of success, despite the opposition from the French authorities in Lebanon, who suspected a British plot. Meanwhile the war broke out, and the project had to be shelved.

I wrote today to Corm and promised to look up his brother-in-law, a wealthy businessman active in Arab cir-

[79]Victor Jacobson (1869–1934); manager of Beirut office of the Anglo-Palestine Company (1906); political representative of the World Zionist Organization in Constantinople and director of Anglo-Levantine Banking (1908); member of the Zionist executive (1913–21, 1933); WZO representative at the League of Nations (1925); in a secret memorandum (1932) suggested the partition of Palestine.

cles in the United States, and his friend, the editor of *Al-Akhlaq*.

I met a number of correspondents from the New York Yiddish press and spoke to them about the great importance of keeping their readers well informed on the grave problems facing the Yishuv, both political and economic. In explaining the character of our relations with the British government, I stressed the vital and urgent need for the abolition of all restrictions on immigration, to enable us to receive the survivors of the Holocaust in the shortest possible time and to integrate them constructively into our social and economic fabric. I was especially interested in getting the *Forward* to publish what I said, since it has a wide circulation and is influential among Jewish labor groups and organizations associated with the AFL.

I attended a press conference called by the Indian delegation. The advertised speakers were to be Sir A. Ramaswami Mudaliar, the delegation's chairman, and Sir Firoz Khan Noon. However, before Mudaliar had finished his introductory remarks, members of the American Committee for an Independent India caused a disturbance and prevented the conference from continuing. They regard Mudaliar and Firoz Khan Noon as "lackeys of British imperialism," subverting the unity of the Indian people in its fight for independence.

My Indian journalist friend, Singh, told me after the press conference that the Indian Congress party is about to mount a broad information campaign in the United States, and to this end is sending over Vijaya Lakshmi Pandit, Nehru's elder sister, a highly cultured person and an excellent speaker. Mrs. Pandit will try to win the support of American public opinion, including the editors of the country's leading newspapers, for the political struggle by Gandhi and his followers. Singh claims that many American politicians support the Congress party, and no doubt Mrs. Pandit will use their influence with the White House and the State Department to get them to put pressure on Britain to leave India. The chief opponent of Indian independence, in Singh's opinion, is Churchill, and as long as he is prime minister the Congress party's chances of success are poor. Congress party leaders look forward to the election of a Labour government in Britain. Only then, they think, can India win the sort of settlement Gandhi is striving for.

Singh knows Mrs. Pandit personally and suggested that I meet her if I am still in America when she arrives. The Indian national movement, Singh believes, would appreciate any help it might receive from the Jewish public and press in America. Singh mentioned that Congressman Emanuel Celler of New York, who in a number of speeches in the House of Representatives had expressed his warm support for Indian independence, is widely popular and respected in India.

Si Kenen told us about a tour of San Francisco Bay organized by the Saudi Arabian delegation for leading American journalists covering the conference. The entertainment was lavish beyond description, and only at the end of the spree did it emerge that the occasion had been arranged and paid for by the oil companies. The seagoing merriment was certainly not in keeping with traditional Wahhabi puritanism, but this did not seem to bother the Arabs aboard, who toasted the journalists drink for drink with something rather stronger than lemonade or Coca-Cola. The party was a huge success.

I had a pleasant conversation with Louis Lipsky, who asked me which books I felt had influenced Zionist thought the most. I mentioned the historical novel *Ahavat Tzion* (The Love of Zion) by Abraham Mapu, Leo Pinsker's *Auto-Emancipation,* and Theodor Herzl's *Der Judenstaat* (The Jewish State). To these Lipsky added Louis Brandeis's book on Zionism. The fact that so eminent and respected an American figure as Justice Brandeis was a Zionist, and that his Zionist convictions did not infringe upon his American loyalties, has had a great impact, Lipsky believes, on many sections of American Jewry, including the youth.[80]

Lipsky asked me about Mapu. I told him that my maternal great-grandfather, Rabbi Eliahu Ragoler (Kalisher), a rabbi in Ragoleh in Lithuania and then in Kalish, had been Mapu's teacher. My great-grandfather was the author of several religious works. He attached great importance to a close study of the Bible. This could well have contributed to Mapu's prodigious knowledge of Scripture and to the development of his style.[81]

[80]Brandeis had written: "Let no American imagine that Zionism is inconsistent with patriotism. . . . There is no inconsistency between loyalty to America and loyalty to Jewry. The Jewish spirit, the product of our religion and experiences, is essentially modern and essentially American. . . . Indeed, loyalty to America demands rather that each American Jew become a Zionist. For only through the ennobling effect of its strivings can we develop the best that is in us and give to this country the full benefit of our great inheritance" (Louis D. Brandeis, *Brandeis on Zionism,* New York, 1942, pp. 28–29).

[81]Ben-Zion Dinur wrote about the connection between Rabbi Eliahu Ragoler (1794–1850) and Mapu (1808–67): "[Mapu] was a dedicated pupil, and a frequent visitor in the home of Rabbi Eliahu Kalisher, one of the most famous rabbis of the day. . . . The lad was gifted and excelled in his application to Torah studies" (*Letters of Abraham Mapu* [in Hebrew]), (Jerusalem: Mosad Bialik), 1970, p. 12.

Thursday, June 7

In our consultations this morning Goldmann and Lipsky reported on their contacts with delegation leaders and with the chairman of the Trusteeship Committee. They were told that there is not the smallest chance of the Russian-Arab proposals on paragraph 5 being adopted by the conference at any stage of further deliberations, including the plenary session of the General Assembly. The American, British, and French delegations, in suppressing the Russian and Arab attempts to undermine the position of mandatory regimes whose futures have not been determined, are moved by considerations of self-interest. It is our good fortune that in so vital a matter for us we have found not only the United States and France but also Great Britain firm in their demand for the integrity of the existing mandates, particularly considering the British hostility to us on countless occasions in discharging its Mandate responsibilities. Does the British position in San Francisco signify a change in interpretation of its obligations toward the Jewish national home under the Mandate, or is there nothing behind it except mere selfish considerations—dictated by the introduction of the trusteeship system, which jeopardizes the existing rights of Britain itself in Palestine? Further developments in our relations with the Mandatory government shall make the matter clearer, for better or for worse.

We held a postmortem on our work at the conference. I summarized the contacts I have made since arriving in San Francisco and mentioned some of my conclusions. I stressed the dangers we shall be facing henceforth from the five Arab states in the United Nations and in its various agencies and committees. I remarked on the Arab League's intention of setting up a permanent office in the United States and the threat that this will present, especially since the Arab office will be backed by the immensely rich and politically powerful American oil companies with concessions in Arab territories, whose representatives are in close touch with the State Department section in charge of affairs in our part of the world. Finally, I noted the American dominance in international affairs, now greater than ever, and suggested that we concentrate as much as possible on fully utilizing the opportunities this affords.

Goldmann and Lipsky praised the close cooperation among the major Jewish bodies present in San Francisco in a common and coordinated defense of Jewish rights in Palestine. They also mentioned the contribution made by the Palestine emissaries in different fields of the Jewish Agency's activities during the conference. Dr. Jacob Robinson, who placed his wide-ranging knowledge and rich practical experience in international affairs at the disposal of the Jewish Agency, was paid special tribute.

Lipsky is due to leave San Francisco today and Goldmann tomorrow. We decided that I should stay on a few extra days to follow events of interest to us.

In a letter to Ze'ev Sharef[82] at the Political Department of the Jewish Agency in Jerusalem, sent before the recent crisis in the Trusteeship Committee, I had written:

My view is that we should do all we can to see that a political settlement of the Palestine question is not delayed much

[82]Ze'ev Sharef (1906–); secretary of the cabinet of the Israel government (1948–57); minister of finance, trade and commerce, and housing in several governments; director of the Tefaḥot Bank.

longer. The international outlook as seen from this end is rather gloomy, and there is little sign that it will improve. With the end of the war the Middle East has entered into an era of far-reaching developments of international importance; this in addition to its own internal realities and problems. The Arab world is in ferment and may rely for advancing its objectives on factors operating on the international scene more than on its own ability to achieve these objectives. Events in Syria have again shown that the Western powers are divided among themselves, a fact that the Soviet Union, and especially the Arabs themselves will try to exploit. It is safe to assume, as in the past, that international tensions cannot help us but can only help the Arabs. We learned this in the years before the war, the proof being the white paper.

In the many meetings I have had here with Arab delegates, I have noticed their growing sense of self-importance since the creation of the Arab League. They will return home with a feeling of newly acquired power and prestige on the international scene, even if this time they did not manage to secure their objective as far as Palestine is concerned. Although the Arabs failed completely on the Trusteeship Committee, their unity on the Palestine question undoubtedly impressed other delegations, including those not normally opposed to us. There was much talk at the conference on the need to encourage the establishment of regional organizations and support those already formed. You will remember that at Dumbarton Oaks guidelines like these were agreed on. Despite their failure in San Francisco to secure the UN's recognition of the Arab League as such a body, the Arabs are quite aware of how to utilize the general drift in this direction to their advantage. You have seen abundant evidence of this in Goldmann's exchange of letters with Alger Hiss, the secretary-general of the conference, which I sent on to Jerusalem. They will not give up their efforts to achieve that objective in the future.

It is worth remembering that, apart from the political dangers we face from the Arab League, there is an equally serious economic threat. If only a few of the economic projects the league's spokesmen bandy about come to anything, we will be the losers if we have not by then achieved political independence and become masters of our own economic destiny in our area in circumstances suited to our needs.

First and foremost, however, we should reflect on the condition of world Jewry, a community shocked by what has happened during the war in Europe, yet apparently lacking the power to face the challenge in a determined and large-scale constructive way rather than merely by traditional methods of charity.

There are, it seems to me, two main causes for that: the largest remaining Diaspora Jewish community in the world, that of the United States, has not yet grasped the deeper meaning of the scope of the tragedy that has overtaken our people—not in some remote corner of the world but in the heart of civilized Europe. It will take some time before the shock will lead to the recognition of what Palestine, and Palestine alone, can do. But the unsettled state of affairs regarding the future of Palestine may discourage even many who wish our cause well from looking to Palestine for the solution to the problem of resettling the survivors of Hitler's Holocaust.

In the present situation we face demands and responsibilities whose future significance cannot be exaggerated. Time could well prove the decisive factor in our ability to solve the problem of the Holocaust survivors by bringing them to Palestine. The moral and material strength of the Zionist movement will be judged by this more than by anything else, by our own and by future generations of our people. It is obvious, however, that bound as we are by the provisions of the 1939 white paper, we cannot hope to solve the problem unless a radical change in the political situation takes place.

In these circumstances we should not put off the solution of the Palestine question for long, nor should we wait for a peace conference, since nobody can even guess when it might take place or what it might deal with. As I have said, time will merely intensify Arab opposition to our claims and postpone the chances of substantial immigration to Palestine. If they cannot gain entry to Palestine within a specified period of time, the survivors of the Holocaust will have no choice but to look for other places to go to. We must also be aware of the fact that our ability to get financial help from American Jewry and elsewhere will largely depend on our practical capacity to absorb these people: the greater our contribution, the more financial help we can expect to receive.

I fear, therefore, that we cannot go on running our policy in our present manner for much longer—not because of the difficulties and embarrassment in repeatedly knocking on other people's doors, but because organized political and diplomatic activity can only function in terms of a "club" in which members are equal, a "club" that maintains an established register of general norms and a code of defined and strictly observed relations between its members. Five Arab states now sit on all international committees, enjoying free and direct access to all other members of these bodies; they can therefore exploit their normal status as sovereign states, and in addition their numerical advantage at the United Nations in negotiating and bargaining with other states. How much longer we can afford to be outside the "club" without appearing to be—even to our best friends—a nuisance?

I was rather late in getting to San Francisco. It would have been better if I had arrived here at least a week earlier, so that I might have taken part in the preliminary discussions on our agenda. I have tried to use my time as best I can: I spent little of it listening to the debates at the plenary session of the General Assembly, and instead have done much "field work" —meetings with delegates, journalists, and representatives of public bodies, some of whom, like us, have no official standing at the conference and work, as the Jewish representatives do, on its fringes, in the corridors and hotel lobbies. I have spent considerable time with Arabs, many of whom I had already known personally, and I was able to make contact with some of the Arab delegates on the basis of the personal ties between us. I also scored because in my frequent visits to neighboring countries I have made good friends in Turkey and Iran. I have been able to broaden my contacts with the official representatives of a number of European, Asian, and Latin American states, and in meeting journalists from many countries I learned a great deal about world problems. My contacts here with State Department personnel concerned with the Middle East I find particularly valuable. All in all, my few weeks in San Francisco have been very worthwhile from every point of view.

I talked to Goldmann before his return to New York. He thinks that we must fight any future attempts to exchange the Mandatory regime in Palestine for a trusteeship and that we should present the Biltmore Program to the world as the only solution to the Palestine question. Years of the mandates system under the League of Nations have taught us to expect nothing better from any other international system of government. We succeeded this time in preventing changes in the terms of the Palestine Mandate and will therefore be able to enter the next round of the political struggle resting our claims on the rights we enjoy under the Mandate. There is not much comfort in this, however, because Great Britain's anti-Zionist policies restrict our ability to meet our immigration and settlement needs (which are of vital and urgent importance to our cause) and impede our progress toward political independence.

Goldmann thinks that the broad, comprehensive information campaign we have mounted during the conference has done much to create a better understanding of our claims and has helped clear the way for gaining the support of a number of prominent delegations and men of standing and influence in international affairs. Goldmann believes that the work in San Francisco will bear fruit in future stages of our struggle and will prove no less important for us than the concrete achievement at the conference: frustrating the attempt to alter the Mandate's terms.

After the latest upheavals in the Middle East, in Goldmann's opinion there is no doubt that Palestine cannot remain for long in its present state, with independent Syria and Lebanon next door. We have to concentrate all our efforts on the political struggle for a Jewish state. Although in many ways London holds the key, we must also labor energetically in other capitals, especially in Washington, Paris, and Moscow. Particular emphasis has to be given to Washington because of the growing importance of the United States in world affairs and the Jewish community's influence in American public life. The Jewish Agency has to conduct its political work in the American capital in close contact and coordination with American Jewish organizations. Their principal task should be to assist us in mustering support and gaining friends for our cause among members of Congress and in the White House, and in winning the wider American public over to our side.

Goldmann repeated his suggestion that I stay on in America for some time and move to Washington without delay. He promised to help in every possible way to organize the political work of the Jewish Agency in the capital by setting up for that purpose a properly staffed and efficiently run office.

Goldmann suggested that on my return to New York I should discuss the matter with Kaplan, and with Ben-Gurion when he arrives in America. I would also have to ask Shertok for his opinion, of course. It is in fact Shertok who will have the last word on Goldmann's proposal.

———————

This evening I again addressed members of Hadassah, this time on the role played by the Yishuv in raising the living standards of Palestinian Arabs. I mentioned the valuable contribution of Hadassah in improving the health of the entire population of Palestine, including the Arabs. There were many questions, betraying much interest—and much ignorance! Our friends' lack of proper information on many of our basic problems could cause a great deal of damage to the Zionist movement, just when it faces a series of fateful decisions. I realized this danger when a woman asked, in good faith: "Why don't Zionist and Yishuv leaders want a settlement with the Arabs, like Dr. Magnes and his supporters do?"

Friday, June 8

My last day in San Francisco. So much has happened here, and the pace of life has been so "American," that months seem to have passed since I arrived in the United States. In the morning I bade farewell by telephone and by lightning visits to a large number of people who have been helpful to me in one way or another. I arranged to meet Foy Kohler and Charles Malik in Washington after the conference and to remain in touch with a number of others: delegates and journalists. Zev Brenner will send to me in New York, via Palcor, regular reports on conference news for as long as it lasts. This afternoon, I flew from San Francisco to New York.

New York, June 11–July 3, 1945

III *Politics and Public Relations*

Monday, June 11

Because of a shortage of hotel accommodations, I am staying in the apartment of Dorothy Thompson, who is abroad. The first of us to be put up here was Eliezer Kaplan, and I have now joined him. It is a beautiful place, packed with books and pictures of her friends. She seems to be on familiar terms with scores of famous people in different walks of life, to judge from the warm dedications written on their photographs. One such friend was the late President Roosevelt, whom Dorothy Thompson had served faithfully in his election campaigns. She also did us a valuable service in depicting the white paper as a breach of Britain's historic obligation to the Jewish people and as part of the Chamberlain government's policy of appeasing the enemies of freedom and democracy—Hitler, Mussolini, and the ex-mufti of Jerusalem, Haj Amin el-Husseini.

Kaplan and I will be using Miss Thompson's apartment for only a few days. This week she is returning to the United States, and we will have to look for other accommodations.

This morning Kaplan and I discussed Goldmann's proposal that I stay on in America to take charge of the Jewish Agency's Political Office in Washington. His immediate reaction was that there is no doubt of the United States' growing importance on the international scene or the influence it will command on major issues in world affairs, including Palestine. It demands our closest attention, he said, to determine what we should do to face the challenge.

I gave Kaplan my impressions of my meetings with Arabs in San Francisco and told him about their self-confidence, which has grown with the establishment of the Arab League and with the position they enjoy at the United Nations conference. I also noted that the Turkish, Iranian, and Greek delegations are afraid of any move in our favor that might upset the Arabs. I said that the danger for us lies not so much in what the Arabs themselves may do to harm our cause, but in how strongly Britain will back them and whether the United States will remain indifferent to our pleas. I mentioned disturbing signs I detected in my talks with State Department officials, the judgments they have made on the problems in the Middle East, and the role of oil as one of the main factors in determining United States policy there. In addition, the Arab League's Washington information office will undoubtedly lead and coordinate the activities of the Arab embassies against us, relying on the moral and material support of Arab friends in the country.

Kaplan expressed full support for Goldmann's plan and proposed that I stay on for at least eight months or even a year. He suggested that I consult Ben-Gurion, who will soon arrive in America, on the matter and that I inform Shertok. In Kaplan's opinion the matter must not be put off; we have to strengthen our representation in Washington without further delay. Goldmann comes to Washington only rarely and stays briefly. There is not a single Palestinian in the office of the American Zionist Emergency Council in Washington who can present our case with either the requisite knowledge or the proper authority. Since the Arabs will soon have a Washington office specifically organized to mount anti-Zionist propaganda, the Jewish Agency representative has to be an expert in Arab affairs and au fait with Arab developments. Kaplan went on to emphasize the importance of fostering close social relations with influential people in Washington, including government officials.

When we met later at the Jewish Agency's offices in Madison Avenue, I heard Kaplan telling Goldmann that he favors the broadening of agency activity in Washington. Both will speak to Lipsky and to Ben-Gurion about my staying on in Washington for some time, as proposed by Goldmann.

I spent the late afternoon and evening with Hayim Greenberg. In the course of our long conversation he told me what the American government did, or rather how much it did not do, both before and during the war, to save Jews in Nazi hands. Much of the blame for what happened falls on President Roosevelt, his administration, and public organizations of all kinds. They all share the responsibility to various degrees for the appalling course of events. Of course, it is still difficult to reach a final conclusion on the subject, and it will certainly be a long time before all the evidence and documents come to light and allow a full investigation of what took place. However, one can already point to grievous omissions in easing the position of German Jews after Hitler's rise to power and in rescuing many by helping them to leave Germany before war broke out.

Greenberg said that when Hitler became chancellor in 1933, the leading American Jewish organizations grasped the seriousness of the threat facing German Jewry. The American Jewish Congress, the American Jewish Committee, and B'nai B'rith all asked the State Department to use diplomatic means to protect Jews from the attacks of the Nazi regime. But Secretary of State Cordell Hull regarded a diplomatic demarche, of the kind the Jewish organizations sought, to be interference in the internal affairs of Germany. It is true that under pressure from many members of Congress, particularly those representing centers of large Jewish population, sharp words of criticism were occasionally voiced by administration officials, including the president. Jewish organizations pressed repeatedly, however, for a clear and declared policy that would make Hitler realize that the United States government would not remain indifferent to what was going on—but their demands came to nothing.

Of the bodies active in marshaling American public opinion and pressuring the government on the issue, Greenberg particularly mentioned the American Jewish Congress. Its president, Dr. Stephen Wise, was aided in his endeavors by people in different walks of life, Jews and non-Jews, including leading churchmen and prominent journalists. Wise, who after 1935 was also president of the Committee of Jewish Delegations in Geneva, knew the problem better than other American Jewish leaders. After Hitler's rise to power he tried to impress his grave evaluation of the situation on the American Jewish public. The fact, however, that United States Jewry had no central body to speak on its behalf prevented agreement and joint action by Jewish organizations. The division in the Jewish camp weakened the efforts to concentrate greater public pressure on the authorities in order to get prompt and tangible results.[83]

[83]Nathan Feinberg, who was active in the Committee of Jewish Delegations at Geneva in the interwar period, in commenting on Jewish political activities against the Nazi regime in the years 1933–39, writes: "In the face of Hitler's iniquitous assault upon one of the most deeply rooted Jewish communities in Europe, . . . it might have been assumed that the central Jewish institutions set up to defend Jewish rights would rally together instantaneously and undertake joint action to repel the savage onslaught. . . . But this is not how matters developed: for . . . differences of opinion as how to react arose between the institutions. . . . Thus, the Committee of Jewish Delegations, the American Jewish Congress, and the like advocated an open and unflinching fight against the Nazi regime, . . . while institutions such as the American Jewish Committee, the Board of Deputies of British Jews, and the Anglo-Jewish Association in Great Britain and the Alliance Israélite Universelle in France were

One factor that blocked the saving of large numbers of Jews was the strict American immigration policy, which prohibited them from coming to the United States. The many and continuous efforts by American public bodies and influential individuals—both Jews and non-Jews—to change these laws failed. There were a number of reasons for this: President Roosevelt feared that by supporting the demanded changes in the immigration laws he would lose votes; William Green, president of the AFL, was afraid that large-scale immigration might lead to heavy unemployment; the conservative press was apprehensive about undesirable changes in American society; and anti-Semites in all walks of American life did little to conceal their opposition to Jews "flooding" the country.

In 1933 the League of Nations, with the official support of the United States government, had appointed an American, Professor James G. McDonald,[84] president of the American Foreign Policy Association, as high commissioner for refugees, and a fellow American, Joseph Chamberlain, was elected to the league's Council for Refugees. However, the two men soon realized that there was little point in their efforts as long as their own government refused to set an example by admitting substantial numbers of refugees from Nazi persecution. Professor McDonald resigned in 1935; Chamberlain resigned sometime later.

---

opposed to these methods; making a lot of 'noise and uproar' would, they believed, not merely not help, but would even make matters worse. . . . The state of affairs described will to a large extent explain why the political activities of the Jews in the international arena in the years 1933–39 were almost entirely carried out by the Committee of Jewish Delegations, to which the American Jewish Congress was affiliated, and subsequently—from August 1936—by its successor, the World Jewish Congress" (*Jewish Resistance during the Holocaust, Proceedings of the Conference on Manifestation of Jewish Resistance* [Jerusalem: Yad Vashem, 1971], pp. 75–76).

[84]Subsequently first United States ambassador to Israel.

Greenberg particularly cited the attempts to ease the immigration laws by Senators Robert Wagner and Edith Rogers and the Jewish members of the House of Representatives, Emanuel Celler and Samuel Dickstein. However, when they proposed legislation to this end, it was rejected in both houses of Congress since it did not have the support of the administration. President Roosevelt himself was largely responsible for the situation: from time to time he publicly expressed his regret at the suffering of German Jews but did not lift a finger to do anything concrete to help the lot of the persecuted, either by energetic diplomatic action or by supporting the easing of immigration to the United States. Greenberg went on to say that not only Palestine but also Great Britain and several South American countries each accepted more Jewish refugees, including children, than did the United States.

Not all State Department personnel, according to Greenberg, had opposed appropriate diplomatic action in defense of German Jewry. There were officials who would have been prepared to help if their superiors, and particularly their chief, the secretary of state, had backed them up. Cordell Hull, however, remained intransigent during his entire term of office on that matter, as on so many other matters connected with American policy of interest to Jews, including the question of Palestine.

Greenberg thinks that the energy expended by the Jewish public in organizing a boycott of German goods (whose effect in the end was small) would have been better spent in applying more pressure on the White House. This was especially true after the failure of the Evian Conference in July 1938, which demonstrated the impotence of the international community, principally the United States, in assisting the persecuted Jews in Europe. The conference had been summoned at the initiative of the United States, but because the American government presented the delegates with no tangible proposals proportional to the problem either in scale or substance, no other government stirred itself to do so. At this juncture there was an opportunity for Jewish organizations to reveal President Roosevelt's two-facedness and to try to rouse American public opinion against what was going on. The emergency demanded radical, effective action, but nothing of this kind emerged and each Jewish organization continued, as in the past, on its own separate way without even coordinating what it did with other Jewish bodies. The American Jewish Committee strove for worthless programs for the settlement of Jews outside the United States, while Zionists, naturally enough, fought against the 1939 white paper and for the opening of Palestine's doors to large-scale immigration "by right and not on sufferance."

As for what happened during the war, Greenberg thinks it is still hard to get the full story. It will probably be a long time before the whole truth is revealed, before we can judge the responsibility of America and the Allies in not coming to the rescue of Jews in German-occupied Europe when it was still possible to save many of them.

After I left Greenberg, I thought long and hard about what he had said. I reflected that from 1933 on, the small and struggling Yishuv has absorbed more Jews than any other country—despite the Arab revolt and obstruction by the British authorities. Who knows how many more lives we could have saved if a Jewish state had come into being before 1939?

Tuesday, June 12

Zev Brenner wired from San Francisco that the Arab delegations are for the moment preoccupied with the question of Syria and Lebanon and are not concerning themselves with Palestine. An apparent rift has opened between the Syrian and Lebanese delegations over the question of tactics vis-à-vis France, and Arab League members have forced Charles Malik to issue a statement indicating that there is "complete understanding" between the Syrians and Lebanese in their assessments of the situation in their respective countries. Brenner also apprised me of the activity of Carlos Romulo of the Philippines, who has been calling for clauses in the Trusteeship Chapter of the United Nations Charter which, if adopted, would be to our detriment.

I had lunch with Judge Joseph M. Proskauer at the Harmony Club, one of the most prestigious—and wealthiest—private Jewish clubs in the United States. Before we even sat down my host remarked, whether in jest or in earnest, that I am one of the very few non-German Jews whom he has ever invited to a meal at the club. Nearly all the club's six hundred members belong to Jewish families of German origin, and, as in most private clubs founded by German Jews, the Harmony Club's official language was German until World War I. The admission of new members is a complicated procedure, and there is a long waiting list, evidence of the club's status and public importance.

I expressed surprise at the name "Harmony," a term signi-
fying, it seems to me, the very opposite of the club's exclusive character. Proskauer replied with a question, again half
serious, half joking: is there no discrimination in the Zionist
movement, for is it not run by East Europeans—Weizmann,
Ben-Gurion, and Stephen Wise, who were born in Russia,
Poland, and Hungary respectively? I recalled the strained
relations between Proskauer and Wise and was not surprised
by this kind of allusion to one of the most courageous and
dedicated figures in public American Jewish life.

We discussed American politics, and Proskauer told me
that he had been a friend of and worker for Alfred E. Smith,
the former governor of New York and Democratic presidential candidate in 1928; now, however, he doubts the party's
chances of remaining in power. He thinks that President
Truman has little prospect of election when his present term
as Roosevelt's successor ends. After a long period of radical
New Deal policies, America needs balance and stability, particularly in the economic and financial spheres. He advocates
less government interference in the life of the individual and
society and greater freedom for personal initiative.

I asked Proskauer whether he thinks the Yishuv will suffer
if the Republican party comes to power. He replied that this
might be to our advantage since the Republicans will be
more independent of British influence than the Democrats.
There are many leading personalities in the Democratic
party, he believes, who are inclined to accept uncritically any
idea emanating from London—probably not Truman himself
but some of his advisers, especially people in policy-making
positions in the State Department.

Proskauer is obviously pleased with his own and the
American Jewish Committee's work in San Francisco, describing it as one of the major contributions to the needs of
the Jewish people at this time by a Jewish organization. He
again said he will pursue his opposition to the white paper,

but without linking his fight to any special political ideology. I tried to explain—this time with greater emphasis on the fact that the origins of the white paper lay primarily in British political considerations—that there will be no prospect of the restrictions contained in the white paper being lifted without a radical change in the British government's entire Palestine policy. He retorted that there is no point in making it more difficult for the British government to come toward us on practical issues by presenting political demands stemming from the Biltmore Program, especially now that Arab pressure has grown with the establishment of the Arab League. I charged that the league itself is the outcome of British policy, but Proskauer seemed puzzled by my approach. He is quite ignorant, it appears, about the background of the league's formation and about Britain's role in the matter.

Once again I discovered how necessary it is to enlighten even as prominent and influential a Jewish leader as Proskauer on major points connected with the Palestine question. I also suspect that the views of many people in different, and especially opposing, camps are often colored by their personal jealousies and rivalries and not merely by political differences. This holds true, as I have already learned, in the Zionist camp as well.

Abraham Dickenstein, founder of the Ampal Company and its U.S. representative, introduced me to Edmund Kaufmann, former president of the Zionist Organization of America. He has given up his official position in the ZOA but continues to help the movement's efforts in any way he can. Kaufmann is practically the only Zionist leader who lives in Washington, and he has many contacts in the administration. I was glad to be introduced to him, because if I move to Washington I will certainly have to rely on the assistance of local people.

Chatting with Kaufmann, I learned that he is a descendant of Karl Marx and that his family still has in its possession some of the personal effects of the author of *Das Kapital*. Dickenstein told me that Kaufmann, who has strayed quite a distance from the ideological precepts of his illustrious forebear, has amassed a substantial *Kapital* of his own through his chain of jewelry and watch shops, and is regarded as a pillar of the Jewish community of Washington. Kaufmann seemed affable and friendly, but his questions and remarks showed that, like many other good and dedicated Zionists in this country, he knows very little about Palestine.

During our long talk this evening, Arthur Lourie reviewed with me the situation in the American Zionist Emergency Council. Dr. Abba Hillel Silver's resignation from the presidency has weakened the AZEC just when the Zionist movement in this country has to close ranks and rally all its forces to meet the challenge it is facing vis-à-vis the Palestine problem. Silver is close to Republican party circles and has very influential friends among its leadership. These ties are of great importance, for most Zionist leaders have good relations with the Democratic party, and only a few have any worthwhile connections with the Republicans. Lourie favors Goldmann's plan to broaden the Jewish Agency's political arm in Washington and to put me in charge of its office there. He told me of the AZEC's Washington activities and described the people in charge of the activities.

Friday, June 15

I spent the past few days as a guest at the Long Island estate of the parents of Archibald Roosevelt, a quiet and pleasant retreat a short distance from New York City. Archie, as everybody calls him, holds the post of assistant military attaché at the American legation in Iraq, and has been a member of the party accompanying the Iraqi regent on his visit to the United States. Archie's father, the only surviving son of former president Theodore Roosevelt, is presently with the army in the Pacific. His mother greeted me. She showed me around the lovely house, which, she explained, used to belong to Theodore Roosevelt, who spent most of his life here. I glanced around the large living room at the photographs of the young Teddy Roosevelt and was struck by the resemblance that Archie bears to his grandfather.

The colonial-style house, surrounded by a large and beautiful garden, dates from before the American War of Independence. Mrs. Roosevelt told me, with some measure of pride, that in his memoirs George Washington mentioned the big tree that still stands beside the stream running through the estate. Indeed, the past is a palpable presence everywhere here. On the walls of all the rooms and hallways hang portraits of the first Roosevelts to reach America from Holland. Behind the glass in one of the cupboards is a display of gifts given by George Washington to the Roosevelt family in recognition of their help during the Revolution. One room contains a display of objects connected with the action-filled life of Theodore Roosevelt.

Archie's parents, Republican Roosevelts, are very conservative. So I was not surprised when, in the course of a dinner discussion on America's postwar role, my hostess commented that she hopes that in the future the United States will get involved abroad only when its vital security is at stake.

I found Mrs. Roosevelt's views quite interesting. During my stay in the United States I have encountered mostly Democratic supporters, and it would be easy to make the mistake of assuming that isolationism has disappeared from the American scene. Apparently, Republican senator Arthur Vandenberg's support for FDR's foreign policy is not universal among members of his party.

Archie spoke to me about tensions in Iraq. The government there does not have enough control over events or over the communal and social processes that more than ever threaten the country's political and general stability. He thinks that the Soviet Union will seek to play the role once played by Nazi Germany in exploiting Iraq's internal problems—the country is wracked by conflicts between Shi'ites and Sunnites, Arabs and Kurds, villagers and city dwellers. Archie also mentioned the Kurdish problem, which, in his opinion, constitutes a threat to the stability of the northern and eastern flanks of the Fertile Crescent as great as that posed by Palestine in the western and southern flanks. These two problems, Kurdish nationalism and Jewish aspirations in Palestine, he concluded, will probably bring on severe crises in the entire area unless acceptable solutions can be found.

I went to dinner this evening to the home of Emanuel Neumann[85] and his wife. We discussed the problem of our relations with the Arabs and the difficulties we may encounter
with the Arab camp united and Egypt ambitious to run the
Arab League's affairs.Neumann also talked about the American public's lack of understanding regarding Arab intentions,
and he stressed the importance of Zionist educational efforts
to counter the growing propaganda of Arab sympathizers in
the United States.

Theirs is a warm and hospitable Jewish home. Mrs. Neumann is a gracious hostess and her husband a very knowledgeable and shrewd man. He speaks perfect Hebrew and
has a distinguished record as a Zionist leader in America. The
few years he spent in Palestine have contributed much to his
practical perception of our problems.

Sunday, June 17

This afternoon I addressed the conference of the Geverk-
shaften Campaign of the Histadrut on the political situation.
I spoke in Yiddish, not without considerable difficulty. However, perhaps because of my effort to use a language so dear
to the hearts of many of the listeners, I received a warm
reception. Eliezer Kaplan also addressed the gathering,

[85]Emanuel Neumann (1893–   ); president of the ZOA
(1947–49, 1956–58); member of the Jewish Agency executive (in the
1930s) in Jerusalem; member of American Section (from 1946), its
permanent chairman (from 1968); president of the World Union of
General Zionists (from 1963).

speaking on the Yishuv's current needs and tasks—above all, the rescue of the remnant of the Holocaust, who must find a home in Palestine. There were many other speeches too, about what Histadrut efforts have achieved in the U.S., but I came away with the feeling that some of the prominent Jewish leaders in the American trade-union movement play no direct part in the Histadrut's activities. The position of influence attained by the trade unions in the era of the New Deal, and the important role that people like Sidney Hillman and David Dubinsky, who are Jews, play in the labor organizations and in political affairs in general, including the formulation of U.S. foreign policy—all this makes it imperative to try to win their active personal support for our cause. I detected certain signs at San Francisco and again at this conference that lead me to hope that, with the right approach, we may break down many of the barriers which have kept apart the Zionists and the various Jewish workers' groups in America. The influence of the anti-Zionist Bund is still certainly being felt in these circles, but there is apparently no longer the same boundless hostility between the Bund and its supporters and the members of the Labor Zionist movement as in the past.

Monday, June 18

This morning, at Dr. Stephen Wise's suggestion, I visited Senator Robert Wagner at his New York office. Dr. Wise has spoken highly of him and of his dedicated work as chairman of the American Committee for Palestine. Wagner is close to President Truman, and when the latter was in the Senate,

Wagner on a number of occasions gained his support on Zionist issues.

The senator greeted me warmly, but some of his questions about the Palestine situation soon betrayed the fact that he too does not realize fully the grave difficulties that the white-paper policies have been causing us, or the threat that the white paper represents to our endeavors to secure our future. I tried to get him to see that without political independence we cannot hope to make progress in the two essential aspects of our work: immigration and settlement. It is these that the Arabs oppose, and British policy has been tailored to Arab desires to strangle Zionist aspirations. I told him that the present trends in British foreign policy in the Middle East and the creation (with active British assistance) of the Arab League do not increase the prospects in our favor.

Wagner listened closely, and then said: "It is well known all over the world that Jews cherish democracy and human rights. All that you have said is serious enough, but what about the protection of the rights of the minority in Palestine?" I thought he meant that in the final settlement of the Palestine problem the status of the Jewish community in Palestine would remain that of a permanent minority and that proper guarantees should be incorporated in the settlement to secure its rights. I explained that for the Jewish community to remain a permanent minority in Palestine was contrary to our national aspirations and conflicted with the promises of the Balfour Declaration, which formed part of the terms of the Mandate.

The senator heard me out, then persisted with his question: "That is all very well, but why will you not grant minority rights to the Arabs?" I naturally thought he meant in the future, when we become the majority in the country, and I referred to the decisions of the Zionist Congresses on that point and the numerous official statements made by

Zionist leaders regarding the rights of the Arabs in the future Jewish state.

At this point Wagner began to show some impatience. "From what you tell me, it looks as though your intentions to deal with the rights of the Arab minority in Palestine is not a matter for your present concern but to be put off into the future." Only then did I grasp that the chairman of the American Committee for Palestine was not at all sure who constitutes the majority in the country, Jews or Arabs. I cautiously explained the present demographic composition of the country, taking care not to offend him by alluding to his ignorance in this vital matter.

We then spoke about developments in the Arab camp. Wagner asked me what has become of the Arab "who caused the Jews so much misery and cooperated with the Nazis." I gathered that he meant the ex-mufti of Jerusalem, Haj Amin el-Husseini, and I told him what I know of his whereabouts. The senator promised to speak to the secretary of state on the subject, to ask that the United States government not remain indifferent to the ex-mufti's fate and demand that French authorities hold him in custody until he stands trial alongside other war criminals.

Wagner mentioned his efforts to assist victims of Nazi persecution prior to the war, when it was still possible to save many of them by an easing of American immigration laws. During the war, too, he tried to secure entry for Jews whose lives were in jeopardy in Europe. He went on to say, smilingly, that in his lifetime he had certainly committed many sins, but he still hoped to get to heaven because of the staunch advocacy of Jews whom he had saved and who would testify before the Almighty in his favor.

When I rose to take my leave, Wagner said that all his life he has supported the free rights of every individual group and people. As a good Christian, he feels it to be his duty to do all he can to assist the return of Jews to their homeland; he added that we can continue to depend on his help in the future. He also said that President Truman is endowed with a keen sense of humanity and justice, and after what has happened to the Jews under Hitler, we will find the president an attentive listener to our just claims and appeals.

I lunched with Louis Lipsky. I gathered that both Goldmann and Kaplan had already told him of the plan to put me in charge of the Political Office of the Jewish Agency in Washington. Lipsky fully supports the idea, stressing the value of my experience in Arab affairs, which he thinks will help me in meetings with Arab experts in the State Department and elsewhere in the administration, and also in presenting our case to public figures and the press. I told Lipsky of my talk with Wagner, and he said he is not surprised in the least. Wagner's speeches, as so often happens in American public life, are usually written for him by others more knowledgeable than he on a particular subject: he merely reads what is put in front of him. Lipsky does not doubt Wagner's sincerity toward Zionism, but his value to us does not lie in the degree of his knowledge about Palestine, but in the status he enjoys as a highly respected and influential senator.

I spent the evening with emissaries of Yishuv organizations and political parties attached to general Jewish and Zionist youth associations in America. I told them about the situation in Palestine and about my impressions of the San Francisco conference. Moshe Furmansky, from Kibbutz Mishmar Ha-emek, spoke to me after the meeting about the growing interest of American Jewish youth in Jewish subjects, a development prompted, in his opinion, by their shock at events in Europe and by their recognition that Palestine is the only solution to the problem of the survivors. Furmansky has found a great interest in the social problems of the Yishuv, and especially in the kibbutz movement, among Jewish students. He thinks we stand a good chance of turning many young Jews in this country into Zionists, some of whom may decide to settle in Palestine. But our success will depend on systematic, continuous, and comprehensive educational work, calling for suitable, high-level instructors from Palestine with a fluent command of English. I heard many words of praise for Furmansky, who has won the respect of all the Zionist circles in New York.[86]

Tuesday, June 19

I spent much of the morning in the offices of the AZEC, where I read political material that had apparently not reached Jerusalem before I left. In one of the files I found a copy of the letter Senator Wagner sent to President Truman on April 18, 1945, expressing appreciation for the help President Roosevelt had given Zionism. The letter highlighted the late president's support for a Jewish commonwealth in Palestine, mentioning that on March 16, 1945, on his return from Yalta, President Roosevelt had declared to the Zionist leader Dr. Stephen Wise his continuing adherence to his previously stated position on the Palestine question. Senator Wagner hoped that President Truman would follow the same path. I did not find the president's reply to Wagner's letter.

In another file I came across interesting material on the

[86]After his return to Palestine, Furmansky was killed during an Arab attack on his kibbutz in 1948.

stand taken personally by President Truman on Palestine and on his attitude to Zionism when he was still a senator. On May 25, 1939, he had attacked the white paper on the floor of the Senate, saying: "It made a scrap of paper out of Balfour's promise to the Jews. It has just added another to the long list of surrenders to the Axis powers."

On May 2, 1944, the Zionist Organization of America had appealed to Senator Truman for his support for Jewish claims in Palestine, the cancellation of restrictions on immigration, and the establishment of a Jewish commonwealth in Palestine in the spirit of the Biltmore Program. Truman had replied that as a member of the subcommittee charged with the task of writing the platform for the Democratic party's convention in Chicago, he had taken part in the drafting of the clause stating the party's stand on the Palestine question. At the same time, Truman wrote, his eyes had been on the bitter fate of Europe's Jews, and this had persuaded him to include in the platform's clause on Palestine the following sentence: "We favor the opening of Palestine to unrestricted Jewish immigration and colonization, and such a policy as would result in the establishment there of a free and democratic Jewish commonwealth." Truman's letter ended with a phrase pregnant with meaning: "When the right time comes, I am willing to help make the fight for a Jewish homeland in Palestine."

When he wrote those words Truman was still a senator, not yet elected vice-president. The crucial question: had he spoken and written then only as the representative of a party seeking Jewish votes, or as someone who recognized the justice of the Jewish case in Palestine and was a convinced supporter of the Zionist cause? I was struck by the sentence referring to the fate of European Jewry, indicating his humanitarian approach to the Palestine issue and not simply his wish to derive a political advantage from it. I was impressed, too, by the final sentence containing his explicit promise to assist, "when the right time comes," in the struggle for the Jewish homeland in Palestine.

Another even more crucial question comes to mind: will Truman adhere to his promise now, when one can hardly doubt that the "right time" has come and he himself is in the White House? At any rate, there is reasonable ground for us to be cautiously optimistic about the president's character and his attitude to the Zionist question.

Cyrus Sulzberger, the *New York Times* chief foreign correspondent whom I first met in Ankara during the war, invited me to lunch. Following a short stint in Moscow, he has come home for a few days to receive instructions from his editor on the countries he is to visit next. He told me he will probably be based in Paris, serving as the paper's roving correspondent, primarily in Europe. He has asked his uncle, Arthur Hays Sulzberger, the publisher of the *Times,* to have the Middle East included in his sphere of duty, since he knows it from the war years, most of which he spent in Turkey. His wife, Marina, is in Greece, the country of her origin, with her family. I assured him that he will receive all the help we can give him if he ever visits Palestine. He commented smilingly that Stalin, a Georgian, was responsible for raising the patriotic spirit of the Russian people in their struggle against the German invader, while Ilya Ehrenburg, a Jew, excelled in information and propaganda activity to this end. In Sulzberger's opinion, the spirit of Russian patriotism will not necessarily disappear now that the war is over. Stalin may find it a useful tool for his peacetime plan of Kremlin control over the expanded Soviet Union, symbolizing not only the heart of world Communism but of "Greater Russia" as well.

After lunch I met Dr. Stephen Wise in the AZEC office and mentioned my call on Senator Wagner. Wise thinks we obviously had a linguistic misunderstanding over the matter of minority rights in Palestine. It is hard to believe, he said, that a man who has been involved for years on the Palestine question does not know that we—and not the Arabs—are in the minority. I saw no point in starting an argument that might hurt Wise's feelings, and I avoided telling him the details of that part of my talk with Wagner.

I told Wise that I was greatly struck by what I read this morning about President Truman's attitude to Zionism and asked him to what extent, in his opinion, it is a sincere expression of Truman's views on the subject.

Wise met Truman on April 20, soon after he became president. On that occasion he detected no difference whatsoever between Truman the senator and Truman the president, regarding his views on Zionist affairs, except that he now is in a position to act rather than simply to speak or promise. Wise believes that the president's problem, and ours, will be to overcome the opposition of State Department officials. As a matter of fact, Wise said, the president referred to this in no uncertain terms during their conversation.

As to Goldmann's plan for my work in Washington, Wise is in complete agreement and offered his full cooperation. He promised to arrange for me to meet some of his influential Washington friends, including one or two on the staff of the White House. One of the first people I will have to meet is Supreme Court Justice Felix Frankfurter.[87] There isn't a sin-

***

[87]Felix Frankfurter (1882–1965); justice on the Supreme Court of the United States from 1919 until his death; professor of law at Harvard University; friend and colleague of Justice Louis Brandeis in his Zionist work in America; acted as legal adviser to the Zionist delegation at the Paris Peace Conference (1919); an intimate friend of Dr. Chaim Weizmann, whom he assisted in his contacts with Emir Feisal, later the first king of Iraq.

gle important figure in the leadership of the country, Wise said, whom Frankfurter does not know. Many are personal friends of his, and quite a number were his students when he taught at Harvard Law School. Wise thinks that President Truman is bound to replace the important members of the White House staff left from Roosevelt's time, but even among the new faces there will certainly be acquaintances and friends of Frankfurter's. One such man is David K. Niles,[88] President Truman's adviser on several important matters, including those affecting the American Jewish community. Niles held this post under Roosevelt, but Wise has just learned that President Truman has asked him to stay on in the position. Niles is very close to Frankfurter, and Wise thinks this could be important if I succeed in gaining Frankfurter's trust and he proves ready to help me. He warned me, however, that Frankfurter can only open doors for me; I will have to strengthen the contacts, build on them, and make use of them myself. As usual, Wise was warm and affable. I was again impressed by his ability to charm everyone he meets.

Wednesday, June 20

I received a telegram from Zev Brenner, containing details of a press conference called by Fraser, at which, among other things, he replied to questions on Palestine. Fraser stated that

[88]David K. Niles (1890–1952); administrative assistant to Presidents Roosevelt and Truman (1942–51); played an important role in Truman's decisions in support of Zionist demands and United States recognition of Israel.

in his view there is no fundamental contradiction between the interests of Arabs and Jews in Palestine and said that it should be possible to find a peaceful solution to the problem. The Mandatory government, he believes, should assist in the task, as well as the Trusteeship Council of the United Nations if necessary. Fraser concluded by describing the Palestine question as "difficult and complex" but one that ought to be approached with hope and faith.

The political secretary of the Jewish Agency's London office, Joseph Linton, wrote me from London of the agency's work in the political sphere. The agency's position was clearly set out in the memorandum signed by Dr. Chaim Weizmann and submitted to Prime Minister Churchill on May 22, 1945. It described the urgent plight of the Holocaust survivors and of the Jews in Arab lands, who look to Palestine as their only haven. For this reason Palestine must become a Jewish state, and the agency must be granted full powers to decide matters concerning immigration and the country's development. Linton also mentioned that, after consulting with the Jewish Agency executive in Jerusalem, it was decided to ask the British high commissioner to grant immediately 100,000 entry permits to Palestine, to be placed at the agency's disposal. Churchill has not yet replied to the memorandum.

Linton also reported that Jewish Agency people have been in contact with British Liberal and Labour party leaders to win their support for our cause. The Labour party's stand on the Palestine issue was confirmed at the meeting of the party's executive on April 25, 1945. The executive reaffirmed the decisions taken by the party conference in London in 1944, calling on the British government to cancel the unjust restrictions on immigration and suggesting that proposals be put forward at once regarding the future of Palestine. The Liberal party, too, has been sympathetic to our claims. The agency's London office, says Linton, regards the broadening of our Washington activities as of prime importance. A promise of the American government's support and assistance might strengthen Churchill's hand if he resolves to abolish the policy based on the white paper and embark on a course more attuned to our needs.

Henry Atkinson invited me to lunch with Reinhold Niebuhr, considered to be one of the greatest living Christian thinkers, as well as a brave fighter for human liberty and a courageous spokesman for the principles of American democracy. Niebuhr asked about the mood in Palestine and about possible solutions to the Palestine question. He expressed his unqualified support for the establishment of a Jewish state in the country, adding that he doubts whether any other solution can ultimately bring about understanding and stability in the relations between Jews and Arabs. He has no faith in a binational state as a solution. The experience in Europe in the years between the wars, he said, ought to serve as a warning to those who favor this particular solution for Palestine. The situation in a binational state would be an explosive one: the Jews would be dissatisfied with its limitations and would demand free entry for their brethren, which the Arabs in turn would be bound to resist. Niebuhr thinks that without large immigration of Jews to Palestine there can be no future there for the Jewish people.

Atkinson spoke of the importance of rallying world Christian opinion—especially in the United States—behind the demand for a Jewish state in Palestine. Both Atkinson and Niebuhr believe that the matter should be presented to the world as something not only of concern to Jews, but also as the responsibility of Christians, in atonement for the horrors that were perpetrated against European Jewry. Both regard the slaughter of European Jewry as the grimmest chapter in the history of Christian civilization.

I attended the meeting of the Central Committee of Poalei Zion and reported my impressions of the San Francisco conference. I was asked about the latest Arab developments and the chances for a Jewish-Arab settlement. I stressed the importance of working to gain public support for the idea that we seek political independence in Palestine not for national reasons alone, but in order to preserve and develop the progressive, democratic character of the society we have built in Palestine. We are surrounded by feudal and reactionary neighbors who are hostile to Zionism and who see in the Zionist venture a threat to their oppressive regimes. We can ensure our future only when we become masters of our own destiny.

Another telegram arrived from Zev Brenner, informing me that paragraph 5 in the "Working Paper for a Chapter of the Charter on Dependent Territories and Arrangements for International Trusteeship" has been adopted in its entirety by Commission II of the General Assembly and is certain to be passed by the plenary session and incorporated without amendment into the United Nations Charter.[89] The Egyptian proposal to deny trusteeships to states guilty of aggression was not discussed. Arshad al-Omari, chairman of the Iraqi delegation, sharply attacked the paragraph, saying that it does not guarantee the rights of the majority population in

[89]Subject only to unsubstantial amendments, paragraph 5 was approved by the plenary session of the General Assembly and was included in the United Nations Charter (chapter XII, article 80, paragraph 1).

the mandated territories, because guidelines are lacking for the winding up of trusteeship regimes and because the voice of countries to be placed under such regimes were not heard in the discussions. Mohammed Awad, the Egyptian representative, supported his Iraqi colleague, although he spoke in a more moderate vein. In reply, Fraser, apparently acting on behalf of Smuts, president of Commission II, said that all peoples and nationalities in trusteeship territories who have grievances, of whatever kind, will have several ways open to them to state their views and complaints, including the submission of petitions. In his remarks Fraser more than once used the words "peoples and nationalities" and added that the United Nations will protect their rights and their interests.

The telegram did not mention the position taken by the Soviet delegation, but the press reported that on this occasion, too, the Soviet representative on the commission supported the Arab stand.

With the successful conclusion of the matters referred to in the telegram our work in San Francisco has come to an end, and with it an important chapter in the struggle to preserve Jewish rights under the Palestine Mandate. Without this assurance it would be difficult on legal grounds for us to proceed to the next stage of our political struggle on the international scene. All the signs indicate that in the struggles that lie ahead we may expect a stronger collision with the Arabs than occurred at San Francisco.

I am not sure that our people at home realize sufficiently the significance of what we have achieved at San Francisco. Apart from preserving the integrity of the Palestine Mandate, we have accomplished something very important by cementing Jewish solidarity on Palestine. This has found tangible expression in our rallying not only Zionists but the broad American Jewish public (as well as Jews of other countries in the free world) behind an active defense of our rights. Despite all the shortcomings in organization and the divisions in Jewish ranks at the conference, we have blunted, at least morally, the impact of the Arab League. There is good reason to assume that the United States delegation at the conference was impressed by the fact that not only American Zionist organizations and the American Jewish Conference but also the American Jewish Committee have all taken a clear stand in rejecting the white-paper policies of the British government and supporting Jewish rights in Palestine as laid down in the Mandate. At all costs we have to keep American Jewry united on the Palestine question, particularly as this community, the largest, richest, and most powerful Jewish community in the free world, will have to shoulder duties and responsibilities as difficult as any borne by our people in the past.

I met today with Congressman Emanuel Celler of Brooklyn, who has served in the House of Representatives without a break since 1922. He is a member of the Democratic party and belongs to its liberal faction in Congress. He has been a consistent supporter of the New Deal policies of President Roosevelt and took an active part in the congressional deliberations regarding the legislative stages of the New Deal. An active Zionist since youth, Celler has for many years labored in behalf of issues of Jewish concern, endeavoring to secure additional support from his non-Jewish colleagues in both houses of Congress.

Celler told me about his efforts in Congress throughout the war for the repeal of the white paper, and about his publicly voiced criticism (in 1944) of President Roosevelt's stand on the matter. Of course he could not accuse Roosevelt of having endorsed the white paper, which the president had never done,[90] but he did criticize his refusal to take active and significant steps against a British government policy that was contrary to the spirit and letter of Britain's obligations under the Palestine Mandate. And he urged Roosevelt to press the British to agree to the establishment of a Jewish state in Palestine. Celler is proud, too, of his help to other politically oppressed peoples, particularly in India and Ireland, seeking to free themselves from British rule. He has earned the warm appreciation of Jawaharlal Nehru and Eamon de Valera and thinks that his good relations with these leaders may be useful to the Zionist cause someday.

I asked Celler about President Truman. He obviously has great respect for the new president's integrity and dedication to his public duties. Celler finds Truman straightforward and modest, a man who has never pretended to be what he is not. His formal education is limited, and his intellectual interests scarcely go beyond what seems to him reasonable and just. His outlook on life originates more in the progressive social

[90]President Roosevelt, in a memorandum to the secretary of state on May 17, 1939, made the following observations: "I have read with interest and a good deal of dismay the decisions of the British Government regarding its Palestine policy. . . . I do not believe that the British are wholly correct in saying that the framers of the Palestine Mandate 'could not have intended that Palestine should be converted into a Jewish state against the will of the Arab population of the country.' My recollection is that this way of putting it is deceptive for the reason that while the Palestine Mandate undoubtedly did not intend to take away the right of citizenship and of taking part in the Government on the part of the Arab population, it nevertheless did intend to convert Palestine into a Jewish Home which might very possibly become preponderantly Jewish within a comparatively short time. Certainly that was the impression that was given to the whole world at the time of the Mandate. . . . My offhand thought is that while there are some good ideas in regard to actual administration of Government in this new White Paper, *it is something that we cannot give approval to by the United States*" (italics mine, E. E.; from *Papers of President Franklin D. Roosevelt at Hyde Park*, in *Foreign Relations of the United States, 1939*, 4:757–58).

and religious principles of the American founding fathers than in abstract doctrines of a political school of any kind. He is a totally different man from his predecessor, who, for all his mental versatility and large perspectives, lacked certain qualities that Truman possesses. Celler thinks that Roosevelt's basic social and economic policies will not be reversed, but that one should now look for less swift and dramatic developments here as well as in other areas of American life that saw so much change under the previous administration. In reply to my question, Celler said that the new president has decided to maintain Roosevelt's foreign policy: there is no sign whatsoever that he intends to return to the isolationist attitude of the prewar years. We can take encouragement from this, for Celler considers that we may be able to gain Truman's help in arriving at a satisfactory solution to the Palestine question. Celler recalled the positive response of the then Senator Truman to every appeal for his support on Zionist issues and on our demands addressed to the Mandatory government. Celler has many personal recollections of Truman's sincerity on Jewish matters, including his sympathy for Zionism. He warned me, however, not to judge Truman only by his past. As president, Truman will have to take into consideration the professional advice and specialized guidance of the various government departments, and these will certainly include many who have little love for Jews or for Zionism. It is still too early to determine the new president's ability to bear the burden of his office, especially in international relations, where he has not had much involvement either as a senator or as vice-president.

Celler invited me to visit Washington and promised to introduce me to his colleagues in Congress and to other public figures.

I dined at the home of Etta Rosensohn, an active Hadassah leader, where I met her brother, Albert Lasker, a leading expert in the field of public relations. I asked him what influence American newspapers have on public opinion, and he replied that there are no definitive criteria to evaluate the matter scientifically. For example, foreign governments and their representatives in the United States on the whole judge American public opinion by the editorial comment in the *New York Times*, the *New York Herald Tribune*, and a few other select newspapers. Since there is no single national newspaper in the U.S. comparable, say, to the *Times* of London, and since practically every big city in the country, and many small ones too, have their own paper or papers, it is difficult to know to what extent this Babel of print reflects the views of the general American public, or even a substantial part of it. If you were to ask members of Congress, they would say that the measure of a newspaper's influence is its circulation. Thus, the *New York Daily News*, with its circulation of over 2 million, is an important medium in the eyes of politicians and advertisers, since its readership is perhaps more than three times that of the *New York Times*, which sells about 600,000 copies a day, and more than five times that of the *New York Herald Tribune*, with daily sales of 350,000. When government departments carry out surveys of public opinion on various subjects, they too usually give preference to newspapers with large circulations, without regard to the makeup of the newspapers' readership.

I think that we need professional advice from people such as Lasker in our public-relations work. Devotion and enthusiasm alone are no substitute for practical knowledge of the psychology of the public we will be appealing to or for expert understanding of how best to achieve the result we seek. I have not yet had the opportunity to familiarize myself with the publicity evaluation methods used by the Zionist institutions in this country, a subject that will be of great importance if it is decided that I am going to Washington.

Friday, June 22

This morning I called at the editorial offices of *Al-Hudah*, located in the same building as the National Lebanese Association and the Lebanese Progress League. The guiding spirit in all three is Saloum el-Mokarzel, whom I met in San Francisco.

Al-Hudah is the organ of the Maronite community in the United States, and since its founding, before World War I, it has opened its pages to Amin el-Rihani, Jubran Khalil Jubran (Khalil Gibran), Abd el-Masih Hadad, and other writers, most of whom were born in Lebanon and arrived in America as children. Their literary talents have all developed in this country. El-Rihani and Jubran, who have written in both English and Arabic, were influenced by American writers, chiefly Walt Whitman.

I came to know Amin el-Rihani well when I was a student in Beirut. He was living at that time in his native village of el-Freikeh, north of Beirut, built on a steep hill above the Freikeh Valley, one of the most beautiful spots in Lebanon. Among his many Arab readers el-Rihani was known as "the philosopher of el-Freikeh," as his essays and prose poems contained many philosophical ideas about human relations and the role of the individual in society. El-Rihani's popularity among non-Arabic readers was largely a result of his books on his travels in Arab lands in the 1930s, which he himself translated from Arabic into English. El-Rihani was very pleased that some of his works had been translated into Hebrew. I often used to visit him in el-Freikeh and last met him at the start of the war in Tiberias, when he was staying in neighboring el-Hamma for medical reasons. He was killed in a car accident in 1940 and was buried in his native village, which he loved so much.

El-Mokarzel introduced me to his staff. One was born in a village near el-Freikeh, had known Amin el-Rihani, and spoke of him with deep appreciation and respect. He remembered el-Rihani's beginnings as an author and had even proofread an essay of his that *Al-Hudah* had published. He considers el-Rihani to be the pioneer who blazed the trail for others in the new Arabic-American literature.

El-Mokarzel is concerned about events in Lebanon. He repeated his view that Lebanese membership in the Arab League is a disaster for the Christians, particularly the Maronite community. He thinks that the league will encourage further Muslim aggression under the cover of Arab nationalism and undermine the independence of Lebanon, a state that is the national home of Christians—as Palestine is of the Jews—and their refuge in the entire Middle East.

After lunch I went to the Jewish Agency's office, which I found in a state of great excitement because of a White House announcement that Earl G. Harrison,[91] dean of the

[91]Earl G. Harrison (1899–1955); an attorney and expert on demography in the United States; lecturer at the University of Pennsylvania and dean of its law school; United States representative at international conferences on population movements and active within the United States in this field. An important and active role in Harrison's appointment was played by Henry Morgenthau, Jr., who earlier had urged the War Refugee Board, created

law school at the University of Pennsylvania and former United States commissioner of immigration and naturalization, has been appointed by the president "to inquire into the condition and needs of those among the displaced persons in the liberated countries of Western Europe and in the SHAEF area of Germany—with particular reference to the Jewish refugees—who may possibly be stateless or nonrepatriable."

Our friends in Philadelphia have telephoned to say Harrison is deeply interested in the question of refugees and can be relied on to discharge his task with skill and a sense of responsibility.

The general view of our people is that the appointment indicates the humane, lively personal interest of President Truman in the problem of Jewish refugees and his desire to investigate the situation, not through normal bureaucratic channels or through U.S. army authorities in Europe, but by the more speedy and efficient means of a special emissary. The fact that, in outlining the mission, a clearly defined expression of need has been given to the situation of stateless or nonrepatriable Jews is of the highest practical and political importance.

My own feeling in the matter is that whatever immediate, practical results emerge from the Harrison mission, both the British and the Arabs will have to take note of the president's initiative. For our part, we must not wait for the results of Harrison's mission but use the development as a lever to put strong pressure on world opinion to support our urgent demand that Palestine be opened to mass Jewish immigration,

---

in January 1944, to undertake serious rescue work but had found the results disappointing. At Dr. Weizmann's request he prompted the Truman administration to investigate the conditions among Jewish displaced persons and suggested that James McDonald be appointed to the task. At the State Department's suggestion, however, the president appointed Harrison.

and first of all from countries where the conditions require prompt action.

I met Robert Szold[92] for dinner. We spoke about the late Justice Louis Brandeis, with whom Szold was close and whom he greatly admired. He bemoaned the fact that a leader of Brandeis's stature is lacking now, just when American Jewry has a historic role to play in seeing that the Palestine question moves toward a settled and constructive solution. As for the Harrison mission, Szold thinks that it indicates President Truman's readiness to involve himself actively in an enterprise of more than a mere humane character. He would not have taken the step of initiating an inquiry into the problem of refugees unless he is ready to draw practical conclusions from the information and proposals that Harrison brings back with him from Europe. Szold thinks that Harrison's conclusions may have important implications for the future of the Zionist struggle. His findings may contribute substantially to our prospects of winning large segments of American opinion over to our side.

Szold went on to speak of the importance of David Niles's position as the president's adviser on Jewish affairs. Szold knows Niles well and has a high opinion of him, both personally and as a Jew. Niles had been a confidant of Roosevelt's, serving as his chief adviser on labor, Catholic, Negro, and Jewish affairs. Szold mentioned what Wise had told me, that Truman has replaced nearly all the former president's

[92]Robert S. Szold (1889–   ); president of the Zionist Organization of America (1930–31); member of the Brandeis-Mack group in American Zionism and a founder and chairman of the Palestine Economic Corporation; director of many corporations for the economic development of Palestine; member of the Executive Committee of the American Jewish Conference (1943).

advisers but has asked Niles to stay on. This proves that Niles has the president's personal confidence and that Truman has a high opinion of his abilities. Szold is sure that nothing affecting the president's relations with the Jewish community will be done without Niles's views being heard. Niles is not a Zionist. He has been and may still be, said Szold, a member of the American Jewish Committee, although he has never been an active one. The Zionist leader closest to him all these years has been Stephen Wise, and there is much mutual affection between the two. Szold said that he often meets Niles when visiting Washington.

I told Szold about the plan for me to stay for some time in the United States to direct the Jewish Agency office in Washington. He favors the idea, promising, among other things, to arrange a meeting between me and Niles. He advised me that if my planned appointment to Washington materializes, I should approach my task carefully and patiently. My success will depend more than anything else on winning the confidence of the people whose help I will need. I shall have to learn the American character and adjust myself to the style of living and way of doing things in Washington, so that I can move easily in the company of Americans and know how and with whose help I may advance my objectives. From what I told Szold and from other reliable information reaching us from Palestine, it is clear to him that the Yishuv will not suffer the white-paper policies much longer. The remnants of the Holocaust languishing in liberated Europe have forced the Zionist movement to make *aliya* our first priority in the major attack on the white paper. There is, said Szold, a strong moral basis and human involvement, especially in the fight for the personal destiny and national security of the homeless refugees. This point should take top priority in the public-relations efforts we address to both American Jewry and the general American public.

Monday, June 25

A prominent leader arranged for me to meet informally and confidentially with a senior economic consultant to a major American oil company that has interests in Iraq and Saudi Arabia.

In C.'s opinion World War II has radically changed relations between American oil companies and the U.S. government. There has never before been a time when cooperation between the two was as essential for national American interests. Global wartime strategy has made it imperative for the government to hold on to the positions won by American troops, at least until some of the most urgent and pressing of the world's problems have been solved and until a settlement leading to international stability has been secured. The far-flung bases of the United States Army in practically all parts of the world during the war have created, among other things, severe shortages of fuel for its own needs and sometimes, too, for the populations of the countries where its forces have been based, since an army of occupation is normally also responsible for civilian needs. Oil consumption in the United States itself has risen greatly, far above local supplies, and domestic reserves of oil have reached an all-time low, less than the minimum considered vital for security requirements at home. For a long time to come America will need to import oil, and even now is unable to supply from its own limited resources the U.S. fleets operating outside a certain strategic area in the Atlantic and Pacific oceans. The Middle East contains some of the world's richest oilfields, and American oil companies control the most important ones, those in Saudi Arabia. These security and economic considerations are presently of paramount importance to United States interests. America must, and wants to, join the Arabs in programs to achieve the most efficient possible exploitation of Arab oil.

In the past, C. commented, money always did the trick. But in the changed conditions in the world generally and in the Middle East particularly, there is now also a political price for everything, which has to be paid if the goods are to remain safe and be promptly delivered. Hence the problem: Arab oil represents the most serious obstacle to Zionist aspirations and to obtaining United States help in those matters where Zionist interests conflict with Arab interests. We should recognize the problem facing us in its true colors, said C., and not accuse the State Department or the American armed services of anti-Semitism or of hostility to Zionism as such, when all that matters to them is that American interests should not clash with the Arabs on our account.

He hastened to add that anti-Semitism certainly exists in the ranks of the United States government and its different departments and services. It could easily be brought to light in the State Department and the Pentagon. But this is only part of the story. Anti-Semites certainly find it easy to argue against us by stressing "vital United States interests," but equally there are people in the administration who are not prejudiced against Jews; rather, considerations of American self-interest have persuaded them to support the Arabs instead of the Jews when they are forced to choose sides in the Palestine problem.

C. also described the close working relationship between the heads of American oil companies having concessions in Arab countries and the State Department and the army. It can be said without exaggeration that, by and large, official American representatives in Iraq and Saudi Arabia are the representatives just as much of the oil companies as of the president of the United States. A number of American diplomats have recently resigned from government service and become oil company employees, without any diminution in their influence either in the Arab countries or in Washington.

C. told me of the oil companies' new approach to public relations. In the past the companies refrained—and prevented others, as far as they could—from publicizing themselves or their activities. There is a story about a writer who went to the president of a major oil company, proposing to write a book on the company's history and activities. The president replied that the writer would be paid a certain sum of money for a good book, but if he agreed not to write anything he would receive twice as much! Now things have changed. Today every large oil company has its own public-relations staff and employs experts in the field. They earn handsome salaries and enjoy the cooperation of many prominent American journalists. They have large budgets at their disposal. James Duce, vice-president in charge of operations of Aramco, guides the company's activities in this area. He also acts as chief liaison officer of Aramco with the State Department and other government departments in Washington. He is a fanatical anti-Zionist.

The conversation with C. provided me with much valuable information and food for very serious thought about what we should expect on the American front in our political struggle. I later told Goldmann what I had heard and sent the substance on to Jerusalem.

Louis Segal[93] of Poalei Zion told me that the work of the American Zionist Emergency Council (of which he is a member) has been much vitiated by the absence of a clear policy line on basic matters of current Zionist policy. Stephen Wise has little notion of the rapidly increasing seriousness of the situation in Palestine and sees no need to step up pressure on the United States government to defend and advance our claims more vigorously. Wise was practically the only Zionist leader in Roosevelt's time with direct access to the White House, but the very friendliness of his contacts with the president and members of the government often prevented his being firm enough in his demands or clashing with his friends when their actions fell short of what was required. The same may happen again, said Segal, if our contacts with the new president and his administration are handled exclusively by Wise.

Segal thinks that there is a reasonable chance that Dr. Abba Hillel Silver will return to active work on the AZEC. He will if he is assured that there will be support for a more determined and militant line toward the White House. Segal believes many people in Mizrachi, Hadassah, Poalei Zion, and especially the ZOA want Silver's return. Silver is a strong personality, an excellent speaker, and a Republican. With him on AZEC, the Democratic administration may fear that any surrender or retreat before anti-Zionist elements would give Silver ammunition to use to the benefit of the Republican party. The pro-Zionist Yiddish press has repeatedly called for Silver's return to active work in political Zion-

[93]Louis Segal (1894–1964); American Labor Zionist leader; active in trade-union activities; secretary-general of the Jewish National Workers Alliance, or Farband (from 1926 until his death); member of the executive of the Ihud Olami (World Union of Zionists-Socialists); member of the Jewish Agency executive (from 1954 until his death).

ism. The political council of the ZOA, under the leadership of Emanuel Neumann, is no real threat, in Segal's opinion, to the existence or prestige of the AZEC. However, the existence of a rival body to the AZEC is harmful to the Zionist cause at a time when the paramount need is to unite its entire forces within a single organizational framework. Silver's return to Zionist leadership will correct that.

I had the impression from what Segal told me that he expects a crisis in the American Zionist Emergency Council. The fact that he, a Labor Zionist leader, predicts it makes it even more significant for a proper evaluation of the internal trends and possible developments in the Zionist movement in this country, irrespective of party differences and personal loyalties.

Herman Shulman heard from a reliable source that Joseph Grew, acting secretary of state,[94] who is a veteran senior official in the State Department, has hardly welcomed President Truman's initiative on the question of Jewish refugees in Europe and had his doubts about the advisability of Harrison's appointment to investigate the situation, foreseeing a possible link with the Palestine question. Grew believes that America should refrain, for the moment at any rate, from any initiative or action likely to involve it in the Palestine controversy, as well as any step that might encourage Zionists to press for future U.S. intervention. Grew considers that American pressure would damage the standing of the British government and only make it more difficult to reach a solution to the problem. He apparently has no illusions about

[94]Joseph C. Grew served in this position for a short time, from the resignation of Edward Stettinius until July 3, 1945, when James Byrnes became secretary of state in President Truman's administration.

how far direct intervention from the United States on the problem of Jewish refugees would involve it in the Palestine question: U.S. immigration laws will not be eased and large numbers of Jewish refugees will therefore not be allowed into the United States. Their entry into Palestine and settlement there will under the circumstances be looked upon as the logical and natural solution to the problem, whether Harrison proposes something of this kind or not.

Shulman commented that Grew's position, his attempts to prevent America's active and positive intervention in the Palestine problem, is typical of his State Department colleagues, almost all of whom are anti-Zionist without necessarily being pro-British. However, Shulman has heard that in the new State Department section that is responsible for the United States zone of occupation in Germany, whose concerns include the question of stateless refugees, Harrison's mission has been well received. The same source has told him that this section will welcome any solution to the refugee problem that will take the refugees out of its hands as expeditiously as possible.

I attended a meeting of the AZEC. Eliezer Kaplan spoke on the challenges facing American Zionism, emphasizing the refugee problem as the most important and pressing item on the agenda. He stressed that the movement of the refugees to Palestine is not only a political but also a heavy financial undertaking, greater than any we have known. We shall also need large sums of money for the absorption of the immigrants, as well as large sums for our security requirements, which will grow with the increasing Arab opposition to large-scale Jewish immigration. Our political struggle will have a purpose, Kaplan said, if we can translate our political achievements into constructive action, first and foremost through absorbing large numbers of immigrants and integrating them into the social and economic fabric of the Yishuv's life. If we Zionists carry out our responsibilities first, then we can expect active assistance from our fellow Jews as well, Kaplan concluded.

Wise, Lipsky, Shulman, Rose Halprin, Israel Goldstein, and others spoke of the importance of the Harrison mission and underlined the political significance of President Truman's move. Toward the end of the discussion there was talk of expanding our publicity to stress the need for a rapid solution of the Palestine question on the basis of the Biltmore Program. It was agreed that, in the concentrated assault on the white paper, we should call on our sympathizers in all walks of American life, including those in both houses of Congress, to demand a radical revision of British policy in Palestine. President Truman's hand in appointing Harrison should be strengthened, and he should be encouraged to maintain the active political involvement of the United States in the Palestine question. Hayim Greenberg highlighted the importance of Zionist propaganda in the Latin American countries; this political bloc will be of great consequence in the United Nations.

Tuesday, June 26

I had breakfast with Dr. Stephen Wise. Although I had discovered that the American working day often begins with a breakfast meeting, on this occasion there was no agenda. Wise asked me, among other things, about my activity in the

Zionist underground in Soviet Russia, about my studies in Beirut, about the Arabs and their political leaders in Palestine and neighboring countries.

I recounted the continuous efforts of the Political Department of the Jewish Agency in Jerusalem to create Jewish-Arab understanding with the national movements in Arab countries and with their leaders. In this connection I recalled the meeting Ben-Gurion and I had in Beirut with Fuad Hamzah, director general of the Saudi Arabian ministry for foreign Affairs, in 1937.

Wise then told me that when Dr. Weizmann was in the United States in 1942–43, he had suggested to Sumner Welles, then undersecretary of state, that he (Weizmann) should meet with King ibn-Saud to attempt to lay the foundation for Jewish-Arab understanding. In his discussion with Welles, Dr. Weizmann recalled his historic meeting with Emir Feisal at the end of World War I and said that a meeting with ibn-Saud could be even more fateful. Jewish-Arab relations had meanwhile become completely deadlocked, and a just and stable solution to the Palestine problem would benefit not only the parties directly involved but contribute to the peace and progress of the entire area. Welles had reacted favorably to the suggestion and added that, from what he knew of President Roosevelt's attitude to the Palestine question, the president, too, would favor the proposal.

Dr. Weizmann's meeting with the president on June 11, 1943, did not produce any practical results, however, and did not bring about the desired progress in Zionist-Arab rapprochement through President Roosevelt's intervention with King ibn-Saud.[95]

[95]In President Roosevelt's archives at Hyde Park, New York, there is a letter (PPF 8084) from Undersecretary of State Sumner Welles to President Roosevelt, dated May 19, 1943, which contains the following passage: "Dr. Chaim Weizmann . . . came to see me

I lunched with the publisher of the *New York Times* and his senior editorial colleagues. Anne O'Hare McCormick had arranged for me to meet Arthur Hays Sulzberger, her boss. In addition to Sulzberger and Mrs. McCormick, those attending were Edwin James, Charles Merz, and Lester Markel. Both during and after the meal I was asked many questions about the situation in Palestine and the chances of an agreement with the Arabs. Sulzberger did not conceal his doubts about Zionism and our claim for political independence.

---

yesterday. He asked me if I would find out if you would be willing to receive him some time between May 25 and May 31. I have found Dr. Weizmann the most constructive of all the Jewish leaders with regard to the Palestine question. He believes, as I think you do, that the solution of this problem should, if possible, be found by agreement between the Jews and Arabs, and it is his present hope that the way can be prepared for him to meet with King ibn-Saud and to try to work out the basis for an agreement which would obviate in the future the dangers and difficulties of the past twenty-five years."

In his autobiography, *Trial and Error* (New York: Harper and Brothers, 1949), p. 427, Dr. Weizmann tells about his meeting with Prime Minister Churchill, before Weizmann's visit to the United States in March 1942. In the course of a brief conversation, "or—should I say monologue" by Churchill, as Weizmann describes the meeting, the prime minister said that he had a plan "to see ibn-Saud made lord of the Middle East . . . provided he settles with you [the Jews]." Churchill requested secrecy but had no objection if Weizmann wanted to "talk it over" with President Roosevelt. Weizmann relates that at his first meeting with the president he had no opportunity to mention the matter at all and that they only talked of Dr. Weizmann's scientific work. Much later, at a meeting with President Roosevelt on June 11, 1943, Dr. Weizmann, in the presence of Sumner Welles who had arranged the meeting, did apparently mention Churchill's "plan," to which "the attitude of Mr. Roosevelt was completely affirmative" (*Trial and Error*, p. 435). As a matter of fact, soon after seeing Dr. Weizmann, Lt. Col. Harold B. Hoskins of the United States Army, who had been temporarily engaged by the State Department as an expert on Arab and Zionist matters, a man whom the president obviously considered the most suitable envoy for exploring the chances for an Arab-Jewish settlement on

James and Merz energetically supported British policy. Only Lester Markel, editor of the Sunday edition of the *Times,* showed considerable knowledge of our affairs and defended the lifting of restrictions on Jewish immigration to Palestine on both humanitarian and political grounds. He added that this could contribute considerably to the solution of the Jewish refugee problem in liberated Europe, especially since no country in the world, the United States included, is in his opinion prepared to accept them in large numbers or look after absorbing them, which the Jews of Palestine—referring to what I had said earlier—are both ready and able to do. Charles Merz, one of the paper's chief editorial writers, went to great lengths to support Sulzberger's anti-Zionist views. I noticed also their strong pro-British sympathies, compared with the critical remarks about France made by Merz and

---

Palestine, was sent by President Roosevelt on a mission to King ibn-Saud. The results were as futile as the previous attempt in the same direction by St. John Philby in 1940. A few months prior to Weizmann's interview with Churchill, Weizmann had met Philby, a confidant of ibn-Saud's. Philby told Weizmann that "only two requirements, perhaps, are necessary to solve your problem: that Mr. Churchill and President Roosevelt should tell ibn-Saud that they wished to see your program carried through; [and] that they should support his overlordship of the Arab countries and raise a loan for him to enable him to develop his territories." Weizmann "fitted together St. John Philby's 'offer' and Mr. Churchill's 'plan' " (*Trial and Error,* pp. 427–28). The Saudi king refused to enter into any negotiations with Dr. Weizmann or any other representative of the Jewish Agency, saying to Hoskins that "he was prepared to receive anyone, of any religion, except a Jew" (Great Britain, Public Record Office, *Papers of the British Prime Minister,* 1943, pp. 192–93). However, while an envoy other than Hoskins might not have achieved any different results from his mission to the fanatical king of Saudi Arabia, having selected an outspoken anti-Zionist who had no consideration whatsoever for the Jewish position on the Palestine question, President Roosevelt could hardly have expected him to bring back conciliatory tidings. More details on the Weizmann-Philby-Hoskins-ibn-Saud "negotiations" are to be found in Elizabeth Monroe, *Philby of Arabia* (London: Faber and Faber, 1973).

others. Sulzberger himself often cited "reliable information" that he had received from British sources on the Palestine situation.

I later passed on to Lipsky my impressions of my conversation with Sulzberger and his colleagues. Lipsky said Sulzberger suffers from a disease that afflicts many assimilated Jews, a condition for which there is no cure. Sulzberger fears that one single word in his paper supporting our cause in Palestine will be attributed to the fact that the paper has a Jewish publisher. Lipsky knows the editorial board and thinks that most Jews and non-Jews on it take the convenient course of agreeing with their boss on the question of Zionism and Palestine. Lipsky found it a pleasant surprise to hear that the only person who dared to disagree with Sulzberger was Lester Markel. Lipsky feels that we have little chance of altering Sulzberger's anti-Zionist views because his mind is closed on the subject. Nevertheless, he urged me to keep up my contacts with the paper's staff, especially with Markel.

Wednesday, June 27

David Ben-Gurion arrived in New York yesterday and lost no time in telling the press that the Yishuv will not tolerate for much longer the provisions of the white paper, which it will oppose "by every means in its power." His statement was prominently featured in the morning newspapers.

This evening I reported to Ben-Gurion on my impressions of the San Francisco conference and described my other work since arriving in the United States. Ben-

Gurion regards the United States as one of the principal arenas of our future political struggles, and considers it urgent and essential to broaden our work here. He believes that American Jewry will have an important role to play in our future operations and that we have to muster all the strength we can. The gravity of the situation demands that we step up our various efforts and devise more effective means to achieve the desired results, particularly in the areas of political support and fund raising. During his stay in the United States Ben-Gurion will be engaging in such activity, and special emissaries will be sent from Palestine to carry on the work.

Ben-Gurion's remarks reminded me of John Stuart Mill's comment that "when the object is to raise the permanent condition of a people, small means do not merely produce small effects: they produce no effects at all."

Monday, July 2

I have spent the last few days laid up in bed at the Hotel Fourteen, which is a center for newly arrived Palestinians in New York. When I got back to the Jewish Agency's office, I found a copy of a cable that Ben-Gurion sent to Moshe Shertok:

KAPLAN, GOLDMANN, LIPSKY, AND MYSELF DECIDED ELIAHU EPSTEIN STAY WASHINGTON FOR A YEAR STOP AGREED ZEHAVA EPSTEIN SHALL JOIN HUSBAND EARLIEST DATE IMPORTANCE THEIR ESTABLISHING HOUSE IN WASHINGTON
DAVID BEN-GURION

Eliezer Kaplan told me officially that the decision has been made to put me in charge of the Jewish Agency's Political Office in Washington. My task will be to see to the expansion and strengthening of our political work in the capital and to run an office in consultation with the agency executive in New York and with Dr. Nahum Goldmann personally. Kaplan is quite sure that Shertok will confirm the decision by Ben-Gurion and his colleagues and that I will have all the help I need from Jerusalem.

I told Kaplan that I am perfectly happy with the arrangement. After my experience in San Francisco I am confident that Goldmann and I can work together with mutual understanding and respect. Kaplan spoke at length about the crucial importance of my new responsibilities and expressed his confidence in my ability to meet them.

I later discussed my duties in Washington with Goldmann. He explained that the Jewish Agency in Washington currently consists of a secretary, Miriam Cohen, who works by herself in a tiny office. Practically all she does is look after Goldmann's appointments when he visits Washington. The American Zionist Emergency Council also has an office in Washington, directed by Dr. Benjamin Akzin, who was a member of the political entourage of the late Vladimir Jabotinsky. The office deals with public relations and information work directed principally toward members of Congress. I will have to maintain contact with this office to coordinate our activities, but I will be acting independently, reporting only to the New York and Jerusalem offices of the Jewish Agency. Goldmann will do his best to see that I am introduced to people in Washington who might be able to assist me in my work.

In view of the stepped-up Arab activity, Goldmann thinks

I should begin work in Washington with the least possible delay. I told him that I am ready to leave for Washington immediately.

I spent the evening reflecting on my situation and on my experiences of the past weeks. In the short time I have been in the United States I have acquired a good deal of information on different aspects of American social and political life and problems. I have met a large number of people among the Jewish leadership and established a good working relationship with their staffs and assistants. I have also established a promising basis for further contacts with people in the State Department dealing with our part of the world, as well as with a number of representatives of foreign countries stationed in Washington. As a former journalist, I have been able to gain the confidence and friendship of many newsmen. Moreover, my background as a graduate of the American University of Beirut may prove to be of considerable value in my contacts both with American officials and with Arab colleagues, fellow students of mine now serving in diplomatic posts in the United States.

These are my thoughts as I take stock of my assets for this new assignment. At the moment there is no one with whom I can share my thoughts, fears, and doubts. I can only hope for the best.

I have written to tell Zehava about the developments of the past few days and my hope that she will join me to help me in my difficult task.

Tuesday, July 3

This morning the Jewish Agency office received a telegram
from Moshe Shertok, addressed to me:

AM CONVINCED YOU WILL DO A GOOD JOB STOP KEEP CHEERFUL STOP
HOPE WIFE JOINS YOU SOON STOP DEPARTMENT WILL RALLY YOUR
ASSISTANCE STOP GREETINGS

MOSHE SHERTOK

 Tomorrow morning I set out for Washington.

Index

323

American Zionist Political Committee, 193
Anglo-American Committee of Inquiry on Palestine, 99n, 234
Anglo-Jewish Association, 274n
Annex Regarding Palestine, 26, 71, 108, 124, 145, 152, 154, 188, 195
Antaki, Naim al-, 148
Antonius, George, 58, 93, 166
Aquinas, Thomas, 48
Arab-American Mining Company Institute, xiii, 167–68
Arab Higher Committee, 55n
Arab League. See Pact of the League of Arab States
Aramco, 134–35, 309
Arida, Antoine, 137, 200
Askari, Ja'afar Pasha al-, 57
Aslan, Samuel, 55
Atkinson, Henry, 56, 111–12, 234–36, 295–96
Awad, Mohammed, 297
Ayubi, Ali Jawdat Pasha al-, xvii, 57, 60

Badawi, Abdel Hamid Pasha, 141, 171, 188
Bailey, Josiah, 168
Balfour, A. J., 92, 290
Balfour Declaration, x, 4, 5n, 6, 23, 31n, 39, 45, 52, 104–6, 139, 142, 151, 166, 202, 286
Baroody, Jamil, 255
Barth, Karl, 236
Baydur, Huseyin Ragip, 127, 196–97
Bech, Joseph, 161
Bedr Khan, Jaladat, 242–43, 244
Bedr Khan, Kamuran Ali, 242–44
Beeley, Harold, xvii, 99–100, 162–65, 201, 209–11, 216, 249–50
Bell, Gertrude, 99
Belt Ramirez, Guillermo, 74
Ben-Gurion, David, xiv, xix, 4, 82, 223, 247, 266, 272–73, 279, 314, 317–19
Ben-Zvi, Rachel, 99
Ben-Zvi, Yitzhak, 99
Bergson, Henri, 48–49, 98
Bergson, Peter. See Kook, Hillel
Bidault, Georges, 215, 231n

Biltmore Program, x, xiv, 4–5, 17, 31, 53, 59, 61, 74, 83, 126, 128–29, 143, 151, 179, 183, 192, 224, 234–35, 248, 265, 280, 290, 313
Bishlani, Antonius el-, 198
Bloom, Sol, 69, 156
B'nai B'rith, xiii, 30, 37, 42, 90n, 149–51, 241, 273
Board of Deputies of British Jews, 15, 36, 63, 113, 274n
Bondarchuk, Vladimir, 180
Bonnet, Henri, 228, 231–32
Bowman, Isaiah, 69
Brandeis, Louis, 259, 292n, 305
Brenner, Zev, 114, 237, 267, 278, 293, 296
Bridges, Harry, 104
British Mandate for Palestine, x–xi, 3n, 4–6, 8–13, 17, 20n, 31n, 38–40, 52–54, 79–80, 86, 100, 104–8, 124, 126–27, 129, 131, 138–40, 142, 146–47, 151–52, 154, 163, 173, 175–76, 178–79, 187, 190, 201, 210–12, 214, 218, 223–24, 240, 260, 265, 286, 297–99
British Trade Unions Congress, 67
B'rit Shalom, 248
Bronfman, Samuel, 37, 110
Brook, Ray, 42–44, 97, 160, 177–78, 229–30
Brownsdon, Edward, 97
Buck, Pearl, 220
Bulgaris, Demetrios, 87
Burton, Richard F., 99
Byrnes, James, 311n

Cambon, Jules, 221n
Canadian Jewish Congress, 15, 36–37
Celler, Emanuel, 258, 276, 298–300
Chamberlain, Joseph, 275
Chamberlain, Neville, 250, 271
Chamoun, Camille, 102
Charter. See United Nations Charter
Chiang Kai-shek, 17, 251
Churchill, Winston, x, 6, 9, 72, 175, 210n, 233, 246, 258, 294–95, 315–16n

Fraser, Peter, 38–39, 105, 140, 155, 161–62, 171–73, 179, 211–15, 218, 227, 230–31, 238, 293–94, 297
French Consultative Assembly, 75
Friedrich, Carl, 235
Furmansky, Moshe, 288–89

Gandhi, Mohandas K., 258
Gavrilovic, Stojan, 54–55, 189, 225, 233
Gellman, Leon, 33n
General Assembly. See United Nations General Assembly
General Zionists, xiii, 37
George VI, 99
Gerig, Benjamin, 212
Gildersleeve, Virginia, 69, 156
Glueck, Nelson, 41
Goldmann, Nahum, xiii–xiv, 27, 31, 33n, 34, 39–40, 68, 70, 78, 81, 84–85, 87, 94–95, 98, 105–8, 115, 119, 123, 131, 135, 138, 145–46, 153–55, 161, 169, 173–76, 178–79, 183, 187–89, 193, 202, 211–12, 214–15, 217–18, 220–23, 225, 230–32, 237–38, 248, 255, 260–62, 265–66, 271–73, 281, 288, 292, 309, 318–20
Goldstein, Herbert, 113
Goldstein, Israel, 33n, 35, 38, 174, 313
Golomb, Eliahu, 26
Gonzalez-Videla, Gabriel, 126
Gorse, Georges, 75–77, 101–2, 180, 228
Goulimis, Constantine, 115
Green, William, 37, 67, 109, 235, 275
Greenberg, Hayim, 33n, 120–23, 273–74, 276–77, 313
Grew, Joseph, 311–12
Gromyko, Andrei A., 11, 75
Gruenbaum, Yitzhak, 87

Hadassah, xiii, 33n, 35n, 37, 103n, 112, 192, 200, 248, 266, 301, 310
Haganah, 26n, 87n, 96
Haidari, Daoud Pasha al-, 124, 196
Haile Selassie, 130, 181
Halifax, Lord, 206

Halprin, Rose, 33n, 35, 248, 313
Hamzah, Fuad, 314
Hapsburg, Otto, 222
Harris, Adele, 49, 103
Harrison, Earl G., 303–5, 311–13
Hashomer Ha-tza'ir, 103n
Hassan, Mahmoud Pasha, 141
Hayes, Saul, 37
Hebrew Committee of National Liberation, 36, 170n
Hehalutz, xvi, 50–51
Heine, Heinrich, 132
Herzl, Theodor, 259
Hillman, Sidney, 67, 285
Hiram (biblical), 256
Hisar, Sinasi, 119–20
Hiss, Alger, 70, 107–8, 123–24, 145, 154, 187–88, 262
Histadrut, 103n, 104, 109–10, 156, 284–85
Hitler, Adolf, 10, 55, 65n, 97, 178, 222, 224, 232, 251–52, 263, 271, 273–74, 288
Hitti, Philip, 167
Hocking, W. E., 168
Holmes, John Haynes, 234
Hoskins, Halford, 167
Hoskins, Harold, 315–16n
House of Representatives (U. S.), 69, 168, 192, 235, 258, 276, 298
Hu Lin, 251–52
Hull, Cordell, 273, 276
Human Rights Commission, 31n
Husseini, Haj Amin el-, 55, 141, 166, 234, 271, 287

ibn-Khaldun, 253
ibn-Saud, Abdul-Aziz, 14, 45–46, 125, 135, 166, 168, 202–4, 229, 314–16n
Ickes, Harold, 135, 235
Ihud Association, 62n
Ihud Olami (World Union of Zionists-Socialists), 310n
Imam Yahya, 166
İnönü, İzmet, 197
Institute of Arab-American Affairs, xiii, 116, 168–69
Institute of Jewish Affairs, 31–32
Institute of Oriental Studies, 167

Instituto Mexico-Israel, 90n
Interior Department (U. S.), 132–33, 135
International Conference of Labor Organizations, 67
International Labor Office, 67
Ireland, Philip, xii, 88–89
Irgun Tzvai Leumi, 87n, 170n
Israeli-German Reparations Agreement, 32n

Jabotinsky, Vladimir, 116n, 319
Jacobson, Victor, 256
Jamali, Fadhil al-, xvii, 56, 58–60, 124–25, 178, 194–96
Jamal Pasha, 128
James, Edwin, 315–16
Jawad, Hashim, xvii, 46–48
Jewish Agency for Palestine, xiii, xv–xvi, xix, 3–7, 14–17, 19, 25, 27–28, 30–31, 32n–33n, 34–37, 43, 46, 52–54, 64, 71, 82, 87, 94, 98, 103n, 105–8, 120, 124, 127, 138, 142, 154, 169–70, 173–74, 183, 187–88, 191, 193, 214, 222–23, 248, 261, 266, 271–73, 281, 284n, 288, 294–95, 303, 306, 310n, 314, 318–19, 321
Jewish Institute of Religion, 35n
Jewish Labor Committee, 36, 63, 109
Jewish Legion, 106n
Jewish National Fund, 35n, 103n
Jinnah, Mohammed Ali, 91
Joint Distribution Committee, 88, 247
Jouve, A., 75, 77, 180, 202, 227–28, 231, 246
Jubran, Jubran Khalil, 302

Kalisher, Eliahu, 259n
Kaplan, Eliezer, 32, 71, 87–88, 223, 226–27, 233, 247–48, 266, 271–73, 284–85, 288, 312–13, 318–19
Kaufmann, Edmund, 280–81
Keilani, Rashid Ali al-, 229
Kemal Atatürk (Mustafa Kemal), 64, 66, 124, 243
Kenen, Isaiah, 37–38, 81, 110, 153, 174, 176, 208–9, 216–17, 220, 230, 258

Keren Hayesod, 27n
Khalidi, Ismail, 168
Khouri, Abdallah, 137
Khouri, Faiz al-, 142
Khouri, Faris al-, xviii, 44–45, 136, 142–43, 148–49, 216
Kipling, Rudyard, 74
Kissinger, Henry, xvii
Kleffens, Eelko N. van, 106
Kohler, Foy, xii, xv, xvii, 70–72, 88–89, 112, 157–59, 165, 206–7, 254, 267
Kohn, Hans, 93, 166
Koo, V. K. Wellington, 152–53
Kook, Hillel, 170
Koudsi, Nazem al-, 148
Krasovec, Stane, 233
Kuznetsov, V. V., 67, 75

Lasker, Albert, 301
Laski, Harold, 47, 246
Lavrentiev, A. I., 75
Lawrence, T. E., 99, 118, 166
League for Labor Palestine, 103n
League of American-Arabs Committee for Democracy, 168
League of Nations, 3, 5–6, 16, 25, 27n, 29, 32, 33n, 34, 38–40, 79–80, 100, 107, 115, 119, 131, 139, 152–53, 171, 175, 183, 209–11, 213–14, 218, 221, 252, 256, 275
Lebanese Progress League, 302
Lenin, Nikolai, 65
Lindheim, Irma, 103
Linton, Joseph, 294–95
Li Ping-heng, 67
Lipsky, Louis, 27, 31, 33n, 35, 45–46, 81, 110, 183, 190–93, 212, 220, 230–31, 237–38, 259–61, 273, 288, 313, 317–18
Liu Chieh, 218
Louis XIV, 216
Lourie, Arthur, 32, 54, 98, 169, 189, 191, 281
Lowdermilk, Walter, 235
Luce, Clare Boothe, 205
Luce, Henry, 205
Lyautey, Louis H., 117–18

MacCallum, Elizabeth, 116
McCormick, Anne O'Hare, 61–62, 97, 168, 205, 315
McDonald, James G., 275, 304n
Magnes, Judah, 62, 112, 200–201, 248, 266
Malik, Charles, xviii, 48–49, 98–99, 102, 136, 148–49, 267, 278
Malouf, Faris, 168
Mandate for Palestine. See British Mandate for Palestine
Mandatory Power(s), 6, 9, 12–13, 30, 39, 80, 94, 108, 139, 146, 180, 218, 250, 260, 265, 294, 300
Manuilsky, Dmitry, 180–81
Mapu, Abraham, 259
Mara, Mikulas, 245–46
Maritain, Jacques, 48, 236
Markel, Lester, 315–17
Marsh, Daniel, 235
Marshall, George, xiv
Marshall, Louis, 150
Marx, Karl, 65, 280–81
Masaryk, Jan, 84–85, 106, 189, 225, 245
Menemencioglu, Nauman, 127
Mereminsky, Israel, 109, 156
Merz, Charles, 315–16
Mihailovitch, Draja, 222
Mikve Israel, 96
Mill, John Stuart, xix, 64, 318
Mishmar Ha'emek, 103n
Mizrachi, xiii, 33n, 37, 192, 310
Mokarzel, Naim el-, 198
Mokarzel, Saloum el-, xviii, 198–200, 302–3
Molotov, V. M., 65n, 74–75, 180–81, 230n
Monsky, Henry, 30, 35, 38, 81, 95, 105, 107, 138, 149–51, 155, 161, 173–75, 182, 189, 212
Mora, Marcial, 74
Mordecai (biblical), 132
Morgenthau, Henry, Jr., 303n
Moss, Abraham, 37
Moyne, Lord, 39
Mudaliar, A. Ramaswami, 257
Murray, John Courtenay, 236
Murray, Philip, 36, 67–68, 235
Murray, Wallace, 206

Mussolini, Benito, 55, 65, 178, 224, 271

Naggiar, Paul-Émile, 77, 102, 115, 202, 218–19, 228
Nahas Pasha, Mustafa el-, 48
Naim, Wadih, 148
Naqqash, Albert, 255–56
Nash, Richard H., 250–51
Nasser, Gamal Abdel, 141n
National Lebanese Association, 302
National Lebanese Society of America, xviii, 198, 200
Near East College Association, xii, 165–66
Near East Foundation, xiii, 166
Nehru, Jawaharlal, 257, 299
Neumann, Emanuel, 284, 311
New Zionist Organization, 36, 116
Niebuhr, Reinhold, 234–36, 295–96
Niles, David K., 293, 305–6
Noon, Firoz Khan, 96–97, 257
Nordau, Max, 116n
Novikov, K. V., 223–25

Ochs, Adolf, 97
Office of Near Eastern and African Affairs, 70–72, 88, 112, 206–7. See also State Department (U. S.)
O'Mahoney, Joseph, 134
Omari, Arshad al-, 47, 296
Organization of American States, 160

Pact of the League of Arab States, 26, 108, 113, 119, 123–24, 127–29, 131, 137–38, 143, 145, 149, 152, 154, 157–61, 164, 166, 176–77, 182, 187–88, 195, 199–200, 212, 215–16, 219–20, 224, 232–33, 242, 247, 253–54, 261–62, 272, 278, 280, 284, 298, 303
Palestine Commission, 58n
Palestine Economic Corporation, 256, 305n
Palestine Mandate. See British Mandate for Palestine
Palgrave, F. T., 99
Pan American Union, 9, 16, 138, 157

Weisgal, Meyer, 30
Weizmann, Chaim, 23, 26, 30n, 52, 82, 116n, 118, 137, 152, 190, 240, 279, 292n, 294, 304n, 314–16n
Welles, Sumner, 160, 314–15n
White Paper (May 1939), x, 5, 41–42, 45, 69n, 82, 104, 107, 145–46, 183, 206, 250, 263, 271, 279–80, 286, 290, 298, 298n, 306, 317
Whitman, Walt, 302
Wilentchuk, Isaac, 256
Willkie, Wendell, 227
Wilson, Evan, 69n
Wilson, John, 167
Wilson, Woodrow, 13, 31n, 120
Wingate, Orde, 130, 181
Wise, Stephen S., xiv, 33n, 34–35, 43, 45–46, 69, 74, 81–83, 95, 103, 113, 130, 155, 161, 173–76, 183, 190–93, 274, 279, 285, 289, 292–93, 306, 310, 313
"Working Paper for a Chapter of the Charter on Dependent Territories and Arrangements for International Trusteeship," 9, 139–40, 146–48, 161, 171, 201, 209–10, 213, 296–97
World Conference of Trade Unions, 104
World Council of Jewish Women, 15, 36
World Court, 32
World Jewish Congress, xiii, 15, 27, 32, 35n, 36, 37, 63, 275n
World Organization of Protestant Churches, 111

World Union of General Zionists, 284n
World Union of Zionists-Socialists (Ihud Olami), 310n
World Zionist Congress, 5, 35, 32–33n, 97, 116n, 286
World Zionist Organization, 26n, 27n, 82, 109n, 256
Wright, Michael, 206
Wu Yi-fang, 45

Yad Vashem, 32n
Yafi, Abdallah, 136
Yahuda, Abraham S., 116–19
Yalçin, Husseyin Cahit, 64–67, 77–78, 127, 196–97, 252–53
Yalta Conference, 52
Yishuv (Jewish community of Palestine, pre-1948), xix, 27, 39–40, 43, 66, 71, 99, 104, 114, 116n, 121, 130, 132, 140–41, 150, 169, 200, 202, 225, 233, 239, 250, 253, 256–57, 266, 277, 279, 285, 288–89, 306, 313
YIVO, 32n

Zacks, Samuel, 37
Zaritsky, Max, 36
Zaslani, Reuven. See Shiloah, Reuven
Zeineddine, Farid, xvii, 57–60, 142
Zionist Congresses. See World Zionist Congress
Zionist Federation, 90n
Zionist Organization of America (ZOA), 27n, 30n, 33n, 35n, 103n, 166, 192–93, 280, 284n, 290, 305n, 310–11

וקראתם

נברכם דרור

Proclaim liberty through-
out the land unto all the
inhabitants thereof *Leviticus 25:10*

Published in Philadelphia in the two-hun-
dredth year of American Independence by
The Jewish Publication Society of America

בארץ לכל